MARXIST SOCIAL THOUGHT

Also by Robert Freedman

MARX ON ECONOMICS

Marxist

Social Thought

EDITED BY **Robert Freedman**

INTRODUCTION BY JEROME BALMUTH

AN ORIGINAL HARVEST BOOK

Harcourt, Brace & World, Inc., New York

First edition

Library of Congress Catalog Card Number: 68-13362

Printed in the United States of America

TO MY MOTHER AND FATHER:

PAULINE AND ROBERT, SR.

Preface

The purpose of this book is to provide in readily available form a comprehensive view of Marx's social thought, as presented in the writings of both Marx and Engels. The works of these two men are too widely scattered for easy access. Here their major writings are brought together in logical order.

I have attempted to present a chronology of their ideas rather than of their writings. Chapter I, "From Hegel to Feuerbach to Marx," deals with Marx's conversion from the idealism of Hegel to an adaptation of the materialism of Feuerbach. Chapter II, "The Theory of Alienation," taken largely from the recently translated *Economic and Philosophic Manuscripts of 1844,* demonstrates Marx's fundamentally moral concern for the effects of capitalism on the quality of life and human personality. Chapter III, "The Materialist Conception of History," develops Marx's theory of social change and documents the materialist conception of history, from the standpoint of his understanding of the social order, its problems and evolution. Chapter IV, "The Economic Interpretation of History—Classes," contains Marx's application of the materialist conception of history under the special economic form he called capitalism. Chapter V, "Superstructure and Substructure," shows the relationship of capitalism and its supporting values to the institutions of the state, law, religion, marriage, and family life. Chapter VI, "From Capitalism to Communism," traces the decline of capitalism and the emergence of the revolutionary dictatorship of the proletariat and, finally, describes the communist state. Several of the chapters have appendices to illustrate how Marx used history to make comprehensible the events of the world.

Here Marx's theory of economics is subordinated to his epic interpretation of the historical process.[1] Here Marx is shown as philosopher, moralist, historian, sociologist, as well as economist. Despite his far-ranging inquiries, an essential unity of thought can be seen in his theory and practice.

In this book, as in my earlier *Marx on Economics,* I have left critical judgment to the reader. Yet it is difficult to hide my admiration for this giant of the nineteenth century. It is not that I wish to promulgate his ideas or that I necessarily think them valid but that I consider them grand in conception, humane, and seminal. Modern social science owes a great deal to Marx. Much modern social analysis of both ideological Marxists and nonideological non-Marxists is informed by Marx, as the introduction will suggest.

I have tried to show Marx in his best light, in spite of the fact that he was not always consistent over the years. Also there is some question as to whether he and Engels understood "materialism" in the same way. In this book, however, Engels and Marx are assumed to be of one mind. They never disagreed publicly, they wrote many books and articles together, and Engels acknowledges their complete agreement, while bowing to the primacy of Marx.

The short introductory essay that follows is something of a misnomer. It is more an appreciation than an introduction. There

[1] In my edited volume *Marx on Economics* (New York: Harcourt, Brace & World, 1961), Marx's economics is made available to the reader in logical and, hopefully, coherent form.

I argue that Marx had some interesting and important ideas. The second introductory essay, written by Jerome Balmuth, will trace Marx's theory of alienation from its philosophical source in Hegel. The reader is encouraged to discover Marx for himself and, if necessary, to supplement this book with one of the innumerable critical works that still flow copiously from the pens of Marxist scholars. All the footnotes appear in the original works, and are included here to maintain fidelity to those works.

My colleagues Jerome Balmuth, in philosophy, and Arnold Sio, in sociology, have read drafts of the various introductions and have offered criticism, for which I am grateful. My wife, Evelyn, has read most of the manuscript with a critical eye to see whether it could be of value to the nonspecialist. My children, Ross and Laurie, have borne their neglect with the degree of patience usual for their ages. Patricia Ryan, who typed the manuscript for *Marx on Economics,* prepared this one with her usual skill and speed. Finally, I wish to acknowledge my indebtedness to the Colgate University Research Fund for financial aid in the typing of this manuscript.

Robert Freedman, Jr.

Colgate University
Hamilton, New York
September, 1967

Contents

Editor's Introduction

At the graveside of Karl Marx, his friend and lifelong collaborator Frederick Engels credited him with two discoveries of surpassing importance—"the law of development of human history [and] the special law of motion governing present-day capitalist mode of production and the bourgeois society that this mode of production has created." [1]

The first discovery, the materialist conception of history, holds that man must satisfy his basic needs for food, shelter, and clothing before he can pursue matters of the mind and spirit. Indeed, the level of subsistence "form[s] the foundation upon which state institutions, the legal conceptions, art, and even ideas on religion" rest.[2]

[1] Speech at the graveside of Karl Marx, by Frederick Engels. Delivered March 17, 1883. *MESW II,* p. 167.

[2] *Ibid.*

The second discovery, the elucidation of the relation between capital and labor, was a "demonstration how, within present society . . . the exploitation of the worker by the capitalist took place." [3]

The materialist interpretation of history, emphasizing the primacy of economics, has often been taken as a denigration of the human race. Marx is charged with asserting that man is *motivated* solely by the desire for "monetary gain and comforts," [4] and that he has no genuine ethical, moral, or spiritual needs. But Engels ridiculed critics who claimed that Marx defended or advocated "materialism [understood as] gluttony, drunkenness, lust of the eye, lust of the flesh, arrogance . . . miserliness, profit-hunting and stock exchange swindles—in short, all the filthy vices in which [the critic] indulges in private." [5]

On the contrary, Marx held the human race in high esteem. He was certain that with the achievement of communism, which in the fullness of historical time lay beyond capitalism, man could be released from his environment and so freed to develop his spiritual nature. Marx the historical materialist stood for the ideal of the moral perfection of the human being in a world of peace and plenty. He believed in the fundamental goodness of human nature and held out the prospect that man would one day live in a world that would enable him to achieve his full potential. But the "real" or "material" world of nature had to be mastered and man's basic physical needs satisfied before his spiritual needs could be met. To this end society had to organize to produce.

Marx argued that the form of productive organization was always related to the level of technological development. The advent of machinery that could vastly increase the productive ability of workers ushered in a form of economic organization that Marx termed "capitalism." But capitalism, Marx saw, was a system of organization at once social and economic in its effects. As an economic system, it required the division of labor for efficient pro-

[3] "Karl Marx," by Frederick Engels, *MESW II,* p. 165.

[4] Erich Fromm, *Marx's Concept of Man* (New York: Frederick Ungar Publishing Co., 1961), p. 2.

[5] *Infra* p. 22.

duction. The goad of hunger that drove man to work and the division of labor that separated him from nature and from his own creativity led to alienation from his true self.

Capitalism was responsible also for the emergence of the class system. Capitalists owned tools while laborers possessed only their own labor power. The laborer, to live, was forced to sell his services to the tool owner on unfavorable terms. The differences in power between those who owned the means of production and those who did not mark the distinction between the two classes—the bourgeoisie and the proletariat. Inequality of economic condition had its analogue in inequality of political and social condition; the bourgeoisie dominated every aspect of social life. What was probably most important about this fact for Marx was that exploitive relationships degraded and dehumanized men, making them selfish and cruel to one another. Man's fundamentally noble nature was thereby corrupted.

Yet Marx eulogized capitalism. He argued that only this system could produce the wealth and productive capacity necessary to set men free. Only this system, harnessing the greed of the capitalist to the engine of economic growth through capital accumulation, could provide the environment within which man could become truly human. The intense and ever increasing suffering of the proletariat, therefore, had a historic purpose. Suffering became the precondition of ultimate freedom.

The bourgeoisie, enjoying their dominant position, not unsurprisingly confused their temporary and transient role in the great plan of history with an ideal and permanent social order. They accepted as natural and right the class system and its supporting institutions. They looked upon the existing constitutions of state, law, religion, and the family as ideal. Marx tried to prove that institutional forms, too, reflected the "real" conditions that lay beneath, and that these conditions were always changing. Capitalism was only the last, albeit the most important, phase in the continuous evolution of history toward the ideal society.

In Marx's view the bourgeoisie developed ideologies (false conceptions of the real world) in support and justification of their class position. They utilized political institutions such as the state and law to ameliorate class conflict, to enforce discipline and to suppress disorder. The bourgeoisie, supported by ideology and all the power of the state, resisted change. In time the proletariat, aroused by their own suffering and taught by revolutionary intellectuals, would perceive the world correctly, seize power, and usher in the ideal social order toward which all history pointed.

While Marx believed in the promise of history, he believed more strongly that man had to act on his own behalf, unlike the European materialists, who regarded him as the passive recipient of external stimuli. Marx believed that it was possible to know the real world only by acting upon it, and by acting one changed it.

Marx's theory of history was evolutionary and optimistic. He did not subscribe to a conspiracy theory. His system required no scapegoats. Capitalist and laborer alike were locked together in a symbiotic relationship, fulfilling their historic function of creating ever increasing wealth at the cost of ever increasing misery for the working class. Ultimately, out of the contradictory or dialectical process by which wealth and misery grew together, there was to evolve a new and higher synthesis—a society not driven to work by necessity, a society without a division of labor, class structure, and exploitive human relationships.

> Only then will the separate individuals be liberated . . . [and] put in a position to acquire the capacity to enjoy this all-sided production of the whole earth the creations of man . . . [and] control . . . those powers, which . . . till now overawed and governed men as powers completely alien to them. . . .[6]

Engels's claim that Marx had discovered "the laws of human history" meant that Marx's socialism was "scientific" in contrast with the "utopian" socialism of his predecessors and contemporaries, a point illuminated by Engels's analysis of the ideas of Robert Owen, Saint Simon, Proudhon, the German communist Weitling, and others. "[All] these [men saw] socialism [as] the expression of absolute truth, reason and justice, [which] has only

[6] Karl Marx and Frederick Engels, *The German Ideology* (New York: International Publishers, 1939), p. 28.

to be discovered to conquer all the world by virtue of its own power." [7] Marxism, by contrast, made socialism scientific by placing it on a "real basis." To discover the causes and cures of misery and strife required an analysis of the events of economic history. Marxism was scientific, wrote Engels, because it tried to extrapolate trends in history by utilizing a model derived from a study of the "real" world. While Marx was studying the etiology of the ills of his day, "utopian" socialists were merely crying out against them. While the "utopians" were mentally constructing ideal social systems to be effected by men of reason and good will through persuasive argument, Marx was organizing the latent power of the working class for political action. Whereas the utopians assumed that "reason" guided men's behavior, Marx taught that "interests" compelled men's actions. While utopians examined their own thoughts for the solution to social problems, Marx examined society. Marx hurled some of his most devastating invective at what he considered the fruitless daydreams of the do-gooders, reformers, and romantic revolutionaries of his day.[8] For both bourgeois Pollyannas, like the economist J. B. Say, and Cassandras, like Thomas Malthus, he had nothing but contempt.

If Engels's claim for Marx's contribution was exaggerated, many of Marx's insights were permanently valuable. If Marx failed to discover "the laws of human history"—if, indeed, they existed to be discovered—he added greatly to our understanding of social processes. If Marx overemphasized the technological and economic environment and its effects on social and human relationships, he still focused the attention of social scientists on the problems of disorganization that derived from the industrial revolution. If Marx's predictions as to the course of capitalist development went awry, what critic of that day was closer to the mark? Whatever unrest Marxist thought provoked in nineteenth-century Europe must be weighed against the callous rationalizations of suffering offered

[7] Engels, "Socialism: Utopian and Scientific," *MESW II,* p. 128.

[8] After 1848 Marx spent much of his political life opposing proposed revolutionary violence. He abhorred senseless bloodshed, which could only fail in its objective and bring hardship and suffering to the people.

by the declining feudal nobility and the emerging industrial class.[9]

While Marx's conclusions were in a scientific sense less than fully verifiable, we must consider the scope of the effort. He tried, after all, to encompass all of history and to explain all social relations and even the structure of human personality. Theories of society and philosophy, economics and politics, art and morality were enveloped by his system. Though Marx's "functionalism" tied institutional and ideological change too closely to technological change, at least he recognized that in *this* epoch, as contrasted with earlier historical epochs, dynamic change was the norm rather than the exception.

For social scientists his analysis of dynamic change has contemporary relevance. In economics, business cycle theory and growth theory are indebted to Marx's understanding that the capitalist process, in Joseph Schumpeter's phrase, revolutionizes society from within.[10] Marx saw that the rhythm of capital accumulation was uneven (under laissez faire), that periods of accumulation and expansion were followed by periods of contraction and unemployment. Though Marx's theory of business cycles was incomplete,[11] he pointed out that the variability of profits accounted for the unevenness of economic activity. He took the position that business cycles were an inherent part of capitalism.[12] Not only did profits account for the business cycle but they accounted for economic growth. Growth could continue, despite cyclical hesitations, so long as the possibility of profit existed. The centrality of profits

[9] My own view is that Marxism then as now became the name and the slogan by which discontent found its voice. Marx wrote about real evils. Much of Marx's descriptive writing in *Capital* and Engels's work in *The Condition of the Working Class* came out of official government documents.

[10] Marx was not entirely original as an economist. He learned basic economic theory from Ricardo, whom he admired. Also, like all other economists before and since, he was deeply in the debt of Adam Smith.

[11] He had no theory of turning points in business cycles. Joseph Schumpeter, an apostle of capitalism, was able to build a lasting and sophisticated explanation of the business cycle upon a Marxist base. His remarkable appreciation of Marx is found in *Capitalism, Socialism and Democracy* (New York: Harper and Bros., 1942), Part I. His monumental work, which shows the influence of Marx, is *Business Cycles* (New York: McGraw-Hill, 1939).

[12] To Schumpeter and others the cyclical aspect of capitalism was a necessary feature of the process of economic growth.

to growth was not new with Marx; classical economics had always taught this. But that profits, over time, were uniquely related to technological innovation (for Marx almost always of a labor-saving type) was the discovery that converted much of economics from a study of conditions of static equilibrium to a study of the process of dynamic change. All important models of economic growth today place technological improvement at their center.[13]

Marx's economics required a sociology. Economic activity occurs within a social structure that must support it in various ways. Marx's theory of classes provided an explanation of both the source of power and the source of values[14] to explain group behavior under capitalism. The bourgeoisie as a social class had the power derived from property ownership to create the social environment necessary to a capitalistic civilization. The bourgeoisie also provided the ideology to justify the use of that power. Out of Marx's theory of classes, which explains differential power, comes the often observed truth that those holding power will generally use it in their own interests. That important branch of sociology which deals with class structure—from the work of Max Weber to that of Lloyd Warner and C. Wright Mills—owes much to Marx's original insights.

Marx's two-class analysis[15] has grown in modern times to a five-

[13] Economics still utilizes comparative statics for many important purposes. But so far as business cycles and economic growth are concerned, Marx's dynamic system represents an important advance over most classical writings.

[14] Values, "the traditions which haunt human minds," were not entirely derived from class relationships. Values and political institutions were often seen as independent forces. See "Engels to Bloch," September 21–22, 1890, *Marx-Engels Selected Correspondence* (Moscow: Foreign Language Publishing House, 1953). There is also internal evidence for this conclusion from the discussion in Engels, *Socialism: Utopian and Scientific* (Chicago: C. H. Kerr and Co., 1912), pp. 37–43.

[15] In *The Eighteenth Brumaire of Louis Bonaparte* (Appendix to Chapter IV) Marx divided the bourgeoisie into "Capital and Landed Property." He also distinguished the "aristocracy of finance" from other bourgeois elements. Further, Marx divided farmers into "Landed Property" and "allotment [small holder] farmers" with conflicting interests. Allotment farmers would be driven out of business by large-scale farming enterprises just as small businessmen would be driven out of business by large monopolists. Further, Marx differentiates the small trading class and larger capitalists.

or even seven-class system, but his original concept remains valuable. Studies show that class position is closely (though not uniquely) related to occupation and wealth and is an important factor in an individual's political, social, and economic outlook and behavior. There can be little doubt that much of political and social life is dominated by the middle and upper middle classes, who tend to interpret events from the perspective of their class. Our capacity to understand political behavior, the sources and uses of power, and the requirements of a democratic political order have benefited enormously from class analysis. If Marx exaggerated the role of class in determining outlook and social policy, if he underestimated our capacity to transcend selfish interests for the public interest, he was explaining by means of group theory the same phenomenon that classical economists had approvingly noted with regard to individuals. While Malthus and others had assumed that selfishness was an inherent human quality, Marx believed that it was socially induced. His emphasis on the social base of values was certainly scientifically more defensible than the earlier, and still popular, assumption of the "natural" depravity of man.[16]

After we have duly credited Marx with important contributions to modern social science, we are compelled to say that his critique of social organization was only peripheral to his basic concern for the quality of human life. His theory of alienation, as expressed in the recently translated *Economic and Philosophic Manuscripts of 1844* (which predate the Communist Manifesto of 1848), is a case in point. According to this theory, man's soul was destroyed by the necessity to wrest a living from nature, particularly under capitalism, where the division of labor reached its ultimate development and man's inhumanity to man, its zenith. The division of labor resulted in the production of objects (goods) in which human labor became congealed. Human labor became an object separated from its human source. Since the objects produced were for exchange or sale rather than for the use of the producer, they were not the expression of an act of creativity but rather an expression

[16] Of course, Marx did assume without scientific justification that under favorable circumstances the "natural" goodness of man would emerge. He did emphasize the plasticity of character as against the view that man was inherently evil and therefore had to be held in constant check.

of the bondage of men that destroyed the creative capacities of men. Because the products of men's labor were appropriated by others for the use of others, producers became alienated. Alienation occurred when men became means rather than ends. When men were manipulated by other men, or by the "system," or by harsh necessity, they were unable to function spontaneously as human beings.

Such thinking continues to be influential. One current explanation of crime, juvenile delinquency, certain mental illnesses, and apathy is that the withdrawn, hostile, or rebellious individual is alienated. He resents his lack of freedom or capacity to seek his own goals successfully. Similarly, a persistent social criticism of the affluent middle class is that it substitutes the acquisition of objects, prestige, and power, which are corrupting and unsatisfying, for the true gratification of man's creative impulses. Marx thought that eliminating private property and producing for "use" rather than for profit could restore men to their true selves. The true self enjoyed positive freedom, the freedom for spontaneous creativity. Such a condition was possible only when men were free from the compulsion to work and free of the coercion of other men. Marx, in common with social reformers of his day, believed that if only the environment could be made perfect, men would live satisfying and happy lives. Today we are more likely to say that a favorable environment is a necessary precondition for positive freedom rather than a guarantee of it. Nevertheless, Marx emphasized the quality of human life, rather than its comforts, and, in the best Western humanist tradition, the inviolability of the human spirit.

It is because Marx expected communism to bring an end to alienation that he has been scornfully characterized as utopian. Marx certainly held man to a higher standard than history has thus far expected him to reach. Marx may have underestimated the permanent necessity for and even desirability of political organization and the division of labor. He may also have failed to see the possibilities for creative activity within the hierarchical structures of modern industrial life. Nevertheless, humanists of his vision often offer us moral goals that elevate our sights and provide exhilarating, if not easily attainable, prospects.

Introduction: Marx and The Philosophers

JEROME BALMUTH

Marx's thought continues to engross men. It retains the fascination of all seminal thought, in that it exhibits a different relevance at different times. In the early part of this century, particularly in the 1920's and 1930's, Marx's work seemed peculiarly prophetic of the profound economic depression of those times. In it was found a clear explanation for the apparent bankruptcy of Western capitalism. Capitalism was doomed to destroy itself because of the contradiction at its heart: its system of private ownership of the social means of production, for private profit. Inevitably this created and sanctioned the concentration of wealth and the exploitation of the mass of propertyless laborers. Capitalism thus germinated its own destruction; for in seeking to maximize private profit it restricted ruthlessly the wages of workers. This produced, paradoxically, surplus goods amid poverty and underconsumption. This was the root of modern economic misery. Its inevitable fruits were social revolution and a new society.

For those difficult decades, Marx's economic thought seemed a wholly persuasive diagnosis of social ills and a clear forecast. In its apparent relevance to all problems, and in its exciting insight into the ever-present conspiratorial forces affecting economic and political conditions, it stirred the imagination and motivated the actions (as it still does) of countless thoughtful men. For these men it satisfied completely the search for a single clue to the real nature of society and change.

But Marx's description of economic and political institutions is no longer pertinent. It is not that it has been shown to be false, at least for the times in which he wrote, but that neither the prophecy nor the ideological ambitions based on it have materialized. The changing nature of capitalism and its continued vitality have deprived the economic analysis of much of its power as the solely significant explanation for social change. But this has not emptied Marx's work of relevance. Seen anew, Marxist thought addresses itself *less* to the inevitable bankruptcy of a defeated capitalism than to the multifarious problems emerging from a triumphant industrialism. In particular, Marx's work provides an important hypothesis about the intimate relationship between the economic conditions of industrial capitalism and the moral and social structure of the society in which it functions. Here Marx emerges, not as a historical or political analyst, but as a social theorist and moral revolutionary whose concern is basically the institutional conditions that threaten human freedom and individuality.

In this role, certain of Marx's claims become particularly significant for this time of modern industrial society. A new pertinence is discovered in his central thesis that to understand the nature of a society—not merely its past, but its present, and the movement of one to the other—one must look carefully at the prevailing social relations for the production and the exchange of goods and services. In the case of modern industrial society, an examination of the various systems of ownership, management, and profit reveal how the socioeconomic structures have affected the noneconomic character of the society: the state, with its political and legal processes, the moral sanctions of that society, as well as its religious, family, and urban institutions. This reinforces the relevance of Marx's distinction between "superstructure" and "substructure," his thesis that social and ideological institutions not only are built on, but necessarily reflect, economic institutions. Such an insight remains valuable whatever the truth of Marxist theory of the historical fate of capitalism.

More significant than ever remains Marx's view of alienation or estrangement. This concept appears in the early *Economic-Philosophical Manuscripts of 1844* and reappears somewhat modified in *Capital.* In this context the claim is that the capitalistic system of production inevitably creates conditions—such as division of labor and private appropriation of goods—in which men find themselves in conflict with the very products they produce, as well as with their fellow producers and the institutions of the society in which they produce. Not merely is man separated from the fruits of his own work, and alienated by competition from his fellow men, but finally, because he has been led to see himself as a commodity, he becomes a non-person, estranged from himself. This diagnosis of the "products" of a society applies not simply to capitalism, but more generally to any organization of industrial production in which men are separated from their products and their fellows. It provides a new insight into the critical ills affecting modern society.

This role of Marx as moral diagnostician and social prophet is hardly surprising if we consider the impact of Marx's thought over the last hundred years. No mere student of political economy, as Marx described himself, could have inspired such a movement were there not implicit in his doctrine a prescription for change and a *telos:* an ideal of a morally perfect world. Marx and Marxists have proclaimed and invited both commitment and action to his vision of a new understanding and a new world. In this book we can find the sources of the critical and moral prescription for mankind. And, because of its continuing relevance, Marx's thought is more than mere intellectual history; it plays an omnipresent role in our contemporary world.

II

It is apparent that in the history of philosophy Marx fits into the school of nineteenth-century critical philosophy emerging from Kant (1724–1804). Though the immediate influences on Marx's thought are Hegel (1770–1831) and Feuerbach (1804–1872), it was Kant who posed the major epistemological and metaphysical questions of that period. Essential to Kant and Kantianism was the revitalized role for reason in the understanding of man and nature. This was a direct rebuttal to Hume's thesis that human reason is essentially a mechanical reflector and collator—a slave of perceptions, both external sensations and internal passions. Kant argued persuasively that no human judgment is without some necessary conceptual form, whether that judgment be on the lowest level of sensibility—mere perceptions of individual objects—or on a higher level of experience where permanence, duration, and relationships are attributed to perceived objects. On each level certain forms or categories are necessarily prior to what is experienced in nature. In perception, these a priori forms are those of space and time. On the level of experience, the understanding utilizes logical categories. It is the understanding that judges what we see before us, *as one thing*—a stone; and *that* object, in the sky, *as* the sun; and the sun as *causing* the warmth of the stone. It is by virtue of such judgments of experience that we have a science of nature: the rational ordering of experiences, culminating in the laws of natural science. Thus science—the objective order of nature—is possible only because of the categories of the human understanding.

Moreover these two levels of reason—perception and understanding—are not enough. The human mind requires an ultimate level of metaphysical or dialectical thought, in which reason strives to uncover totally the conditions of the possibility of all experience. At this point, Kant argued, reason convicts itself of intellectual overambitiousness, and threatens its own coherence. For though reason seeks to explicate all the conditions of experience, one of the conditions it cannot display is the nonrational circumstances that lie behind that to which the categories apply: those "things-in-themselves" which are logically prior to phenomena as experienced. Reason cannot describe such a world independent of the forms and categories, without self-contradiction; thus it displays only a world bounded by reason. It follows that if reason is limited, the world that reason displays must itself be a limited world. This suggests that "world" itself is a rational conception or idea: a construction of reason rather than something to be discovered. To put it briefly, the world is an idea, a limiting concept of reason; it is not a thing or object, for such things are in or part of the world, and the world is not identical with the things that compose it.

Here is a main root of idealism, in general, and Hegelian and Marxian idealism in particular. For if philosophical reflection shows that the world is an idea, so also does it imply that everything in the world—nature and the sciences describing it—are rational reflections of the ideas of men. And if "nature" and "world" are ideas, so too is man's understanding of himself and the freedom he requires to act as a person. Thus the philosopher, through reason, becomes philosophically aware of the limits of the consciousness of man; he becomes *self*-conscious. With the realization of the limits of reason, the philosopher attains clearer understanding of the nature of world and mind. He grows in self-awareness, exemplifying the role of reason realizing its own limits.

The idea that reason can grow in its awareness of its own character and limits is basic to understanding Hegel's so-called dialectical method, which both Feuerbach and Marx adapted for their own uses. Though Hegel's thought is notoriously unclear, the key idea of the dialectic is that of the Socratic dialogue, in which the method of assertion and critical counterassertion or denial develops a new affirmation, expressing the question, and the tentative answer, more clearly than before. In dialogue, the process of verbal interaction develops, for the participants, a higher level of comprehensiveness as well as of clarity and of understanding. Hegel's thought is that Kant's critical understanding of the limits of reason *itself* reflects a new and higher stage in the development of reason. The mistake is to think that this process of philosophic awareness must halt at any one point in time, rather than continue to even higher forms. For reason is not a fixed faculty; it is a constantly changing and developing method of self-realization and discovery. Its absolute movement is from the particular and exclusive to the universal or inclusive, and from the partial to the whole or concrete. Moreover, since new forms of ideas are necessarily new forms of things (for Hegel, ontology reflects ideology), so there is a corresponding growth and development of all reality. We can illustrate this by comparing our present idea of nature, the world of Einsteinian relativity, with the far different earth-centered world of Ptolemy. The process of arriving at this new conception of the world was a dialectical one, occurring in history. Incompatible observations and reflections were, in time, reconciled into a new cosmology. This process can hold as well for the science of man, psychology, as for the study of society.

We might summarize Hegel's view, and its connection with Kant, as follows: There is an absolute movement, in consciousness and reality, of the idea of "world." Hegel calls this movement and its end the Absolute Idea, World Spirit, or "Geist." The historical movement of the Absolute Idea follows the dialectical form of a continuous triadic development to rational fulfillment. The nature of this concrete whole is understandable only by philosophic reflection.

In this way, Kant's logical analysis of the limits of reason is given an historical interpretation by Hegel. What Kant saw to be revealed immediately and finally by his transcendental analysis, Hegel held to be only a stage in the progressively unfolding revelation of man's ideas of himself and nature. In the case of nature, the highest—most universal and concrete, though not final—realization of reason is in the growing natural sciences; in the case of the self or spirit, it is the renewing forms of art, religion, and ultimately philosophy. Two principles essential to Hegel's logic of dialectical development are worth emphasizing for the part they play for Marx. The first is that nothing in the world just *is;* everything has to be of a certain *sort.* But characterizing the sort of a thing is not merely saying what it is, but what it is *not.* Thus nothing—no event, no state of affairs—can be understood apart from its negation, or what it is not. Moreover, in so far as something comes out of something else, in time, it is necessarily different from its predecessor. Thus dialectical movement seems to involve a change from one thing to its contrary or contradiction, to a higher level of development. Here is an important source for Marx's claim that social institutions develop out of antecedent, even if apparently opposite, social institutions, and evolve to more advanced states.

Secondly, no event or circumstance—indeed, no person or thing—is completely unrelated to any other, either immediate or remote. The occurrence or nonoccurrence of one part of a whole affects and changes other parts, and so the whole. Thus a complete explanation of the meaning of an event, e.g., a particular political or social event, requires the relating, both in space and time, of the effects of that event on others, and on the whole. It follows that no historical event is without economic, social, or political effects, and vice versa.

These two principles suggest the force of Hegel's rationalism on Marx. If no occurrence is without some relationship to the whole, and is explicable only by showing its connection in space and time with other occurrences, then there are no *wholly* independent, totally accidental events either in the universe or in society. Reality is rationally connected in a concrete whole; the real is rational, and what is rational is real. It follows that nothing in reality, whether physical, human, or social in nature, changes without a cause. Moreover we can uncover the causes for human and social events, as we can for physical events, by studying the whole phenomenon. Thus we can discover the laws of society, as we have those of nature, by observing the historical changes in society. This theory of social change is the real legacy to Marx of Hegel's rationalism. Instead of the Absolute Idea, Marx held that it was human society that develops in history, in a dialectical pattern and in accord with laws that can be discovered by its students—the social scientists. In this respect Marx might be termed the first great social scientist.

III

Ludwig Feuerbach is a somewhat neglected figure in philosophy, and were his acknowledged influence on Marx not so important as to be ranked with Hegel's, his work would have even less attention than it deserves on its own. He did, however, arrive on the scene at an appropriate time and with an important doctrine, which allowed Hegelianism to be turned to the analysis of man and society. What Feuerbach argued was that Hegel's emphasis on man as mind or self-consciousness put the focus in the wrong place: for man realizes his own identity only in his awareness of the objects to which he relates as subject.

> In the object which he contemplates, . . . man becomes acquainted with himself; consciousness of the objective is the self-consciousness of man. We know the man by the object, by his conception of what is external to himself; in it his nature becomes evident; this object is his manifested nature, his true objective *ego*. And this is true not merely of spiritual but also of sensuous objects.[1]

It is principally spiritual objects with which Feuerbach is concerned in his masterwork *The Essence of Christianity*. His thesis is that religion and Christianity, as well as specific doctrines and rituals are, at their heart, idealized projections of man's own human nature. Thus, in reality, man worships himself—not as he is, but as feeling tells him he would like to be, fully and finally. God is simply man's Ideal Self conceived impersonally and objectively, and worshiped absolutely as Ultimate Substance. Man, in fact, requires God to express objectively, as Being, his own consciousness and sense of personal identity. The fact is, Feuerbach says, "consciousness of God is self-consciousness, knowledge of God is self-knowledge . . . religion is man's earliest and also indirect form of self-knowledge."[2] This is the anthropological essence of religion that reveals the nature of God as man's projection of himself.

Feuerbach is described, usually, as a materialist, and is credited

[1] Ludwig Feuerbach, *The Essence of Christianity,* trans. G. Eliot (New York: Harper & Row [Harper Torchbook], 1957), page 5.
[2] *Ibid.,* pp. 12–13.

by Engels with turning Marx's Hegelianism from its emphasis on the dialectical development of the Absolute Idea to the historical development of man and society. But this characterization, while correct, understates Feuerbach's own debt to Hegel. It is true that Feuerbach argues that religion, and its central ideas, are wholly reducible to anthropology, i.e., to man's psychical and ultimately physical nature. But the force of his work is still theoretical and speculative: to show that the idea of "God" is an ideal expression of man's self-awareness as universal species. Feuerbach thus shares with Hegel the presumption that religion must and can be explained best, philosophically, as an epiphenomenal manifestation of the universal Idea. In his "Theses on Feuerbach," Marx argued that this Hegelian form of explanation was inadequate, for a thoroughgoing materialism requires that the cleavage that Feuerbach describes between religion and the real world must *itself* be explicable on a nonidealistic, i.e., a materialistic basis.

Now, Marx argued, a true materialistic basis is not the simplistic world of "sensuous objects" or pure matter. This is the world that early materialists conceived, ideally, as existing independent of spirit or mind. Such a material world, Marx says, is merely another product of "the theoretical attitude," of a defective "contemplative materialism." On the contrary, the true material basis of the world is the world of practical activity, of economic and social action. The real world is not a philosophical concoction, but is rather the world of direct engagement, in which mind interacts with human society and physical nature. In the real world the human spirit is expressed in actions.

Thus, Marx is both less Hegelian than Feuerbach but more Hegelian than the materialism of Engels would admit. If, as Hegel said, "world" is a developing idea or "spirit," it cannot, contrary to Hegel, be *fixed abstractly* by any philosopher who is in the world only at one time. Rather the task of philosophy—or mind—is to free man from speculative, idle metaphysics so that he can engage in social action and *produce* his world. Engels's and Feuerbach's claim that mind is a product of the process of nature is as much a half truth for Marx as is the idealist's view that nature is a pure product of mind. Both of these beliefs are, Marx says, purely "scholastic"; they are typical results of attitudes that neglect the possibility of "revolutionary practical-critical activity." The correct role of philosophy is to show that the world is a *social product;* both reflected in, and changed by, man's ideas and practices. Once this is seen clearly, philosophy has nothing more to contribute. The rest is social action. Thus Marx says "philosophers have only *interpreted* the world in various ways; the point, however, is to *change it*" (*Theses on Feuerbach*).

From that point on, Marx had no further use for contemplative or theoretical philosophy. Having arrived at a philosophical position in which direct engagement and change—to produce—is the purpose of human thought, Marx's subsequent work was directed toward the analysis of society to effect such change. It is here that his theory of social change is pertinent. He argues that the economic mode of production and exchange produces social classes, so that class distinctions have their source and rationale in economic relationships. The culmination of this thought for action is the Communist Manifesto, with its call for the abolition of classes.

In spite of this frontal attack on speculative philosophy, however, we must not think that Marx had no philosophical commitment. We should not confuse Marx's philosophical view that human thought must be expressed in action with the idea that Marx abandoned philosophy. He abandoned only philosophy that conceived of thought as, in principle, contemplation divorced from social action. Moreover, whether or not he abandoned contemplative philosophy, it is clear that he had philosophical presuppositions. For the injunction "Change the world!" can have point only where there is certainty of some philosophical ideal or end, to be brought about practically, either immediately or ultimately. In Marx's case such a clear practical purpose permeates his writing: to bring about a world in which men are no longer separated from their products, their fellow men, or themselves. In the following pages the reader will see how this idea for action illuminates Marx's thought.

Department of Philosophy
Colgate University
Hamilton, New York
September, 1967

MARXIST SOCIAL THOUGHT

I

From Hegel to Feuerbach to Marx

Introduction

This chapter will enable the reader to trace, in part, the Hegelian sources of Marx's thought. The opening selection of the section entitled "Critique of Hegel and Feuerbach," which was written by Frederick Engels, suggests the historical context in which Marx wrote and provides a concise statement of his criticism of Hegel and Feuerbach.

Hegelian idealism gripped the imagination of an entire generation of brilliant intellectuals, including Marx and Engels. But it was Ludwig Feuerbach's Essence of Christianity *that provided the necessary breakthrough enabling Marx to transform Hegelian idealism into a form of materialism, a form that some philosophers today speak of as "historical naturalism" or "dialectical materialism." The remaining selections in Chapter I contain Marx's own critical evaluation of Hegel and Feuerbach, and the appendix to the chapter, entitled "The Dialectic Method," is Marx's own state-*

ment of the meaning of the term "dialectical," which plays so important a role in Marx's theory of change.

In the autocratic Russia of the 1830's and 1840's social issues could not be discussed directly but could be argued only behind the cloak of religious disputes. Although Hegel's greatest work, The Phenomenology of Mind, *was concerned with theological questions, it became for Marx the vehicle for questioning the entire social order. In the book Hegel dealt critically with the aspect of the Hebraic-Christian tradition—"absolute religion"—that placed a supermundane God above man. In Hegel's work the traditional dualism between God and the world disappears.*

For Hegel, as for revealed religion, God is incarnate: spirit revealed in the world. God is thus the unity of spirit and world thought (or essence) and existence, knowledge and self-knowledge. He is Absolute Spirit: the self-conscious mind revealing Himself in the actions of men in history. World history is the actual stage on which God—Infinite Being—fulfills Himself, becoming thereby self-conscious.

This process of developing self-consciousness follows the characteristic dialectical confrontation of Spirit, revealed in man and Nature—the world apart from man. Each is an incomplete aspect of reason: the Idea. The Idea is, in this sense, alienated from its own self, much as a man's actions may be alien to his own idea of himself, to his own self-understanding. Such an alienation is overcome by self-knowledge. For the World-Idea dichotomy is bridged by the philosophical understanding of the character and meaning of human history: the growth of the consciousness of freedom. World history is, in reality, the tortured history of man's progressive liberation through self-realization. Through his understanding of world history man gains his freedom. In this freedom lies his fulfillment and his understanding of God's plan. When this fulfillment is final or absolute, men know what it is for God to be God; he is free, and history presumably comes to an end. Hegel and Marx had in common, then, this idea of the Ideal fulfillment of history—an eschatology—with the liberation of man as its end.

It is because world history, as the actualization of freedom, takes place, so to speak, within the mind of man that Hegel's philosophy is referred to as "idealism." Ultimate reality is found in the "Absolute Idea" in the "Universe of Reason." The objective world, which needs to be overcome through self-knowledge, has reality only in our ideas about it.

Engels also explains in the first selection how the Prussian authorities saw in Hegelian idealism a justification of the status quo. Hegel's statement that "all that is real is rational; and all that is rational is real," which is a statement about unity of spirit as man, and spirit as object, was taken to mean that whatever exists (here, the Prussian state) is necessary and rational. In this fashion a very conservative political conclusion was drawn from a nominally radical religious statement.

Engels credits Ludwig Feuerbach with providing Marx the key to converting Hegel's apparently conservative doctrine to revolutionary purposes. Feuerbach argued that reality was rooted in the world rather than in the mind. Feuerbach turned Hegel "upside down." Whereas Hegel thought of man as God revealed, the essence of Feuerbach's message was the reverse—God is man revealed.

Feuerbach argued that God is simply an idealization of that perfect condition for which religious men yearn. Since God was infinite and man finite, religious man suffered because of his finiteness. Suffering expressed itself as a form of self-alienation: man critical of his own shortcomings. The central idea, taken over whole by Marx, was that the objective world was real and that man's alienation from his true self was due, not to his sinful failure to realize his ultimate self in God, but rather to the miserable conditions of his life in the world.

Thus Hegel's dialectical method, his theory of history and progress, and his belief in the perfectibility of man, were enlisted by Marx in the revolutionary movement, with all the Messianic fervor of an Old Testament prophet.

Critique of Hegel and Feuerbach

I

The volume[1] before us carries us back to a period which, although in time no more than a generation behind us, has become as foreign to the present generation in Germany as if it were already a hundred years old. Yet it was the period of Germany's preparation for the Revolution of 1848; and all that has happened since then in our country has been merely a continuation of 1848, merely the execution of the last will and testament of the revolution.

Just as in France in the eighteenth century, so in Germany in the nineteenth, a philosophical revolution ushered in the political collapse. But how different the two looked! The French were in open combat against all official science, against the church and often also against the state; their writings were printed across the frontier, in Holland or England, while they themselves were often in jeopardy of imprisonment in the Bastille. On the other hand, the Germans were professors, state-appointed instructors of youth; their writings were recognized textbooks, and the terminating system of the whole development—the Hegelian system—was even raised, as it were, to the rank of a royal Prussian philosophy of state! Was it possible that a revolution could hide behind these professors, behind their obscure, pedantic phrases, their ponderous, wearisome sentences? Were not precisely those people who were then regarded as the representatives of the revolution, the liberals, the bitterest opponents of this brain-confusing philosophy? But what neither the government nor the liberals saw was seen at least by one man as early as 1833, and this man was indeed none other than Heinrich Heine.

Let us take an example. No philosophical proposition has earned

[1] *Ludwig Feuerbach,* by K. N. Starcke, Ph.D., Stuttgart. Ferd. Enke. 1885 [*note by Engels*].

more gratitude from narrow-minded governments and wrath from equally narrow-minded liberals than Hegel's famous statement: "All that is real is rational; and all that is rational is real." That was tangibly a sanctification of things that be, a philosophical benediction bestowed upon despotism, police government, Star Chamber proceedings and censorship. That is how Frederick William III and how his subjects understood it. But according to Hegel certainly not everything that exists is also real, without further qualification. For Hegel the attribute of reality belongs only to that which at the same time is necessary: "in the course of its development reality proves to be necessity." A particular governmental measure—Hegel himself cites the example of "a certain tax regulation"—is therefore for him by no means real without qualification. That which is necessary, however, proves itself in the last resort to be also rational; and, applied to the Prussian state of that time, the Hegelian proposition, therefore, merely means: this state is rational, corresponds to reason, in so far as it is necessary; and if it nevertheless appears to us to be evil, but still, in spite of its evil character, continues to exist, then the evil character of the government is justified and explained by the corresponding evil character of its subjects. The Prussians of that day had the government that they deserved.

Now, according to Hegel, reality is, however, in no way an attribute predicable of any given state of affairs, social or political, in all circumstances and at all times. On the contrary. The Roman Republic was real, but so was the Roman Empire, which superseded it. In 1789 the French monarchy had become so unreal, that is to say, so robbed of all necessity, so irrational, that it had to be destroyed by the Great Revolution, of which Hegel always speaks with the greatest enthusiasm. In this case, therefore, the monarchy was the unreal and the revolution the real. And so, in the course of development, all that was previously real becomes unreal, loses its necessity, its right of existence, its rationality. And in the place of moribund reality comes a new, viable reality—peacefully if the old has enough intelligence to go to its death without a struggle; forcibly if it resists this necessity. Thus the Hegelian proposition turns into its opposite through Hegelian dialectics itself: All that is real in the sphere of human history becomes irrational in the process of time, is therefore irrational by its very destination, is tainted beforehand with irrationality; and everything which is rational in the minds of men is destined to become real, however much it may contradict existing apparent reality. In accordance with all the rules of the Hegelian method of thought, the proposition of the rationality of everything which is real resolves itself into the other proposition: All that exists deserves to perish.

But precisely therein lay the true significance and the revolutionary character of the Hegelian philosophy (to which, as the close of the whole movement since Kant, we must here confine ourselves), that it once for all dealt the death blow to the finality of all products of human thought and action. Truth, the cognition of which is the business of philosophy, was in the hands of Hegel no longer an aggregate of finished dogmatic statements, which, once discovered, had merely to be learned by heart. Truth lay now in the process of cognition itself, in the long historical development of science, which mounts from lower to ever higher levels of knowledge without ever reaching, by discovering so-called absolute truth, a point at which it can proceed no further, where it would have nothing more to do than to fold its hands and gaze with wonder at the absolute truth to which it had attained. And what holds good for the realm of philosophical knowledge holds good also for that of every other kind of knowledge and also for practical action. Just as knowledge is unable to reach a complete conclusion in a perfect, ideal condition of humanity, so is history unable to do so; a perfect society, a perfect "state," are things which can only exist in imagination. On the contrary, all successive historical systems are only transitory stages in the endless course of development of human society from the lower to the higher. Each stage is necessary, and therefore justified for the time and conditions to which it owes its origin. But in the face of new, higher conditions which gradually develop in its own womb, it loses its validity and justification. It must give way to a higher stage which will also in its turn decay and perish. Just as the bourgeoisie by large-scale industry, competition and the world market dissolves in practice all stable time-honoured institutions, so this dialectical philosophy dissolves all conceptions of final, absolute truth and of absolute states of humanity corresponding to it. For it [dialectical philosophy] nothing is final, absolute, sacred. It reveals the transitory character of everything and in everything; nothing can endure before it except the uninterrupted process of becoming and passing away, of endless ascendancy from the lower to the higher. And dialectical philosophy itself is nothing more than the mere reflection of this process in the thinking brain. It has, of course, also a conservative side: it recognizes that definite stages of knowledge and society are justified for their time and circumstances; but only so far. The conservatism of this mode of outlook is relative; its revolutionary character is absolute—the only absolute dialectical philosophy admits.

It is not necessary, here, to go into the question of whether this mode of outlook is thoroughly in accord with the present state of natural science, which predicts a possible end even for the earth, and for its habitability a fairly certain one; which therefore recognizes that for the history of mankind, too, there is not only an ascending but also a descending branch. At any rate we still find ourselves a considerable distance from the turning-point at which the historical course of society becomes one of descent, and we cannot expect Hegelian philosophy to be concerned with a subject which natural science, in its time, had not at all placed upon the agenda as yet.

But what must, in fact, be said here is this: that in Hegel the views developed above are not so sharply delineated. They are a necessary conclusion from his method, but one which he himself never drew with such explicitness. And this, indeed, for the simple reason that he was compelled to make a system and, in accordance with traditional requirements, a system of philosophy must conclude with some sort of absolute truth. Therefore, however much Hegel, especially in his *Logic,* emphasized that this eternal truth is nothing but the logical, or, the historical, process itself, he nevertheless finds himself compelled to supply this process with an end, just because he has to bring his system to a termination at some point or other. In his *Logic* he can make this end a beginning again, since here the point of conclusion, the absolute idea—which is only absolute in so far as he has absolutely nothing to say about it—"alienates," that is, transforms, itself into nature and comes to itself again later in the mind, that is, in thought and in history. But at the end of the whole philosophy a similar return to the beginning is possible only in one way. Namely, by conceiving of the end of history as follows: mankind arrives at the cognition of this selfsame absolute idea, and declares that this cognition of the absolute idea is reached in Hegelian philosophy. In this way, however, the whole dogmatic content of the Hegelian system is declared to be absolute truth, in contradiction to his dialectical method, which dissolves all dogmatism. Thus the revolutionary side is smothered beneath the overgrowth of the conservative side. And what applies to philosophical cognition applies also to historical practice. Mankind, which, in the person of Hegel, has reached the point of working out the absolute idea, must also in practice have gotten so far that it can carry out this absolute idea in reality. Hence the practical political demands of the absolute idea on contemporaries may not be stretched too far. And so we find at the conclusion of the *Philosophy of Right* that the absolute idea is to be realized in that monarchy based on social estates which Frederick William III so persistently but vainly promised to his subjects, that is, in a limited, moderate, indirect rule of the possessing classes suited to the petty-bourgeois German conditions of that time; and, moreover, the necessity of the nobility is demonstrated to us in a speculative fashion.

The inner necessities of the system are, therefore, of themselves sufficient to explain why a thoroughly revolutionary method of thinking produced an extremely tame political conclusion. As a matter of fact the specific form of this conclusion springs from this, that Hegel was a German, and like his contemporary Goethe had a bit of the Philistine's queue dangling behind. Each of them was an Olympian Zeus in his own sphere, yet neither of them ever quite freed himself from German Philistinism.

But all this did not prevent the Hegelian system from covering an incomparably greater domain than any earlier system, nor from developing in this domain a wealth of thought which is astounding even today. The phenomenology of mind (which one may call a parallel of the embryology and palaeontology of the mind, a development of individual consciousness through its different stages, set in the form of an abbreviated reproduction of the stages through which the consciousness of man has passed in the course of history), logic, natural philosophy, philosophy of mind, and the latter worked out in its separate, historical subdivisions: philosophy of history, of right, of religion, history of philosophy, aesthetics, etc. —in all these different historical fields Hegel laboured to discover and demonstrate the pervading thread of development. And as he was not only a creative genius but also a man of encyclopaedic erudition, he played an epoch-making role in every sphere. It is self-evident that owing to the needs of the "system" he very often had to resort to those forced constructions about which his pigmy opponents make such a terrible fuss even today. But these constructions are only the frame and scaffolding of his work. If one does not loiter here needlessly, but presses on farther into the immense building, one finds innumerable treasures which today still possess undiminished value. With all philosophers it is precisely the "system" which is perishable; and for the simple reason that it springs from an imperishable desire of the human mind—the desire to overcome all contradictions. But if all contradictions are once for all disposed of, we shall have arrived at so-called absolute truth—world history will be at an end. And yet it has to continue, although there is nothing left for it to do—hence, a new, insoluble contradiction. As soon as we have once realized—and in the long run no one has helped us to realize it more than Hegel himself—that the task of philosophy thus stated means nothing but the task that a single philosopher should accomplish that which can only be accomplished by the entire human race in its progressive development—as soon as we realize that, there is an end to all philosophy in the hitherto accepted sense of the word. One leaves alone "absolute truth," which is unattainable along this path or by any single individual; instead, one pursues attainable relative truths along the path of the positive sciences, and the summation of their results by means of dialectical thinking. At any rate, with Hegel philosophy comes to an end: on the one hand, because in his system he summed up its whole development in the most splendid fashion; and on the other hand, because, even though unconsciously, he showed us the way out of the labyrinth of systems to real positive knowledge of the world.

One can imagine what a tremendous effect this Hegelian system must have produced in the philosophy-tinged atmosphere of Germany. It was a triumphal procession which lasted for decades and which by no means came to a standstill on the death of Hegel. On the contrary, it was precisely from 1830 to 1840 that "Hegelianism" reigned most exclusively, and to a greater or lesser extent infected even its opponents. It was precisely in this period that Hegelian views, consciously or unconsciously, most extensively penetrated the most diversified sciences and leavened even popular literature and the daily press, from which the average "educated consciousness" drives its mental pabulum. But this victory along the whole front was only the prelude to an internal struggle.

As we have seen, the doctrine of Hegel, taken as a whole, left plenty of room for giving shelter to the most diverse practical party views. And in the theoretical Germany of that time, two things above all were practical: religion and politics. Whoever placed the chief emphasis on the Hegelian *system* could be fairly conservative in both spheres; whoever regarded the dialectical *method* as the main thing could belong to the most extreme opposition, both in politics and religion. Hegel himself, despite the fairly frequent outbursts of revolutionary wrath in his works, seemed on the whole to be more inclined to the conservative side. Indeed, his system had cost him much more "hard mental plugging" than his method. Towards the end of the thirties, the cleavage in the school became more and more apparent. The Left wing, the so-called Young Hegelians, in their fight with the pietist orthodox and the feudal reactionaries, abandoned bit by bit that philosophical-genteel reserve in regard to the burning questions of the day which up to that time had secured state toleration and even protection for their teachings. And when, in 1840, orthodox pietism and absolutist feudal reaction ascended the throne with Frederick William IV, open partisanship became unavoidable. The fight was still carried on with philosophical weapons, but no longer for abstract philosophical aims. It turned directly on the destruction of traditional religion and of the existing state. And while in the *Deutsche Jahrbücher* the practical ends were still predominantly put forward in philosophical disguise, in the *Rheinische Zeitung* of 1842 the Young Hegelian school revealed itself directly as the philosophy of the aspiring radical bourgeoisie and used the meagre cloak of philosophy only to deceive the censorship.

. . .

Then came *Feuerbach's Essence of Christianity*. With one blow it pulverized the contradiction, in that without circumlocutions it placed materialism on the throne again. Nature exists independently of all philosophy. It is the foundation upon which we human beings, ourselves products of nature, have grown up. Nothing exists outside nature and man, and the higher beings our religious fantasies have created are only the fantastic reflection of our own essence. The spell was broken; the "system" was exploded and cast aside, and the contradiction, shown to exist only in our imagination, was dissolved. One must himself have experienced the liberating effect of this book to get an idea of it. Enthusiasm was general; we all became at once Feuerbachians. How enthusiastically Marx greeted the new conception and how much—in spite of all critical reservations—he was influenced by it, one may read in *The Holy Family*.

Even the shortcomings of the book contributed to its immediate effect. Its literary, sometimes even high-flown, style secured for it a large public and was at any rate refreshing after long years of abstract and abstruse Hegelianizing. The same is true of its extravagant deification of love, which, coming after the now intolerable sovereign rule of "pure reason," had its excuse, if not justification. But what we must not forget is that it was precisely these two weaknesses of Feuerbach that "true Socialism," which had been spreading like a plague in "educated" Germany since 1844, took as its starting-point, putting literary phrases in the place of scientific knowledge, the liberation of mankind by means of "love" in place of the emancipation of the proletariat through the economic transformation of production—in short, losing itself in the nauseous fine writing and ecstasies of love typified by Herr Karl Grün.

Another thing we must not forget is this: the Hegelian school disintegrated, but Hegelian philosophy was not overcome through criticism; Strauss and Bauer each took one of its sides and set it polemically against the other. Feuerbach broke through the system and simply discarded it. But a philosophy is not disposed of by the mere assertion that it is false. And so powerful a work as Hegelian philosophy, which had exercised so enormous an influence on the intellectual development of the nation, could not be disposed of by simply being ignored. It had to be "sublated" in its own sense, that is, in the sense that while its form had to be annihilated through criticism, the new content which had been won through it had to be saved. How this was brought about we shall see below.

. . .

II

The great basic question of all philosophy, especially of more recent philosophy, is that concerning the relation of thinking and being. From the very early times when men, still completely ignorant of the structure of their own bodies, under the stimulus of dream apparitions[1] came to believe that their thinking and sensation were not activities of their bodies, but of a distinct soul which inhabits the body and leaves it at death—from this time men have been driven to reflect about the relation between this soul and the outside world. If upon death it took leave of the body and lived on, there was no occasion to invent yet another distinct death for it. Thus arose the idea of its immortality, which at that stage of development appeared not at all as a consolation but as a fate against which it was no use fighting, and often enough, as among the Greeks, as a positive misfortune. Not religious desire for consolation, but the quandary arising from the common universal ignorance of what to do with this soul, once its existence had been accepted, after the death of the body, led in a general way to the

[1] Among savages and lower barbarians the idea is still universal that the human forms which appear in dreams are souls which have temporarily left their bodies; the real man is, therefore, held responsible for acts committed by his dream apparition against the dreamer. Thus Imthurn found this belief current, for example, among the Indians of Guiana in 1884 [*note by Engels*].

tedious notion of personal immortality. In an exactly similar manner the first gods arose through the personification of natural forces. And these gods in the further development of religions assumed more and more an extra-mundane form, until finally by a process of abstraction, I might almost say of distillation, occurring naturally in the course of man's intellectual development, out of the many more or less limited and mutually limiting gods there arose in the minds of men the idea of the one exclusive God of the monotheistic religions.

Thus the question of the relation of thinking to being, the relation of the spirit to nature—the paramount question of the whole of philosophy—has, no less than all religion, its roots in the narrow-minded and ignorant notions of savagery. But this question could for the first time be put forward in its whole acuteness, could achieve its full significance, only after humanity in Europe had awakened from the long hibernation of the Christian Middle Ages. The question of the position of thinking in relation to being, a question which, by the way, had played a great part also in the scholasticism of the Middle Ages, the question: which is primary, spirit or nature—that question, in relation to the church, was sharpened into this: Did God create the world or has the world been in existence eternally?

The answers which the philosophers gave to this question split them into two great camps. Those who asserted the primacy of spirit to nature and, therefore, in the last instance, assumed world creation in some form or other—and among the philosophers, Hegel, for example, this creation often becomes still more intricate and impossible than in Christianity—comprised the camp of idealism. The others, who regarded nature as primary, belong to the various schools of materialism.

These two expressions, idealism and materialism, originally signify nothing else but this; and here too they are not used in any other sense. What confusion arises when some other meaning is put into them will be seen below.

But the question of the relation of thinking and being has yet another side: in what relation do our thoughts about the world surrounding us stand to this world itself? Is our thinking capable of the cognition of the real world? Are we able in our ideas and notions of the real world to produce a correct reflection of reality? In philosophical language this question is called the question of the identity of thinking and being, and the overwhelming majority of philosophers give an affirmative answer to this question. With Hegel, for example, its affirmation is self-evident; for what we cognize in the real world is precisely its thought-content—that which makes the world a gradual realization of the absolute idea, which absolute idea has existed somewhere from eternity, independent of the world and before the world. But it is manifest without further proof that thought can know a content which is from the outset a thought-content. It is equally manifest that what is to be proved here is already tacitly contained in the premises. But that in no way prevents Hegel from drawing the further conclusion from his proof of the identity of thinking and being that his philosophy, because it is correct for his thinking, is therefore the only correct one, and that the identity of thinking and being must prove its validity by mankind immediately translating his philosophy from theory into practice and transforming the whole world according to Hegelian principles. This is an illusion which he shares with well-nigh all philosophers.

In addition there is yet a set of different philosophers—those who question the possibility of any cognition, or at least of an exhaustive cognition, of the world. To them, among the more modern ones, belong Hume and Kant, and they have played a very important role in philosophical development. What is decisive in the refutation of this view has already been said by Hegel, in so far as this was possible from an idealist standpoint. The materialistic additions made by Feuerbach are more ingenious than profound. The most telling refutation of this as of all other philosophical crotchets is practice, namely, experiment and industry. If we are able to prove the correctness of our conception of a natural process by making it ourselves, bringing it into being out of its conditions and making it serve our own purposes into the bargain, then there is an end to the Kantian ungraspable "thing-in-itself."

. . .

The course of evolution of Feuerbach is that of a Hegelian—a never quite orthodox Hegelian, it is true—into a materialist; an evolution which at a definite stage necessitates a complete rupture with the idealist system of his predecessor. With irresistible force Feuerbach is finally driven to the realization that the Hegelian premundane existence of the "absolute idea," the "pre-existence of the logical categories" before the world existed, is nothing more than the fantastic survival of the belief in the existence of an extramundane creator; that the material, sensuously perceptible world to which we ourselves belong is the only reality; and that our consciousness and thinking, however suprasensuous they may seem, are the product of a material, bodily organ, the brain. Matter is not a product of mind, but mind itself is merely the highest product of matter. This is, of course, pure materialism. But, having got so far, Feuerbach stops short. He cannot overcome the customary philosophical prejudice, prejudice not against the thing but against the name materialism. He says: "To me materialism is the foundation of the edifice of human essence and knowledge; but to me it is not what it is to the physiologist, to the natural scientist in the narrower sense, for example, to Moleschott, and necessarily is from their standpoint and profession, namely, the edifice itself. Backwards I fully agree with the materialists; but not forwards."

Here Feuerbach lumps together the materialism that is a general world outlook resting upon a definite conception of the relation between matter and mind, and the special form in which this world outlook was expressed at a definite historical stage, namely, in the eighteenth century. More than that, he lumps it with the shallow, vulgarized form in which the materialism of the eighteenth century continues to exist today in the heads of naturalists and physicians, the form which was preached on their tours in the fifties by Büchner, Vogt and Moleschott. But just as idealism underwent a series of stages of development, so also did materialism. With each epoch-making discovery even in the sphere of natural science it has to change its form; and after history also was subjected to materialistic treatment, a new avenue of development has opened here too.

The materialism of the last century was predominantly mechanical, because at that time, of all natural sciences, only mechanics, and indeed only the mechanics of solid bodies—celestial and terrestrial—in short, the mechanics of gravity, had come to any definite close. Chemistry at that time existed only in its infantile, phlogistic form. Biology still lay in swaddling clothes; vegetable and animal organisms had been only roughly examined and were explained as the result of purely mechanical cause. What the animal was to Descartes, man was to the materialists of the eighteenth century—a machine. This exclusive application of the standards of mechanics to processes of a chemical and organic nature—in which processes the laws of mechanics are, indeed, also valid, but are pushed into the background by other, higher laws—constitutes the first specific but at that time inevitable limitation of classical French materialism.

The second specific limitation of this materialism lay in its inability to comprehend the universe as a process, as matter undergoing uninterrupted historical development. This was in accordance with the level of the natural science of that time, and with the metaphysical, that is, anti-dialectical manner of philosophizing connected with it. Nature, so much was known, was in eternal motion. But according to the ideas of that time, this motion turned, also eternally, in a circle and therefore never moved from the spot; it produced the same results over and over again. This conception was at that time inevitable. The Kantian theory of the origin of the solar system had been put forward but recently and was still regarded merely as a curiosity. The history of the development of the earth, geology, was still totally unknown, and the conception that the animate natural beings of today are the result of a long sequence of development from the simple to the complex could not at that time scientifically be put forward at all. The unhistorical view of nature was therefore inevitable. We have the less reason to reproach the philosophers of the eighteenth century on this account since the same thing is found in Hegel. According to him, nature, as a mere "alienation" of the idea, is incapable of development in time—capable only of extending its manifoldness in space, so that it displays simultaneously and alongside of one another all the stages of development comprised in it, and is condemned to an eternal repetition of the same processes. This absurdity of a development in space, but outside of time—the fundamental condition of all development—Hegel imposes upon nature just at the very time when geology, embryology, the physiology of plants and animals, and organic chemistry were being built up, and when everywhere on the basis of these new sciences brilliant foreshadowings of the later theory of evolution were appearing (for instance, Goethe and Lamarck). But the system demanded it; hence the method, for the sake of the system, had to become untrue to itself.

This same unhistorical conception prevailed also in the domain of history. Here the struggle against the remnants of the Middle Ages blurred the view. The Middle Ages were regarded as a mere interruption of history by a thousand years of universal barbarism. The great progress made in the Middle Ages—the extension of the area of European culture, the viable great nations taking form there next to each other, and finally the enormous technical progress of the fourteenth and fifteenth centuries—all this was not seen. Thus a rational insight into the great historical interconnections was made impossible, and history served at best as a collection of examples and illustrations for the use of philosophers.

The vulgarizing pedlars, who in Germany in the fifties dabbled in materialism, by no means overcame this limitation of their teachers. All the advances of natural science which had been made in the meantime served them only as new proofs against the existence of a creator of the world; and, indeed, they did not in the least make it their business to develop the theory any further. Though idealism was at the end of its tether and was dealt a death-blow by the Revolution of 1848, it had the satisfaction of seeing that materialism had for the moment fallen lower still. Feuerbach was unquestionably right when he refused to take responsibility for this materialism; only he should not have confounded the doctrines of these itinerant preachers with materialism in general.

Here, however, there are two things to be pointed out. First, even during Feuerbach's lifetime, natural science was still in that process of violent fermentation which only during the last fifteen years had reached a clarifying, relative conclusion. New scientific data were acquired to a hitherto unheard-of extent, but the establishing of interrelations, and thereby the bringing of order into this chaos of discoveries following closely upon each other's heels, has only quite recently become possible. It is true that Feuerbach had lived to see all three of the decisive discoveries—that of the cell, the transformation of energy and the theory of evolution named after Darwin. But how could the lonely philosopher, living in rural solitude, be able sufficiently to follow scientific developments in order to appreciate at their full value discoveries which natural scientists themselves at that time either still contested or did not know how to make adequate use of? The blame for this falls solely upon the wretched conditions in Germany, in consequence of which cobweb-spinning eclectic flea-crackers had taken possession of the chairs of philosophy, while Feuerbach, who towered above them all, had to rusticate and grow sour in a little village. It is therefore not Feuerbach's fault that the historical conception of nature, which had now become possible and which removed all the one-sidedness of French materialism, remained inaccessible to him.

Secondly, Feuerbach is quite correct in asserting that exclusively natural-scientific materialism is indeed "the foundation of the edifice of human knowledge, but not the edifice itself." For we live not only in nature but also in human society, and this also no less than nature has its history of development and its science. It was therefore a question of bringing the science of society, that is, the sum total of the so-called historical and philosophical sciences, into harmony with the materialist foundation, and of reconstructing it thereupon. But it did not fall to Feuerbach's lot to do this. In spite of the "foundation," he remained here bound by the traditional idealist fetters, a fact which he recognizes in these words: "Backwards I agree with the materialists, but not forwards!" But it was Feuerbach himself who did not go "forwards" here, in the social domain, who did not get beyond his standpoint of 1840 or 1844. And this was again chiefly due to this reclusion which compelled him, who, of all philosophers, was the most inclined to social intercourse, to produce thoughts out of his solitary head instead of in amicable and hostile encounters with other men of his calibre. Later we shall see in detail how much he remained an idealist in this sphere.

It need only be added here that Starcke looks for Feuerbach's idealism in the wrong place. "Feuerbach is an idealist; he believes in the progress of mankind." (P. 19.) "The foundation, the substructure of the whole, remains nevertheless idealism. Realism for us is nothing more than a protection against aberrations, while we follow our ideal trends. Are not compassion, love and enthusiasm for truth and justice ideal forces?" (P. VIII.)

In the first place, idealism here means nothing but the pursuit of ideal aims. But these necessarily have to do at the most with Kantian idealism and its "categorical imperative"; however, Kant himself called his philosophy "transcendental idealism"; by no means because he dealt therein also with ethical ideals, but for quite other reasons, as Starcke will remember. The superstition that philosophical idealism is pivoted round a belief in ethical, that is, social, ideals, arose outside philosophy, among the German Philistines, who learned by heart from Schiller's poems the few morsels of philosophical culture they needed. No one has criticized more severely the impotent "categorical imperative" of Kant—impotent because it demands the impossible, and therefore never attains to any reality—no one has more cruelly derided the Philistine sentimental enthusiasm for unrealizable ideals purveyed by Schiller than precisely the complete idealist Hegel. (See, for example, his *Phenomenology*.)

In the second place, we simply cannot get away from the fact that everything that sets men acting must find its way through their brains—even eating and drinking, which begins as a consequence of the sensation of hunger or thirst transmitted through the brain, and ends as a result of the sensation of satisfaction likewise transmitted through the brain. The influences of the external world upon man express themselves in his brain, are reflected therein as feelings, thoughts, impulses, volitions—in short, as "ideal tendencies," and in this form become "ideal powers." If, then, a man is to be deemed an idealist because he follows "ideal tendencies" and admits that "ideal powers" have an influence over him, then every person who is at all normally developed is a born idealist and how, in that case, can there still be any materialists?

In the third place, the conviction that humanity, at least at the present moment, moves on the whole in a progressive direction has absolutely nothing to do with the antagonism between materialism and idealism. The French materialists no less than the deists Voltaire and Rousseau held this conviction to an almost fanatical degree, and often enough made the greatest personal sacrifices for it. If ever anybody dedicated his whole life to the "enthusiasm for truth and justice"—using this phrase in the good sense—it was Diderot, for instance. If, therefore, Starcke declares all this to be idealism, this merely proves that the word materialism, and the whole antagonism between the two trends, has lost all meaning for him here.

The fact is that Starcke, although perhaps unconsciously, in this makes an unpardonable concession to the traditional Philistine prejudice against the word materialism resulting from its long-continued defamation by the priests. By the word materialism the Philistine understands gluttony, drunkenness, lust of the eye, lust of the flesh, arrogance, cupidity, avarice, covetousness, profit-hunting and stock-exchange swindling—in short, all the filthy vices in which he himself indulges in private. By the word idealism he understands the belief in virtue, universal philanthropy and in a general way a "better world," of which he boasts before others but in which he himself at the utmost believes only so long as he is having the blues or is going through the bankruptcy consequent upon his customary "materialist" excesses. It is then that he sings his favourite song, What is man?—Half beast, half angel.

. . .

III

The real idealism of Feuerbach becomes evident as soon as we come to his philosophy of religion and ethics. He by no means wishes to abolish religion; he wants to perfect it. Philosophy itself must be absorbed in religion. "The periods of humanity are distinguished only by religious changes. A historical movement is fundamental only when it is rooted in the hearts of men. The heart is not a form of religion, so that the latter should exist *also* in the heart; the heart is the essence of religion." (Quoted by Starcke, p. 168.) According to Feuerbach, religion is the relation between human beings based on the affections, the relation based on the heart, which relation until now has sought its truth in a fantastic mirror image of reality—in the mediation of one or many gods, the fantastic mirror images of human qualities—but now finds it directly and without any mediation in the love between "I" and "Thou." Thus, finally, with Feuerbach sex love becomes one of the highest forms, if not the highest form, of the practice of his new religion.

Now relations between human beings, based on affection, and especially between the two sexes, have existed as long as mankind has. Sex love in particular has undergone a development and won a place during the last eight hundred years which has made it a compulsory pivotal point of all poetry during this period. The existing positive religions have limited themselves to the bestowal of a higher consecration upon state-regulated sex love, that is, upon the marriage laws, and they could all disappear tomorrow without changing in the slightest the practice of love and friendship. Thus the Christian religion in France, as a matter of fact, so completely disappeared in the years 1793–98 that even Napoleon could not re-introduce it without opposition and difficulty; and this without any need for a substitute, in Feuerbach's sense, making itself felt in the interval.

Feuerbach's idealism consists here in this: he does not simply accept mutual relations based on reciprocal inclination between human beings, such as sex love, friendship, compassion, self-sacrifice, etc., as what they are in themselves—without associating them with any particular religion which to him, too, belongs to the past; but instead he asserts that they will attain their full value only when consecrated by the name of religion. The chief thing for him is not that these purely human relations exist, but that they shall be conceived of as the new, true religion. They are to have full value only after they have been marked with a religious stamp.

Religion is derived from *religare* and meant originally a bond. Therefore, every bond between two people is a religion. Such etymological tricks are the last resort of idealist philosophy.

. . .

The possibility of purely human sentiments in our intercourse with other human beings has nowadays been sufficiently curtailed by the society in which we must live, which is based upon class antagonism and class rule. We have no reason to curtail it still more by exalting these sentiments to a religion. And similarly the understanding of the great historical class struggles has already been sufficiently obscured by current historiography, particularly in Germany, so that there is also no need for us to make such an understanding totally impossible by transforming the history of these struggles into a mere appendix of ecclesiastical history. Already here it becomes evident how far today we have moved beyond Feuerbach. His "finest passages" in glorification of his new religion of love are totally unreadable today.

The only religion which Feuerbach examines seriously is Christianity, the world religion of the Occident, based upon monotheism. He proves that the Christian god is only a fantastic reflection, a mirror image, of man. Now, this god is, however, himself the product of a tedious process of abstraction, the concentrated quintessence of the numerous earlier tribal and national gods. And man, whose image this god is, is therefore also not a real man, but likewise the quintessence of the numerous real men, man in the abstract, therefore himself again a mental image. Feuerbach, who on every page preaches sensuousness, absorption in the concrete, in actuality, becomes thoroughly abstract as soon as he begins to talk of any other than mere sex relations between human beings.

Of these relations only one aspect appeals to him: morality. And here we are again struck by Feuerbach's astonishing poverty when compared with Hegel. The latter's ethics, or doctrine of moral conduct, is the philosophy of right and embraces: 1) abstract right; 2) morality; 3) social ethics [*Sittlichkeit*], under which again are comprised: the family, civil society and the state. Here the content is as realistic as the form is idealistic. Besides morality the whole sphere of law, economy, politics is here included. With

Feuerbach it is just the reverse. In form he is realistic since he takes his start from man; but there is absolutely no mention of the world in which this man lives; hence, this man remains always the same abstract man who occupied the field in the philosophy of religion. For this man is not born of woman; he issues, as from a chrysalis, from the god of the monotheistic religions. He therefore does not live in a real world historically come into being and historically determined. True, he has intercourse with other man; however, each one of them is just as much an abstraction as he himself. In his philosophy of religion we still had men and women, but in his ethics even this last distinction disappears. Feuerbach, to be sure, at long intervals makes such statements as: "Man thinks differently in a palace and in a hut." "If because of hunger, of misery, you have no stuff in your body, you likewise have no stuff for morality in your head, in your mind or heart." "Politics must become our religion," etc. But Feuerbach is absolutely incapable of achieving anything with these maxims. They remain mere phrases, and even Starcke has to admit that for Feuerbach politics constituted an impassable frontier and the "science of society, sociology, was *terra incognita* to him."

He appears just as shallow, in comparison with Hegel, in his treatment of the antithesis of good and evil. "One believes one is saying something great," Hegel remarks, "if one says that 'man is naturally good.' But one forgets that one says something far greater when one says 'man is naturally evil.' " With Hegel evil is the form in which the motive force of historical development presents itself. This contains the twofold meaning that, on the one hand, each new advance necessarily appears as a sacrilege against things hallowed, as a rebellion against conditions, though old and moribund, yet sanctified by custom; and that, on the other hand, it is precisely the wicked passions of man—greed and lust for power—which, since the emergence of class antagonisms, serve as levers of historical development—a fact of which the history of feudalism and of the bourgeoisie, for example, constitutes a single continual proof. But it does not occur to Feuerbach to investigate the historical role of moral evil. To him history is altogether an uncanny domain in which he feels ill at ease. Even his dictum: "Man as he sprang originally from nature was only a mere creature of nature, not a man. Man is a product of man, of culture, of history"—with him even this dictum remains absolutely sterile.

What Feuerbach has to tell us about morals can, therefore, only be extremely meagre. The urge towards happiness is innate in man, and must therefore form the basis of all morality. But the urge towards happiness is subject to a double correction. First, by the natural consequences of our actions: after the debauch come the "blues," and habitual excess is followed by illness. Secondly, by its social consequences: if we do not respect the similar urge of other people towards happiness they will defend themselves, and so interfere with our own urge towards happiness. Consequently, in order to satisfy our urge, we must be in a position to appreciate rightly the results of our conduct and must likewise allow others an equal right to seek happiness. Rational self-restraint with regard to ourselves, and love—again and again love!—in our intercourse with others—these are the basic laws of Feuerbach's morality; from them all others are derived. And neither the most spirited utterances of Feuerbach nor the strongest eulogies of Starcke can hide the tenuity and banality of these few propositions.

Only very exceptionally, and by no means to his and other people's profit, can an individual satisfy his urge towards happiness by preoccupation with himself. Rather it requires preoccupation with the outside world, means to satisfy his needs, that is to say, food, an individual of the opposite sex, books, conversation, argument, activities, objects for use and working up. Feuerbach's morality either presupposes that these means and objects of satisfaction are given to every individual as a matter of course, or else it offers only inapplicable good advice and is, therefore, not worth a brass farthing to people who are without these means. And Feuerbach himself states this in plain terms: "Man thinks differently in a palace and in a hut. If because of hunger, of misery, you have no stuff in your body, you likewise have no stuff for morality in your head, in your mind or heart."

Do matters fare any better in regard to the equal right of others to satisfy their urge towards happiness? Feuerbach posed this claim as absolute, as holding good for all times and circumstances.

But since when has it been valid? Was there ever in antiquity between slaves and masters, or in the Middle Ages between serfs and barons, any talk about an equal right to the urge towards happiness? Was not the urge towards happiness of the oppressed class sacrificed ruthlessly and "by right of law" to that of the ruling class? Yes, that was indeed immoral; nowadays, however, equality of rights is recognized. Recognized in words ever since and inasmuch as the bourgeoisie, in its fight against feudalism and in the development of capitalist production, was compelled to abolish all privileges of estate, that is, personal privileges, and to introduce the equality of all individuals before the law, first in the sphere of private law, then gradually also in the sphere of public law. But the urge towards happiness thrives only to a trivial extent on ideal rights. To the greatest extent of all it thrives on material means; and capitalist production takes care to ensure that the great majority of those with equal rights shall get only what is essential for bare existence. Capitalist production has, therefore, little more respect, if indeed any more, for the equal right to the urge towards happiness of the majority than had slavery or serfdom. And are we better off in regard to the mental means of happiness, the educational means? Is not even "the schoolmaster of Sadowa" a mythical person?

More. According to Feuerbach's theory of morals the Stock Exchange is the highest temple of moral conduct, provided only that one always speculates right. If my urge towards happiness leads me to the Stock Exchange, and if there I correctly gauge the consequences of my actions so that only agreeable results and no disadvantages ensue, that is, if I always win, then I am fulfilling Feuerbach's precept. Moreover, I do not thereby interfere with the equal right of another person to pursue his happiness; for that other man went to the Exchange just as voluntarily as I did and in concluding the speculative transaction with me he has followed his urge towards happiness as I have followed mine. If he loses his money, his action is *ipso facto* proved to have been unethical, because of his bad reckoning, and since I have given him the punishment he deserves, I can even slap my chest proudly, like a modern Rhadamanthus. Love, too, rules on the Stock Exchange, in so far as it is not simply a sentimental figure of speech, for each finds in others the satisfaction of his own urge towards happiness, which is just what love ought to achieve and how it acts in practice. And if I gamble with correct prevision of the consequences of my operations, and therefore with success, I fulfil all the strictest injunctions of Feuerbachian morality—and become a rich man into the bargain. In other words, Feuerbach's morality is cut exactly to the pattern of modern capitalist society, little as Feuerbach himself might desire or imagine it.

But love!—yes, with Feuerbach love is everywhere and at all times the wonder-working god who should help to surmount all difficulties of practical life—and at that in a society which is split into classes with diametrically opposite interests. At this point the last relic of its revolutionary character disappears from his philosophy, leaving only the old cant: Love one another—fall into each other's arms regardless of distinctions of sex or estate—a universal orgy of reconciliation!

In short, the Feuerbachian theory of morals fares like all its predecessors. It is designed to suit all periods, all peoples and all conditions, and precisely for that reason it is never and nowhere applicable. It remains, as regards the real world, as powerless as Kant's categorical imperative. In reality every class, even every profession, has its own morality, and even this it violates whenever it can do so with impunity. And love, which is to unite all, manifests itself in wars, altercations, lawsuits, domestic broils, divorces and every possible exploitation of one by another.

Now how was it possible that the powerful impetus given by Feuerbach turned out to be so unfruitful for himself? For the simple reason that Feuerbach himself never contrives to escape from the realm of abstraction—for which he has a deadly hatred—into that of living reality. He clings fiercely to nature and man; but nature and man remain mere words with him. He is incapable of telling us anything definite either about real nature or real men. But from the abstract man of Feuerbach one arrives at real living men only when one considers them as participants in history. And that is what Feuerbach resisted, and therefore the year 1848, which he did not understand, meant to him merely the final break with the real world, retirement into solitude. The blame for this again falls chiefly on the conditions then obtaining in Germany, which condemned him to rot away miserably.

But the step which Feuerbach did not take has nevertheless to be taken. The cult of abstract man, which formed the kernel of Feuerbach's new religion, had to be replaced by the science of real men and of their historical development. This further development of Feuerbach's standpoint beyond Feuerbach was inaugurated by Marx in 1845 in *The Holy Family.*

IV

Strauss, Bauer, Stirner, Feuerbach—these were the offshoots of Hegelian philosophy, in so far as they did not abandon the field of philosophy. Strauss, after his *Life of Jesus* and *Dogmatics,* produced only literary studies in philosophy and ecclesiastical history after the fashion of Renan. Bauer only achieved something in the field of the history of the origin of Christianity, though what he did here was important. Stirner remained a curiosity, even after Bakunin blended him with Proudhon and labelled the blend "anarchism." Feuerbach alone was of significance as a philosopher. But not only did philosophy—claimed to soar above all special sciences and to be the science of sciences connecting them—remain to him an impassable barrier, and inviolable holy thing, but as a philosopher, too, he stopped halfway, was a materialist below and an idealist above. He was incapable of disposing of Hegel through criticism; he simply threw him aside as useless, while he himself, compared with the encyclopaedic wealth of the Hegelian system, achieved nothing positive beyond a turgid religion of love and a meagre, impotent morality.

Out of the dissolution of the Hegelian school, however, there developed still another tendency, the only one which has borne real fruit. And this tendency is essentially connected with the name of Marx.[1]

[1] Here I may be permitted to make a personal explanation. Lately repeated reference has been made to my share in this theory, and so I can hardly avoid saying a few words here to settle this point. I cannot deny that both before and during my forty years' collaboration with Marx I had

The separation from Hegelian philosophy was here also the result of a return to the materialist standpoint. That means it was resolved to comprehend the real world—nature and history—just as it presents itself to everyone who approaches it free from preconceived idealist crotchets. It was decided mercilessly to sacrifice every idealist crotchet which could not be brought into harmony with the facts conceived in their own and not in a fantastic interconnection. And materialism means nothing more than this. But here the materialistic world outlook was taken really seriously for the first time and was carried through consistently—at least in its basic features—in all domains of knowledge concerned.

Hegel was not simply put aside. On the contrary, one started out from his revolutionary side, described above, from the dialectical method. But in its Hegelian form this method was unusable. According to Hegel, dialectics is the self-development of the concept. The absolute concept does not only exist—unknown where—from eternity, it is also the actual living soul of the whole existing world. It develops into itself through all the preliminary stages which are treated at length in the *Logic* and which are all included in it. Then it "alienates" itself by changing into nature, where, without consciousness of itself, disguised as the necessity of nature, it goes through a new development and finally comes again to self-consciousness in man. This self-consciousness then elaborates itself again in history from the crude form until finally the absolute concept again comes to itself completely in the Hegelian philosophy. According to Hegel, therefore, the dialectical development apparent in nature and history, that is, the causal interconnection of the progressive movement from the lower to the higher, which as-

a certain independent share in laying the foundations of the theory, and more particularly in its elaboration. But the greater part of its leading basic principles, especially in the realm of economics and history, and, above all, their final trenchant formulation, belong to Marx. What I contributed—at any rate with the exception of my work in a few special fields—Marx could very well have done without me. What Marx accomplished I would not have achieved. Marx stood higher, saw further, and took a wider and quicker view than all the rest of us. Marx was a genius; we others were at best talented. Without him the theory would not be by far what it is today. It therefore rightly bears his name [*note by Engels*].

serts itself through all zigzag movements and temporary retrogressions, is only a copy [*Abklatsch*] of the self-movement of the concept going on from eternity, no one knows where, but at all events independently of any thinking human brain. This ideological perversion had to be done away with. We comprehended the concepts in our heads once more materialistically—as images [*Abbilder*] of real things instead of regarding the real things as images of this or that stage of the absolute concept. Thus dialectics reduced itself to the science of the general laws of motion, both of the external world and of human thought—two sets of laws which are identical in substance, but differ in their expression in so far as the human mind can apply them consciously, while in nature and also up to now for the most part in human history, these laws assert themselves unconsciously, in the form of external necessity, in the midst of an endless series of seeming accidents. Thereby the dialectic of concepts itself became merely the conscious reflex of the dialectical motion of the real world and thus the dialectic of Hegel was placed upon its head; or rather, turned off its head, on which it was standing, and placed upon its feet. And this materialist dialectic, which for years has been our best working tool and our sharpest weapon, was, remarkably enough, discovered not only by us but also, independently of us and even of Hegel, by a German worker, Joseph Dietzgen.[1]

In this way, however, the revolutionary side of Hegelian philosophy was again taken up and at the same time freed from the idealist trimmings which with Hegel had prevented its consistent execution. The great basic thought that the world is not to be comprehended as a complex of ready-made *things,* but as a complex of *processes,* in which the things apparently stable no less than their mind images in our heads, the concepts, go through an uninterrupted change of coming into being and passing away, in which, in spite of all seeming accidentality and of all temporary retrogression, a progressive development asserts itself in the end—this great fundamental

[1] See *Das Wesen der menschlichen Kopfarbeit, dargestellt von einem Handarbeiter* [*The Nature of Human Brainwork, Described by a Manual Worker*]. Hamburg, Meissner [*note by Engels*].

thought has, especially since the time of Hegel, so thoroughly permeated ordinary consciousness that in this generality it is now scarcely ever contradicted. But to acknowledge this fundamental thought in words and to apply it in reality in detail to each domain of investigation are two different things. If, however, investigation always proceeds from this standpoint, the demand for final solutions and eternal truths ceases once for all; one is always conscious of the necessary limitation of all acquired knowledge, of the fact that it is conditioned by the circumstances in which it was acquired. On the other hand, one no longer permits oneself to be imposed upon by the antitheses, insuperable for the still common old metaphysics, between true and false, good and bad, identical and different, necessary and accidental. One knows that these antitheses have only a relative validity; that that which is recognized now as true has also its latent false side which will later manifest itself, just as that which is now regarded as false has also its true side by virtue of which it could previously be regarded as true. One knows that what is maintained to be necessary is composed of sheer accidents and that the so-called accidental is the form behind which necessity hides itself—and so on.

—Engels, "Ludwig Feuerbach and the End of Classical German Philosophy," *MESW II*, pp. 360–88

I

The chief defect of all hitherto existing materialism—that of Feuerbach included—is that the thing [*Gegenstand*], reality, sensuousness, is conceived only in the form of the *object* [*Objekt*] or of *contemplation* [*Anschauung*], but not as *human sensuous activity, practice,* not subjectively. Hence it happened that the *active* side, in contradistinction to materialism, was developed by idealism—but only abstractly, since, of course, idealism does not know real, sensuous activity as such. Feuerbach wants sensuous objects, really differentiated from the thought objects, but he does not conceive human activity itself as *objective* [*gegenständliche*] activity. Hence, in the *Essence of Christianity,* he regards the theoretical attitude as the only genuinely human attitude, while practice is conceived and fixed only in its dirty-judaical form of appearance. Hence he does not grasp the significance of "revolutionary," of "practical-critical," activity.

II

The question whether objective [*gegenständliche*] truth can be attributed to human thinking is not a question of theory but is a *practical* question. In practice man must prove the truth, that is, the reality and power, the this-sidedness [*Diesseitigkeit*] of his thinking. The dispute over the reality or non-reality of thinking which is isolated from practice is a purely *scholastic* question.

III

The materialist doctrine that men are products of circumstances and upbringing, and that, therefore, changed men are products of other circumstances and changed upbringing, forgets that it is men that change circumstances and that the educator himself needs educating. Hence, this doctrine necessarily arrives at dividing society into two parts, of which one is superior to society (in Robert Owen, for example).

The coincidence of the changing of circumstances and of human activity can be conceived and rationally understood only as *revolutionizing practice.*

IV

Feuerbach starts out from the fact of religious self-alienation, the duplication of the world into a religious, imaginary world and a real one. His work consists in the dissolution of the religious world into its secular basis. He overlooks the fact that after completing this work, the chief thing still remains to be done. For the fact that the secular foundation detaches itself from itself and establishes itself in the clouds as an independent realm is really only to be explained by the self-cleavage and self-contradictoriness of this secular basis. The latter must itself, therefore, first be understood in its contradiction and then, by the removal of the contradiction, revolutionized in practice. Thus, for instance, once the earthly family is discovered to be the secret of the holy family, the former must then itself be criticized in theory and revolutionized in practice.

V

Feuerbach, not satisfied with *abstract thinking,* appeals to *sensuous contemplation;* but he does not conceive sensuousness as *practical,* human-sensuous activity.

VI

Feuerbach resolves the religious essence into the *human* essence. But the human essence is no abstraction inherent in each single individual. In its reality it is the ensemble of the social relations.

Feuerbach, who does not enter upon a criticism of this real essence, is consequently compelled:

1. To abstract from the historical process and to fix the religious sentiment [*Gemüt*] as something by itself and to presuppose an abstract—*isolated*—human individual.
2. The human essence, therefore, can with him be comprehended only as "genus," as an internal, dumb generality which merely *naturally* unites the many individuals.

VII

Feuerbach, consequently, does not see that the "religious sentiment" is itself a *social product,* and that the abstract individual whom he analyses belongs in reality to a particular form of society.

VIII

Social life is essentially *practical.* All mysteries which mislead theory to mysticism find their rational solution in human practice and in the comprehension of this practice.

IX

The highest point attained by *contemplative* materialism, that is, materialism which does not understand sensuousness as practical activity, is the contemplation of single individuals in "civil society."

X

The standpoint of the old materialism is *"civil"* society; the standpoint of the new is *human* society, or socialized humanity.

XI

The philosophers have only *interpreted* the world, in various ways; the point, however, is to *change* it.

—Marx, "Theses on Feuerbach," *MESW II,* pp. 403–405

Feuerbach is the only one who has a *serious, critical* attitude to the Hegelian dialectic and who has made genuine discoveries in this field. He is in fact the true conqueror of the old philosophy. The extent of his achievement, and the unpretentious simplicity with which he, Feuerbach, gives it to the world, stand in striking contrast to the reverse.

Feuerbach's great achievement is:

(1) The proof that philosophy is nothing else but religion rendered into thoughts and thinkingly expounded, and that it has therefore likewise to be condemned as another form and manner of existence of the estrangement of the essence of man;

(2) The establishment of *true materialism* and of *real science,* since Feuerbach also makes the social relationship "of man to man" the basic principle of the theory;

(3) His opposing to the negation of the negation, which claims to be the absolute positive, the self-supporting positive, positively grounded on itself.

Feuerbach explains the Hegelian dialectic (and thereby justifies starting out from the positive, from sense-certainty) as follows:

Hegel sets out from the estrangement of Substance (in Logic, from the Infinite, the abstractly universal)—from the absolute and fixed abstraction; which means, put popularly, that he sets out from religion and theology.

Secondly, he annuls the infinite, and establishes the actual, sensuous, real, finite, particular (philosophy—annulment of religion and theology).

Thirdly, he again annuls the positive and restores the abstraction, the infinite—Restoration of religion and theology.

Feuerbach thus conceives the negation of the negation *only* as a contradiction of philosophy with itself—as the philosophy which affirms theology (the transcendent, etc.) after having denied it, and which it therefore affirms in opposition to itself.

The position or self-affirmation and self-confirmation contained in the negation of the negation is taken to be a position which is not yet sure of itself which is therefore burdened with its opposite, which is doubtful of itself and therefore in need of proof, and which, therefore, is not a position establishing itself by its existence—not a position that justifies itself; hence it is directly and immediately confronted by the self-grounded position of sense-certainty.

But because Hegel has conceived the negation of the negation from the point of view of the positive relation inherent in it as the true and only positive, and from the point of view of the negative relation inherent in it as the only true act and self-realising act of all being, he has only found the *abstract, logical, speculative* expression for the movement of history; and this historical process is not yet the *real* history of man—of man as a given subject, but only man's *act of genesis*—the *story* of man's *origin.* We shall explain both the abstract form of this process and the difference between this process as it is in Hegel in contrast to modern criticism, that is, in contrast to the same process in Feuerbach's *Wesen des Christentums* (*Essence of Christianity*), or rather the *critical* form of this in Hegel's still uncritical process.

Let us take a look at the Hegelian system. One must begin with Hegel's *Phenomenology,* the true point of origin and the secret of the Hegelian philosophy.

PHENOMENOLOGY

A. *Self-consciousness*

I. *Consciousness.* (α) Certainty at the level of sense-experience; or the "This" and *Meaning.* (β) *Perception,* or the Thing with Its Properties, and *Deception.* (γ) Force and Understanding, Appearance and the Supersensible World.

II. *Self-consciousness.* The Truth of Certainty of Self. (a) Independence and Dependence of Self-consciousness; Lordship and Bondage. (b) Freedom of Self-consciousness: Stoicism, Scepticism, the Unhappy Consciousness.

III. *Reason.* Reason's Certainty and Reason's Truth. (a) Observation as a Process of Reason. Observation of Nature and of Self-consciousness. (b) Realisation of Rational Self-consciousness through its own Activity. Pleasure and Necessity. The Law of the Heart and the Frenzy of Self-conceit. Virtue and the Course of the World. (c) The Individuality Which is Real In and For Itself. The Spiritual Animal Kingdom and the Deception, or the Real Fact. Reason as Law-giver. Reason Which Tests Laws.

B. *Mind*

I. *True* Mind; the Ethical Order.
II. Mind in Self-Estrangement—Culture.
III. Mind Certain of Itself, Morality.

C. *Religion*

Natural Religion; *Religion in the Form of Art; Revealed* Religion.

D. *Absolute Knowledge*

Hegel's *Encyclopaedia,* beginning as it does with Logic, with *pure speculative thought*, and ending with *Absolute Knowledge*—with the self-consciousness, self-comprehending, philosophic or absolute (i.e., superhuman) abstract mind—is in its entirety nothing but the *display,* the self-objection, of the *essence* of the philosophic mind, and the philosophic mind is nothing but the estranged mind of the world thinking within its self-estrangement—i.e., comprehending itself abstractly. *Logic* (mind's *coin of the realm,* the speculative or *thought-value* of man and nature—their essence grown totally indifferent to all real determinateness, and hence their unreal essence) is *alienated thinking,* and therefore thinking which abstracts from nature and from real man: *abstract* thinking. Then: *The externality of this abstract thinking . . . nature,* as it is for this abstract thinking. Nature is external to it—its self-loss; and it apprehends nature also in an external fashion, as abstract thinking—but as alienated abstract thinking. Finally, *Mind,* this thinking returning home to its own point of origin—the thinking which, as the anthropological, phenomenological, psychological, ethical, artistic and religious mind is not valid for itself, until ultimately it finds itself, and relates itself to itself, as *absolute* knowledge in the hence absolute, i.e. abstract mind, and so receives its conscious embodiment in a mode of being corresponding to it. For its real mode of being is *abstraction.*

There is a double error in Hegel.

The first emerges most clearly in the *Phenomenology,* the Hegelian philosophy's place of origin. When, for instance, wealth, state-power, etc., are understood by Hegel as entities estranged from the *human* being, this only happens in their form as thoughts. . . . They are thought-entities, and therefore merely an estrangement of *pure,* i.e., abstract, philosophical thinking. The whole process therefore ends with Absolute Knowledge. It is precisely abstract thought from which these objects are estranged and which they confront with their arrogation of reality. The *philosopher* sets up himself (that is one who is himself an abstract form of estranged man) as the *measuring-rod* of the estranged world. The whole *history of the alienation-process* and the whole *process of the retraction* of the alienation is therefore nothing but the *history of the production* of abstract (i.e., absolute) thought—of logical, speculative thought. The *estrangement,* which therefore forms the real interest of this alienation and of the transcendance of this alienation, is the opposition of *in itself* and *for itself,* of *consciousness* and *self-consciousness,* of *object* and *subject*—that is to say, it is the opposition, within thought itself, between abstract thinking and sensuous reality or real sensuousness. All other oppositions and movements of these oppositions are but the *semblance, the cloak, the exoteric* shape of these oppositions which alone matter, and which constitute the *meaning* of these other, profane oppositions. It is not the fact that the human being *objectifies himself inhumanly,* in opposition to himself, but the fact that he *objectifies himself* in *distinction* from and in *opposition* to abstract thinking, that is the posited essence of the estrangement and the thing to be superseded.

The appropriation of man's essential powers, which have become objects—indeed, alien objects—is thus in the *first place* only an *appropriation* occurring in *consciousness,* in *pure thought*—i.e., in *abstraction:* it is the appropriation of these objects as *thoughts* and as *movements of thought.* Consequently, despite its thoroughly negative and critical appearance and despite the criticism really contained in it, which often anticipates far later development, there is already latent in the *Phenomenology* as a germ, a potentiality, a secret, the uncritical positivism and the equally uncritical idealism of Hegel's later works—that philosophic dissolution and restoration of the existing empirical world. In the *second place:* the vindication of the objective world for man—for example, the realisation that *sensuous* consciousness is not an *abstractly* sensuous consciousness but a *humanly* sensuous consciousness—that religion, wealth, etc., are but the estranged world of *human* objectification, of *man's* essential powers given over to work and that they are therefore but the *path* to the true *human* world—this appropriation or the insight into this process consequently appears in Hegel in this form, that *sense, religion,* state-power, etc., are *spiritual* entities; for only *mind* is the *true* essence of man, and the true form of mind is thinking mind, the logical, speculative mind. The *humanness* of nature and of the nature begotten by history—the humanness of man's products—appears in the form that they are *products* of abstract mind and as such, therefore, phases of *mind—thought entities.* The *Phenomenology* is, therefore, an occult critique—still to itself obscure and mystifying criticism; but inasmuch as it keeps steadily in view man's *estrangement,* even though man appears only in the shape of mind, there lie concealed in it *all* the elements of criticism, already *prepared* and *elaborated* in a manner often rising far above the Hegelian standpoint. The "Unhappy Consciousness," the "Honest Consciousness," the struggle of the "Noble and Base Consciousness," etc., etc.,—these separate sections contain, but still in an estranged form, the *critical* elements of whole spheres such as religion, the state, civil life, etc. Just as *entities, objects,* appear as *thought-entities,* so the *subject* is always *consciousness* or *self-consciousness;* or rather the object appears only as *abstract* consciousness, man only as *self-consciousness:* the distinct forms of estrangement which make their appearance are, therefore, only various forms of consciousness and self-consciousness. Just as *in itself* abstract consciousness (the form in which the object is conceived) is merely a moment of distinction of self-consciousness, what appears as the result of the movement is the identity of self-consciousness with consciousness—absolute knowledge—the movement of abstract thought no longer directed outwards but going on now only within its own self: that is to say, the dialectic of pure thought is the result.

The outstanding thing in Hegel's *Phenomenology* and its final outcome—that is, the dialectic of negativity as the moving and generating principle—is thus first that Hegel conceives the self-genesis of man as a process, conceives objectification as loss of the object, as alienation and as transcendence of this alienation; that he thus grasps the essence of *labour* and comprehends objective man—true, because real man—as the outcome of man's *own labour*. The *real,* active orientation of man to himself as a species being, or his manifestation as a real species being (i.e., as a human being), is only possible by his really bringing out of himself all the *powers* that are his as the *species* man—something which in turn is only possible through the totality of man's actions, as the result of history—is only possible by man's treating these generic powers as objects: and this, to begin with, is again only possible in the form of estrangement.

We shall now demonstrate in detail Hegel's one-sidedness and limitations as they are displayed in the final chapter of the *Phenomenology,* "Absolute Knowledge"—a chapter which contains the concentrated spirit of the *Phenomenology,* the relationship of the *Phenomenology* to speculative dialectic, and also Hegel's *consciousness* concerning both and their relationship to one another.

Let us provisionally say just this much in advance: Hegel's standpoint is that of modern political economy. He grasps *labour* as the *essence* of man—as man's essence in the act of proving itself: he sees only the positive, not the negative side of labour. Labour is man's *coming-to-be for himself* within *alienation,* or as *alienated* man. The only labour which Hegel knows and recognises is *abstractly mental* labour. Therefore, that which constitutes the *essence* of philosophy—the *alienation of man in his knowing of himself,* or *alienated* science *thinking itself*—Hegel grasps as its essence; and he is therefore able *vis-a-vis* preceding philosophy to gather together its separate elements and phases, and to present his philosophy as *the* philosophy. What the other philosophers did —that they grasped separate phases of nature and of human life as phases of self-consciousness, and indeed of abstract self-consciousness—is *known* to Hegel as the *doings* of philosophy. Hence his science is absolute.

Let us now turn to our subject.

Absolute Knowledge. The last chapter of the "Phenomenology."

The main point is that the *object of consciousness* is nothing else but *self-consciousness,* or that the object is only *objectified self-consciousness*—self-consciousness as object.

(Positing of man = self-consciousness.)

The issue, therefore, is to surmount the *object of consciousness. Objectivity* as such is regarded as an *estranged* human relationship which does not correspond to the *essence of man,* to self-consciousness. The *re-appropriation* of the objective essence of man, begotten in the form of estrangement as something alien, has the meaning therefore not only to annul *estrangement,* but *objectivity* as well. Man, that is to say, is regarded as a *non-objective, spiritual* being.

The movement of *surmounting the object of consciousness* is now described by Hegel in the following way:

The *object* reveals itself not merely as *returning into the self*—for Hegel that is the *one-sided* way of apprehending this movement, the grasping of only one side. Man is posited as equivalent to self. The self, however, is only the *abstractly* conceived man—man begotten by abstraction. Man *is* egotistic. His eye, his ear, etc., are *egotistic.* In him every one of his essential powers has the quality of *selfhood.* But it is quite false to say on that account, "*Self-consciousness* has eyes, ears, essential powers." Self-consciousness is rather a quality of human nature, of the human eye, etc.; it is not human nature that is a quality of *self-consciousness.*

The self-abstracted and fixed for itself is man as *abstract egoist* —*egoism* raised in its pure abstraction to the level of thought. (We shall return to this point later.)

For Hegel the *essence of man—man*—equals *self-consciousness.* All estrangement of the human essence is therefore *nothing but estrangement of self-consciousness.* The estrangement of self-consciousness is not regarded as an *expression* of the *real* estrangement of the human being—its expression reflected in the realm of knowledge and thought. Instead, the *real* estrangement—that which appears real—is from its *innermost,* hidden nature (a nature only brought to light by philosophy) nothing but the *manifestation* of the estrangement of the real essence of man, of *self-consciousness.* The science which comprehends this is therefore called *Phenomenology.* All re-appropriation of the estranged objective essence appears, therefore, as a process of incorporation into self-consciousness: The man who takes hold of his essential being is *merely* the self-consciousness which takes hold of objective essences. Return of the object into the self is therefore the re-appropriation of the object.

The *surmounting of the object of consciousness, comprehensively* expressed, means:

(1) That the object as such presents itself to consciousness as something vanishing. (2) That it is the alienation of self-consciousness which establishes thinghood. (3) That this externalisation of self-consciousness has not merely a *negative* but a *positive* significance. (4) That it has this meaning not merely *for us* or *intrinsically,* but *for self-consciousness itself.* (5) For *self-consciousness,* the negative of the object, its annulling of itself, has *positive* significance—self-consciousness *knows* this nullity of the object—because self-consciousness itself alienates itself; for in this alienation it establishes *itself* as object, or, for the sake of the indivisible unity of *being-for-self,* establishes the object as itself. (6) On the other hand, there is also this other moment in the process, that self-consciousness has also just as much annulled and superseded this alienation and objectivity and resumed them into itself, being thus at home with *itself* in *its* other-being *as such.* (7) This is the movement of *consciousness* and in this movement consciousness is the totality of its moments. (8) Consciousness must similarly have taken up a relation to the object in all its aspects and phases, and have comprehended it from the point of view of each of them.

This totality of its determinate characteristics makes the object *intrinsically a spiritual being;* and it becomes so in truth for consciousness through the apprehending of each single one of them as *self* or through what was called above the *spiritual* attitude to them.

As to (1): That the object as such presents itself to consciousness as something vanishing—this is the above-mentioned *return of the object into the self.*

As to (2): *The alienation of self-consciousness* establishes *thinghood.* Because man equals self-consciousness, his alienated, objective essence, or *thinghood,* equals *alienated self-consciousness,* and *thinghood* is thus established through this alienation (thinghood being *that* which is an *object for man* and an object for him is really only that which is to him an essential object, therefore his *objective* essence. And since it is not *real Man,* nor therefore *Nature*—Man being *human Nature*—who as such is made the subject, but only the abstraction of man—self-consciousness—thinghood cannot be anything but alienated self-consciousness). It is only to be expected that a living, natural being equipped and endowed with objective (i.e., material) essential powers should have *real natural objects* of his essence; as is the fact that his self-alienation should lead to the establishing of a *real,* objective world—but a world in the form of externality—a world, therefore, not belonging to his own essential being, and an overpowering world. There is nothing incomprehensible or mysterious in this. It would be mysterious, rather, if it were otherwise. But it is equally clear that a *self-consciousness*-can only establish *thinghood* through its alienation—i.e., establish something which itself is only an abstract thing, a thing of abstraction and not a *real* thing. It is clear, further, that thinghood is therefore utterly without any *independence,* any *essentiality vis-a-vis* self-consciousness; that on the contrary it is a mere creature—something *posited* by self-consciousness. And what is posited, instead of confirming itself, is but a confirmation of the act of positing in which is concentrated for a moment the energy of the act as its product, *seeming* to give the de-posit—but only for a moment—the character of an independent, real substance.

Whenever real, corporeal *man,* man with his feet firmly on the solid ground, man exhaling and inhaling all the forces of nature, *establishes* his real, objective *essential powers* as alien objects by his externalisation, it is not the *act of positing* which is the subject in this process: it is the subjectivity of *objective* essential powers, whose action, therefore, must also be something *objective.* A being who is objective acts objectively, and he would not act objectively if the objective did not reside in the very nature of his being. He creates or establishes only *objects, because* he is established by objects—because at bottom he is *nature.* In the act of establishing, therefore, this objective being does not fall from his state of "pure activity" into a *creating of the object;* on the contrary, his *objective* product only confirms his *objective* activity, establishing his activity as the activity of an objective, natural being.

Here we see how consistent naturalism or humanism distinguishes itself both from idealism and materialism, constituting at the same time the unifying truth of both. We see also how only naturalism is capable of comprehending the act of world history.

Man is directly a *natural being.* As a natural being and as a living natural being he is on the one hand furnished with *natural powers of life*—he is an *active* natural being. These forces exist in him as tendencies and abilities—as *impulses.* On the other hand, as a natural, corporeal, sensuous, objective being he is a *suffering,* conditioned and limited creature, like animals and plants. That is to say, the *objects* of his impulses exist outside him, as *objects* independent of him; yet these objects are *objects* of his *need*—essential *objects,* indispensable to the manifestation and confirmation of his essential powers. To say that man is a *corporeal,* living, real, sensuous, objective being full of natural vigour is to say that he has *real, sensuous, objects* as the objects of his being or of his life, or that he can only *express* his life in real, sensuous objects. To be objective, natural and sensuous, and at the same time to have object, nature and sense outside oneself, or oneself to be object, nature and sense for a third party, is one and the same thing. *Hunger* is a natural *need;* it therefore needs a *nature* outside itself, an *object* outside itself, in order to satisfy itself, to be stilled. Hunger is an acknowledged need of my body for an *object* existing outside it, indispensable to its integration and to the expression of its essential being. The sun is the *object* of the plant—an indispensable object to it, confirming its life—just as the plant is an object of the sun, being an *expression* of the life-awakening power of the sun, of the sun's *objective* essential power.

A being which does not have its nature outside itself is not a *natural* being, and plays no part in the system of nature. A being which has no object outside itself is not an objective being. A being which is not itself an object for some third being has no being for its *object;* i.e., it is not objectively related. Its be-ing is not objective.

An unobjective being is a *nullity*—an *un-being.*

Suppose a being which is neither an object itself, nor has an object. Such a being, in the first place, would be the *unique* being: there would exist no being outside it—it would exist solitary and alone. For as soon as there are objects outside me, as soon as I am not *alone,* I am *another—another reality* than the object outside me. For this third object I am thus an *other reality* than it; that is, I am *its* object. Thus, to suppose a being which is not the object of another being is to presuppose that *no* objective being exists. As soon as I have an object, this object has me for an object. But a *non-objective* being is an unreal, nonsensical thing—something merely thought of (merely imagined, that is)—a creature of abstraction. To be *sensuous,* that is, to be an object of sense, to be a *sensuous* object, and thus to have sensuous objects outside oneself—objects of one's sensuousness. To be sensuous is to *suffer.*

Man as an objective, sensuous being is therefore a *suffering* being—and because he feels what he suffers, a *passionate* being. Passion is the essential force of man energetically bent on its object.

But man is not merely a natural being: he is a *human* natural being. That is to say, he is a being for himself. Therefore he is a *species being,* and has to confirm and manifest himself as such both in his being and in his knowing. Therefore, *human* objects are not natural objects as they immediately present themselves, and neither is *human sense* as it immediately *is*—as it is objectively—*human* sensibility, human objectivity. Neither nature objectively nor nature subjectively is directly given in a form adequate to the *human* being. And as everything natural has to have its *beginning, man* too has his act of coming-to-be—*history*—which, however, is for him a known history, and hence as an act of coming-to-be it is a conscious self-transcending act of coming-to-be. History is the true natural history of man (on which more later).

Thirdly, because this establishing of thinghood is itself only a sham, an act contradicting the nature of pure activity, it has to be cancelled again and thinghood denied.

Re 3, 4, 5 and 6. (3) This externalisation of consciousness has not merely a *negative* but a *positive* significance, and (4) it has this meaning not merely *for us* or intrinsically, but for consciousness itself. (5) *For consciousness* the negative of the object, its annulling of itself, has *positive* significance—consciousness *knows* this nullity of the object because it alienates *itself;* for in this alienation it *knows* itself as object, or, for the sake of the indivisible unity of *being-for-itself,* the object as itself. (6) On the other hand, there is also this other moment in the process, that consciousness has also just as much annulled and superseded this alienation and objectivity and resumed them into itself, being thus *at home with itself* in its *other-being as such.*

As we have already seen: the appropriation of what is estranged and objective, or the annulling of objectivity in the form of *estrangement* (which has to advance from indifferent foreignness to real, antagonistic estrangement) means equally or even primarily for Hegel that it is *objectivity* which is to be annulled, because it is not the *determinate* character of the object, but rather its *objective* character that is offensive and constitutes estrangement for self-consciousness. The object is therefore something negative, self-annulling—a *nullity*. This nullity of the object has not only a negative but a *positive* meaning for consciousness, for such a *nullity* of the object is precisely the *self-confirmation* of the non-objectivity, of the *abstraction* of itself. For *consciousness itself* this nullity of the object has a positive meaning because it *knows* this nullity, the objective being, as its *self-alienation;* because it knows that it exists only as a result of its own *self-alienation*. . . .

The way in which consciousness is, and in which something is for it, is *knowing*. Knowing is its sole act. Something therefore comes to be for consciousness in so far as the latter *knows* this *something*. Knowing is its sole objective relation. Consciousness, then, knows the nullity of the object (i.e., knows the non-existence of the distinction between the object and itself, the non-existence of the object for it) because it knows the object as its *self-alienation;* that is, it knows itself—knows knowing as the object—because the object is only the *semblance* of an object, a piece of mystification, which in its essence, however, is nothing else but knowing itself, which has confronted itself with itself and in so doing has confronted itself with a *nullity*—a something which has *no* objectivity outside the knowing. Or: knowing knows that in relating itself to an object it is only *outside* itself—that it only externalises itself; that *it itself appears* to itself only *as an object*—or that which appears to it as an object is only it itself.

On the other hand, says Hegel, there is at the same time this other moment in this process, that consciousness has just as much annulled and superseded this externalisation and objectivity and resumed them into itself, being thus *at home* in its *other-being as such.*

In this discussion are brought together all the illusions of speculation.

First of all: consciousness—self-consciousness—is *at home with itself in its other-being as such.* It is therefore—or if we here abstract from the Hegelian abstraction and put the self-consciousness of man instead of Self-consciousness—*it is at home with itself in its other-being as such.* This implies, for one thing that consciousness (knowing as knowing, thinking as thinking) pretends to be directly the *other* of itself—to be the world of sense, the real world, life—thought over-reaching itself in thought (Feuerbach). This aspect is contained herein, inasmuch as consciousness as mere consciousness takes offence not at estranged objectivity, but at *objectivity as such.*

Secondly, this implies that self-conscious man, in so far as he has recognised and annulled and superseded the spiritual world (or his world's spiritual, general mode of being) as self-alienation, nevertheless again confirms this in its alienated shape and passes it off as his true mode of being—re-establishes it, and pretends to be *at home in his other-being as such.* Thus, for instance, after annulling and superseding religion, after recognising religion to be a product of self-alienation, he yet finds confirmation of himself in *religion as religion.* Here *is* the root of Hegel's *false* positivism, or of his merely *apparent* criticism: this is what Feuerbach designated as the positing, negating and re-establishing of religion or theology—but it has to be grasped in more general terms. Thus reason is at home in unreason as unreason. The man who has recognised that he is leading an alienated life in politics, law, etc., is leading his true human life in this alienated life as such. Self-affirmation, *in contradiction* with itself—in contradiction both with the knowledge of and with the essential being of the object—is thus true *knowledge* and *life.*

There can therefore no longer be any question about an act of accommodation of Hegel's part *vis-a-vis* religion, the state, etc., since this lie is *the* lie of his principle.

If I *know* religion as *alienated* human self-consciousness, then what I know in it as religion is not my self-consciousness, but my alienated self-consciousness confirmed in it. I therefore know my own self, the self-consciousness that belongs to its very nature, confirmed not in *religion* but rather in *annihilated* and *superseded* religion.

In Hegel, therefore, the negation of the negation is not the confirmation of the true essence, effected precisely through negation of the pseudo-essence. With him the negation of the negation is the confirmation of the pseudo-essence, or of the self-estranged essence in its denial; or it is the denial of this pseudo-essence as an objective being dwelling outside man and independent of him, and its transformation into the subject.

A peculiar role, therefore, is played by the act of *superseding* in which denial and preservation—denial and affirmation—are bound together.

Thus, for example, in Hegel's *Philosophy of Right, Private Right* superseded equals *Morality,* Morality superseded equals the *Family,* the Family superseded equals *Civil Society,* Civil Society superseded equals *the State,* the State superseded equals *World History.* In the *actual world* private right, morality, the family, civil society, the state, etc., remain in existence, only they have become *moments* of man—state of his existence and being—which have no validity in isolation, but dissolve and engender one another, etc. They have become *moments of motion.*

In their actual existence this *mobile* nature of theirs is hidden. It first appears and is made manifest in thought, in philosophy. Hence my true religious existence is my existence in the *philosophy of religion;* my true political existence is my existence within the *philosophy of right;* my true natural existence, existence in the *philosophy of nature;* my true artistic existence, existence in the *philosophy of art;* my true *human* existence, my existence in *philosophy.* Likewise the true existence of religion, the state, nature, art, is the *philosophy* of religion, of nature, of the state and of art. If, however, the philosophy of religion, etc., is for me the sole true existence of religion, then, too, it is only as a *philosopher of religion* that I am truly religious, and so I deny *real* religious sentiment and the really *religious* man. But at the same time I *assert* them, in part within my own existence or within the alien existence which I oppose to them—for this *is* only their *philosophic* expression—and in part I assert them in their own original shape, for they have validity for me as merely the *apparent* other-being, as allegories, forms of their own true existence (i.e., of my *philosophical* existence) hidden under sensuous disguises.

In just the same way, *Quality* superseded equals *Quantity,* Quantity superseded equals *Measure,* Measure superseded equals *Essence,* Essence superseded equals *Appearance,* Appearance superseded equals *Actuality,* Actuality superseded equals the *Concept,* the Concept superseded equals *Objectivity,* Objectivity superseded equals the *Absolute Idea,* the Absolute Idea superseded equals *Nature,* Nature superseded equals *Subjective* Mind, Subjective Mind superseded equals *Ethical* Objective Mind, Ethical Mind superseded equals *Art,* Art superseded equals *Religion,* Religion superseded equals *Absolute Knowledge.*

On the one hand, this act of superseding is a transcending of the thought entity; thus, Private Property *as a thought* is transcended in the *thought* of morality. And because thought imagines itself to be directly the other of itself, to be *sensuous reality*—and therefore takes its own action for *sensuous, real action*—this superseding in thought, which leaves its object standing in the real world, believes that it has really overcome it. On the other hand, because the object has now become for it a moment of thought, thought takes it in its reality too to be self-confirmation of itself—of self-consciousness, of abstraction.

From the one point of view the existent which Hegel *supersedes* in philosophy is therefore not *real* religion, the *real* state, or *real* nature, but religion itself already become an object of knowledge, i.e., *Dogmatics;* the same with *Jurisprudence, Political Science* and *Natural Science.* From the one point of view, therefore, he stands in opposition both to the *real thing* and to immediate, unphilosophic *science* or the unphilosophic *conceptions* of this thing. He therefore contradicts their conventional conceptions.

On the other hand, the religious man, etc., can find in Hegel his final confirmation.

It is now time to lay hold of the *positive* aspects of the Hegelian dialectic within the realm of estrangement.

(a) *Annulling* as an objective movement of *retracting* the alienation *into self.* This is the insight, expressed within the estrangement, concerning the *appropriation* of the objective essence through the annulment of its estrangement; it is the estranged insight into the *real objectification* of man, into the real appropriation of his objective essence through the annihilation of the *estranged* character of the objective world, through the annulment of the objective world in its estranged mode of being—just as atheism, being the annulment of God, is the advent of theoretic humanism, and communism, as the annulment of private property, is the justification of real human life as man's possession and thus the advent of practical humanism (or just as atheism is humanism mediated with itself through the annulment of religion, whilst communism is humanism mediated with itself through the annulment of private property). Only through the annulment of this mediation—which is itself, however, a necessary premise—does positively self-deriving humanism, *positive humanism,* come into being.

But atheism and communism are no flight, no abstraction; they are not a losing of the objective world begotten by man—of man's essential powers given over to the realm of objectivity; they are not a returning in poverty to unnatural, primitive simplicity. On the contrary, they are but the first real coming-to-be, the realisation become real for man, of man's essence of the essence of man as something real.

Thus, by grasping the *positive* meaning of self-referred negation (if even again in estranged fashion) Hegel grasps man's self-estrangement, the alienation of man's essence, man's loss of objectivity and his loss of realness as finding of self, change of his nature, his objectification and realisation. In short, within the sphere of abstraction, Hegel conceives labour as man's act of *self-genesis*—conceives man's relation to himself as an alien being and the manifesting of himself as an alien being to be the coming-to-be of *species-consciousness* and *species-life*.

(b) However, apart from, or rather in consequence of, the perverseness already described, this act appears in Hegel:

First of all as a *merely formal,* because abstract, act, because the human essence itself is taken to be only an *abstract, thinking essence,* conceived merely as self-consciousness. And,

secondly, because the conception is *formal* and *abstract,* the annulment of the alienation becomes a confirmation of the alienation; or again, for Hegel this movement of *self-genesis* and *self-objectification* in the form of *self-alienation* and *self-estrangement* is the *absolute,* and hence final, *expression of human life*—of life with itself as its aim, of life at rest in itself, of life that has attained oneness with its essence.

This movement, in its abstract form as dialectic, is therefore regarded as *truly human life,* and because it is nevertheless an abstraction—an estrangement of human life—it is regarded as a *divine process,* but as the divine process of man, a process traversed by man's abstract, pure, absolute essence that is distinct from him.

Thirdly, this process must have a bearer, a subject. But the subject first emerges as a result. This result—the subject knowing itself as absolute self-consciousness—is therefore *God—absolute Spirit—the self-knowing and self-manifesting Idea.* Real man and real nature become mere predicates—symbols of this esoteric, unreal man and of this unreal nature. Subject and predicate are therefore related to each other in absolute inversion—a *mystical subject-object* or a *subjectivity reaching beyond* the *object*—the *absolute subject* as a *process,* as *subject alienating* itself and returning from alienation into itself, but at the same time retracting this alienation into itself, and the subject as this process; a pure, *restless* revolving within itself.

First, the *formal and abstract* conception of man's act of self-genesis or self-objectification.

Hegel having posited man as equivalent to self-consciousness, the estranged object—the estranged essential reality of man—is nothing but *consciousness,* the thought of estrangement merely—estrangement's *abstract* and therefore empty and unreal expression, *negation.* The annulment of the alienation is therefore likewise nothing but an abstract, empty annulment of that empty abstraction—the *negation of the negation.* The rich, living, sensuous, concrete activity of self-objectification is therefore reduced to its mere abstraction, *absolute negativity*—an abstraction which is again fixed as such and thought of as an independent activity—as sheer activity. Because this so-called negativity is nothing but the *abstract, empty* form of that real living act, its content can in consequence be merely a *formal* content begotten by abstraction from all content. As a result there are general, abstract *forms of abstraction* pertaining to every content and on that account indifferent to, and, consequently, valid for, all content—the thought-forms or logical categories torn from *real* mind and from *real* nature. (We shall unfold the *logical* content of absolute negativity further on.)

Hegel's positive achievement here, in his speculative logic, is that the *determinate concepts,* the universal *fixed thought-forms* in their independence *vis-a-vis* nature and mind are a necessary result of the general estrangement of the human essence and therefore also of human thought, and that Hegel has therefore brought these together and presented them as moments of the abstraction-process. For example, superseded Being as Essence, superseded Essence is Concept, the Concept superseded is . . . the Absolute Idea. But what, then, is the Absolute Idea? It supersedes its own self again, if it does not want to traverse once more from the beginning the whole act of abstraction, and to acquiesce in being a totality of abstractions or in being the self-comprehending abstraction. But abstraction comprehending itself as abstraction knows itself to be nothing: it must abandon itself—abandon abstraction—and so it arrives at an entity which is its exact contrary—at *nature.* Thus, the entire *Logic* is the demonstration that abstract thought is nothing in itself; that the Absolute Idea is nothing in itself; that only *Nature* is something.

The absolute idea, the *abstract* idea, which "*considered* with regard to its unity with itself is *intuiting*" (Hegel's *Encyclopaedia,* 3rd edition, p. 222), and which "in its own absolute truth *resolves* to let the moment of its particularity or of initial characterisation and other-being—the *immediate idea,* as its reflection, *go forth freely from itself as nature*" (l.c.)—this whole idea which behaves in such a strange and singular way, and which has given the Hegelians such terrible headaches, is from beginning to end nothing else but *abstraction* (i.e., the abstract thinker)—abstraction which, made wise by experience and enlightened concerning its truth, resolves under various (false and themselves still abstract) conditions to *abandon itself* and to replace its self-absorption, nothingness, generality and indeterminateness by its other-being, the particular, and the determinate; resolves to let *nature,* which it held hidden in itself only as an abstraction, as a thought-entity, *go forth* freely from itself: that is to say, abstraction resolves to forsake abstraction and to have a look at nature *free* of abstraction. The abstract idea, which without mediation becomes *intuiting,* is nothing else through-and-through but abstract thinking that gives itself up and resolves on *intuition.* This entire transition from Logic to Natural Philosophy is nothing else but the transition—so difficult to effect for the abstract thinker and therefore so queer in his description of it—from *abstracting* to *intuiting.* The *mystical* feeling which drives the philosopher forward from abstract thinking to intuiting is *boredom*—the longing for a content.

(The man estranged from himself is also the thinker estranged from his *essence*—that is, from the natural and human essence. His thoughts are therefore fixed mental shapes or ghosts dwelling outside nature and man. Hegel has locked up all these fixed mental forms together in his *Logic,* laying hold of each of them first as negation—that is, as an *alienation* of *human* thought—and then as negation of the negation—that is, as a superseding of this alienation, as a *real* expression of human thought. But as even this still takes place within the confines of the estrangement, this negation of the negation is in part the restoring of these fixed forms in their estrangement; in part a stopping-short at the last act—the act of self-reference in alienation—as the true mode of being of these fixed mental forms;[1] and in part, to the extent that this abstraction apprehends itself and experiences an infinite weariness with itself, there makes its appearance in Hegel, in the form of the resolution to recognise *nature* as the essential being and to go over to intuition, the abandonment of abstract thought—the abandonment of thought revolving solely within the orbit of thought, of thought devoid of eyes, of teeth, of ears, of everything.)

But *nature* too, taken abstractly, for itself—nature fixed in isolation from man—is *nothing* for man. It goes without saying that the abstract thinker who has committed himself to intuiting, intuits nature abstractly. Just as nature lay enclosed in the thinker in the form of the absolute idea, in the form of a thought-entity—in a shape which is his and yet is esoteric and mysterious even to him—so what he has let go forth from himself in truth is only this *abstract nature,* only nature as a *thought-entity*—but with the significance now of being the other-being of thought, of being real, intuited nature—of being nature distinguished from abstract thought. Or, to talk a human language, the abstract thinker learns in his intuition of nature that the entities which he thought to create from nothing, from pure abstraction—the entities he believed he was producing in the divine dialectic as pure products of the labour of thought forever weaving in itself and never looking outward—are nothing else but

[1] This means that what Hegel does is to put in place of these fixed abstractions the act of abstraction which revolves in its own circle. In so doing, he has the merit, in the first place, of having indicated the source of all these inappropriate concepts which, as originally presented, belonged to disparate philosophies; of having brought them together; and of having created the entire compass of abstraction exhaustively set out as the object of criticism, instead of some specific abstraction. (Why Hegel separates thought from the *subject* we shall see later: at this stage it is already clear, however, that when man is not, his characteristic expression also cannot be human, and so neither could thought be grasped as an expression of man as a human and natural subject endowed with eyes, ears, etc., and living in society, in the world, and in nature.)

abstractions from *characteristics of nature.* To him, therefore, the whole of nature merely repeats the logical abstractions in a sensuous, external form. He *analyses* it and these abstractions over again. Thus, his intuition of nature is only the act of confirming his abstraction from the intuition of nature—is only the conscious repetition by him of the process of begetting his abstraction. Thus, for example, Time equals Negativity referred to itself (l.c., p. 238): to the superseded Becoming as Being there corresponds, in natural form, superseded Movement as Matter. Light is *Reflection-in-Itself,* in *natural* form. Body as *Moon* and *Comet* is the *natural* form of the *antithesis* which according to the *Logic* is on the one side the *Positive resting on itself* and on the other side the *Negative* resting on itself. The Earth is the *natural* form of the logical *Ground,* as the negative unity of the antithesis, etc.

Nature as nature—that is to say, in so far as it is still sensuously distinguished from that secret sense hidden within it—nature isolated, distinguished from these abstractions, is *nothing*—a nothing *proving itself to be nothing*—is *devoid of sense,* or has only the sense of being an externality which has to be annulled.

> "In the finite-*teleological* position is to be found the correct premise that nature does not contain within itself the absolute purpose" (p. 225).

Its purpose is the confirmation of abstraction.

> "Nature has shown itself to be the Idea in the *form* of *other-being.* Since the *Idea* is in this form the negative of itself or *external to itself,* nature is not just relatively external *vis-a-vis* this idea, but *externality* constitutes the form in which it exists as nature" (p. 227).

Externality here is not to be understood as the *self-externalising world of sense* open to the light, open to the man endowed with senses. It is to be taken here in the sense of alienation—a mistake, a defect, which ought not to be. For what is true is still the Idea. Nature is only the *form of the Idea's other-being.* And since abstract thought is the *essence,* that which is external to it is by its essence something merely *external*. The abstract thinker recognises at the same time that *sensuousness—externality* in contrast to thought weaving *within itself*—is the essence of nature. But he expresses this contrast in such a way as to make this *externality of nature*, its *contrast* to thought, its *defect*, so that inasmuch as it is distinguished from abstraction, nature is something defective. Something which is defective not merely for me or in my eyes but in itself—intrinsically—has something outside itself which it lacks. That is, its being is something other than it itself. Nature has therefore to supersede itself for the abstract thinker, for it is already posited by him as a potentially *superseded* being.

—Marx, "Critique of the Hegelian Dialectic and Philosophy as a Whole," *Economic and Philosophic Manuscripts of 1844*, pp. 145–71

Hegel's conception of history assumes an *Abstract* or *Absolute Spirit* which develops in such a way that mankind is a mere *mass* bearing it with a varying degree of consciousness or unconsciousness. Within *empiric*, exoteric history he therefore has a *speculative*, esoteric history develop. The history of mankind becomes the history of the *abstract* spirit of mankind, a *spirit beyond all man!*

Parallel with this doctrine of Hegel's there developed in France that of the *Doctrinarians* proclaiming the *sovereignty of reason* in opposition to the *sovereignty of the people* in order to exclude the masses and rule *alone*. This was quite consistent. If the activity of *real* mankind is nothing but the activity of a *mass* of human individuals then *abstract generality, Reason,* the Spirit must contrariwise have an abstract expression restricted to a few individuals. It then depends on the situation and imaginative power of each individual whether he will pass for a representative of that "spirit."

In *Hegel* the *Absolute Spirit* of history already treats the *mass* as material and finds its true expression only in *philosophy*. But with Hegel, *the* philosopher is only the organ through which the creator of history, the Absolute Spirit, arrives at self-consciousness *by retrospection* after the movement has ended. The participation of the philosopher in history is reduced to this retrospective consciousness, for real movement is accomplished by the Absolute Spirit *unconsciously,* so that the philosopher appears *post festum.*

Hegel is doubly inconsistent: first because, while declaring that philosophy constitutes the Absolute Spirit's existence he refuses to recognize the *real philosophical individual* as the *Absolute* Spirit; secondly, because according to him the Absolute Spirit makes history only *in appearance.* For as the Absolute Spirit becomes *conscious* of itself as the creative World Spirit only in the philosopher and *post festum,* its making of history exists only in the consciousness, in the opinion and conception of the philosopher, i.e., only in the speculative imagination.

—Marx and Engels, *The Holy Family or Critique of Critical Critique,* pp. 115–16

To Hegel, the life-process of the human brain, *i.e.,* the process of thinking, which, under the name of "the Idea," he even transforms into an independent subject, is the demiurgos of the real world, and the real world is only the external, phenomenal form of "the Idea." With me, on the contrary, the ideal is nothing else than the material world reflected by the human mind, and translated into forms of thought.

—Marx, *Capital,* Vol. I, p. 25

Appendix: The Dialectic Method

Proletariat and wealth are opposites; as such they form a single whole. They are both forms of the world of private property. The question is what place each occupies in the antithesis. It is not sufficient to declare them two sides of a single whole.

Private property as private property, as wealth, is compelled to maintain *itself,* and thereby its opposite, the proletariat, in *existence.* That is the *positive* side of the contradiction, self-satisfied private property.

The proletariat, on the other hand, is compelled as proletariat to abolish itself and thereby its opposite, the condition for its existence, what makes it the proletariat, i.e., private property. That is the *negative* side of the contradiction, its restlessness within its very self, dissolved and self-dissolving private property.

The propertied class and the class of the proletariat present the same human self-alienation. But the former class finds in this self-alienation its confirmation and its good, *its own power:* it has in it a *semblance* of human existence. The class of the proletariat feels annihilated in its self-alienation; it sees in it its own powerlessness and the reality of an inhuman existence. In the words of Hegel, the class of the proletariat is in abasement *indignation* at that abasement, an indignation to which it is necessarily driven by the contradiction between its human *nature* and its condition of life, which is the outright, decisive and comprehensive negation of that nature.

Within this antithesis the private owner is therefore the *conservative* side, the proletarian, the *destructive* side. From the former arises the action of preserving the antithesis, from the latter, that of annihilating it.

Indeed private property, too, drives itself in its economic movement towards its own dissolution, only, however, through a development which does not depend on it, of which it is unconscious and which takes place against its will, through the very nature of things; only inasmuch as it produces the proletariat *as* proletariat, that misery conscious of its spiritual and physical misery, that dehumanization conscious of its dehumanization and therefore self-abolishing. The proletariat executes the sentence that private property pronounced on itself by begetting the proletariat, just as it carries out the sentence that wage-labour pronounced on itself by bringing forth wealth for others and misery for itself. When the proletariat is victorious, it by no means becomes the absolute side of society, for it is victorious only by abolishing itself and its opposite. Then the proletariat disappears as well as the opposite which determines it, private property.

—Marx and Engels, *The Holy Family or Critique of Critical Critique,* pp. 51–52

To speak Greek, we have the thesis, the antithesis and the synthesis. As to those who are not acquainted with Hegelian language, we would say to them in the sacramental formula, affirmation, negation, and negation of the negation.

. . .

It is of this absolute method that Hegel speaks in these terms: "Method is absolute force, unique, supreme, infinite, which no object can resist; it is the tendency of reason to find itself, to recognise itself, in everything." ("Logic," vol. III.) Everything being reduced to a logical category, and every movement, every act of production, to method, it naturally follows that all masses of products and of production, of objects and of movement, are reduced to an applied metaphysic. What Hegel has done for religion, right, &c., M. Proudhon seeks to do for political economy.

What, then, is this absolute method? The abstraction of movement. What is the abstraction of movement? Movement in the abstract. What is movement in the abstract? The purely logical formula of movement or the movement of pure reason. In what does the movement of pure reason consist? To pose, oppose and compose itself, to be formulated as thesis, antithesis and synthesis, or, better still, to affirm itself, to deny itself and to deny its negation.

How does reason act, in order to affirm itself, to place itself in a given category? That is the affair of reason itself and its apologists.

But once it has placed itself in thesis, this thesis, this thought, opposed to itself, doubles itself into two contradictory thoughts, the positive and the negative, the yes and no. The struggle of these two antagonistic elements, comprised in the antithesis, constitutes the dialectic movement. The yes becoming no, the no becoming yes, the yes becoming at once yes and no, the no becoming at once no and yes, the contraries balance themselves, neutralise themselves, paralyse themselves. The fusion of these two contradictory thoughts constitutes a new thought which is the synthesis of the two. This new thought unfolds itself again in two contradictory thoughts which are confounded in their turn in a new synthesis. From this travail is born a group of thoughts. This group of thoughts follows the same dialectic movement as a simple category, and has for antithesis a contradictory group. From these two groups is born a new group of thoughts which is the synthesis of them.

As from the dialectic movement of simple categories is born the group, so from the dialectic movement of the groups is born the series, and from the dialectic movement of the series is born the whole system.

Apply this method to the categories of political economy, and you will have the logic and the metaphysics of political economy, or, in other words, you will have the economic categories, known to all the world, translated into an almost unknown language, which will give them the appearance of having been freshly hatched in a head of pure reason, so much do these categories seem to engender the one the other, to enchain and entangle the one in the other by the sole labor of the dialectic movement. Let not the reader be alarmed by these metaphysics with all their scaffolding of categories, of groups, of series and of systems.

—Marx, *The Poverty of Philosophy,* pp. 114–15, 116–18

When we consider and reflect upon Nature at large or the history of mankind or our own intellectual activity, at first we see the picture of an endless entanglement of relations and reactions, permutations and combinations, in which nothing remains what, where and as it was, but everything moves, changes, comes into being and passes away. We see, therefore, at first the picture as a whole, with its individual parts still more or less kept in the background; we observe the movements, transitions, connections, rather than the things that move, combine and are connected. This primitive, naive but intrinsically correct conception of the world is that of ancient Greek philosophy, and was first clearly formulated by Heraclitus: everything is and is not, for everything is fluid, is constantly changing, constantly coming into being and passing away.

But this conception, correctly as it expresses the general character of the picture of appearances as a whole, does not suffice to explain the details of which this picture is made up, and so long as we do not understand these, we have not a clear idea of the whole picture. In order to understand these details we must detach them from their natural or historical connection and examine each one separately, its nature, special causes, effects, etc. This is, primarily, the task of natural science and historical research: branches of science which the Greeks of classical times, on very good grounds, relegated to a subordinate position, because they had first of all to collect materials for these sciences to work upon. A certain amount of natural and historical material must be collected before there can be any critical analysis, comparison, and arrangement in classes, orders, and species. The foundations of the exact natural sciences were, therefore, first worked out by the Greeks of the Alexandrian period, and later on, in the Middle Ages, by the Arabs. Real natural science dates from the second half of the fifteenth century, and thence onward it had advanced with constantly increasing rapidity. The analysis of Nature into its individual parts, the grouping of the different natural processes and objects in definite classes, the study of the internal anatomy of organic bodies in their manifold forms—these were the fundamental conditions of the gigantic strides in our knowledge of Nature that have been made during the last four hundred years. But this method of work has also left us as legacy the habit of observing natural objects and processes in isolation, apart from their connection with the vast whole; of observing them in repose, not in motions; as constants, not as essentially variables; in their death, not in their life. And when this way of looking at things was transferred by Bacon and Locke from natural science to philosophy, it begot the narrow, metaphysical mode of thought peculiar to the last century.

To the metaphysician, things and their mental reflexes, ideas, are isolated, are to be considered one after the other and apart from each other, are objects of investigation fixed, rigid, given once for all. He thinks in absolutely irreconcilable antitheses. "His communication is 'yea, yea' 'nay, nay'; for whatsoever is more than these cometh of evil." For him a thing either exists or does not exist; a thing cannot at the same time be itself and something else. Positive and negative absolutely exclude one another; cause and effect stand in a rigid antithesis one to the other.

At first sight this mode of thinking seems to us very luminous, because it is that of so-called sound common sense. Only sound common sense, respectable fellow that he is, in the homely realm of his own four walls, has very wonderful adventures directly he ventures out into the wide world of research. And the metaphysical mode of thought, justifiable and necessary as it is in a number of domains whose extent varies according to the nature of the particular object of investigation, sooner or later reaches a limit, beyond which it becomes one-sided, restricted, abstract, lost in insoluble contradictions. In the contemplation of individual things, it forgets the connection between them; in the contemplation of their existence, it forgets the beginning and end of that existence; of their repose, it forgets their motion. It cannot see the wood for the trees.

For everyday purposes we know and can say, e.g., whether an animal is alive or not. But, upon closer inquiry, we find that this is, in many cases, a very complex question, as the jurists know very well. They have cudgelled their brains in vain to discover a rational limit beyond which the killing of the child in its mother's womb is murder. It is just as impossible to determine absolutely the moment of death, for physiology proves that death is not an instantaneous, momentary phenomenon, but a very protracted process.

In like manner, every organic being is every moment the same and not the same; every moment it assimilates matter supplied from without, and gets rid of other matter; every moment some cells of its body die and others build themselves anew; in a longer or shorter time the matter of its body is completely renewed, and is replaced by other molecules of matter, so that every organic being is always itself, and yet something other than itself.

Further, we find upon closer investigation that the two poles of an antithesis, positive and negative, e.g., are as inseparable as they are opposed, and that despite all their opposition, they mutually interpenetrate. And we find, in like manner, that cause and effect are conceptions which only hold good in their application to individual cases; but as soon as we consider the individual cases in their general connection with the universe as a whole, they run into each other, and they become confounded when we contemplate that universal action and reaction in which causes and effects are eternally changing places, so that what is effect here and now will be cause there and then, and *vice versa.*

None of these processes and modes of thought enters into the framework of metaphysical reasoning. Dialectics, on the other hand, comprehends things and their representations, ideas, in their essential connection, concatenation, motion, origin, and ending. Such processes as those mentioned above are, therefore, so many corroborations of its own method of procedure.

Nature is the proof of dialectics, and it must be said for modern science that it has furnished this proof with very rich materials increasing daily, and thus has shown that, in the last resort, Nature works dialectically and not metaphysically; that she does not move in the eternal oneness of a perpetually recurring circle, but goes through a real historical evolution. In this connection Darwin must be named before all others. He dealt the metaphysical conception of Nature the heaviest blow by his proof that all organic beings, plants, animals, and man himself, are the products of a process of evolution going on through millions of years. But the naturalists who have learned to think dialectically are few and far between, and this conflict of the results of discovery with preconceived modes of thinking explains the endless confusion now reigning in theoretical natural science, the despair of teachers as well as learners, of authors and readers alike.

An exact representation of the universe, of its evolution, of the development of mankind, and of the reflection of this evolution in the minds of men, can therefore only be obtained by the methods of dialectics with its constant regard to the innumerable actions and reactions of life and death, of progressive or retrogressive changes. And in this spirit the new German philosophy has worked. Kant began his career by resolving the stable solar system of Newton and its eternal duration, after the famous initial impulse had once been given, into the result of a historic process, the formation of the sun and all the planets out of a rotating nebulous mass. From this he at the same time drew the conclusion that, given this origin of the solar system, its future death followed of necessity. His theory half a century later was established mathematically by Laplace, and half a century after that the spectroscope proved the existence in space of such incandescent masses of gas in various stages of condensation.

This new German philosophy culminated in the Hegelian system. In this system—and herein is its great merit—for the first time the whole world, natural, historical, intellectual, is represented as a process, i.e., as in constant motion, change, transformation, development; and the attempt is made to trace out the internal connection that makes a continuous whole of all this movement and development. From this point of view the history of mankind no longer appeared as a wild whirl of senseless deeds of violence, all equally condemnable at the judgment-seat of mature philosophic reason and which are best forgotten as quickly as possible, but as the process of evolution of man himself. It was now the task of the intellect to follow the gradual march of this process through all its devious ways, and to trace out the inner law running through all its apparently accidental phenomena.

—Engels, "Socialism, Utopian and Scientific," *MESW II*, pp. 129–32

II

The Theory of Alienation

Introduction

In transforming Hegelian idealism to materialism, Marx converts Hegel's central theme, self-alienation—the dualism of man and the world—to the purposes of revolution. Like Hegel, Marx is passionately concerned with the ultimate unity of man and the world, so that man may achieve his fullest potential.

Marx believed that the roots of man's alienation were found in the necessity for man to earn a living. "The product of labour is labour which has been congealed as an object, which has become material . . . this realization of labour (as a material object) appears as loss of reality . . . object bondage . . . as alienation" (infra *p. 69*).

Political economy, which deals with production of material objects, is then the field of inquiry most essential for an understanding of human alienation. Marx's claim for the centrality of the economic interpretation of history, as well as his life-long study of economics, follows from this position.

According to Marx capitalism is the most highly developed, if temporary, form of social organization that has hitherto evolved out of the basic necessity for men to earn a living. It is not itself the cause of alienation; but its system is rife with symptoms of alienation.

Capitalist economic organization produces alienation in a variety of ways: Man is set against man—capitalist versus worker—a situation from which inhuman exploitative relationships develop; labor is not voluntary but coerced—"it is forced labour"; one man's labor is appropriated by another—the worker's labor by the capitalist; finally, man creates barriers between himself and nature by becoming enclosed by tools and machines in an artificial urban life.

To Marx the pivotal position of the theory of alienation is clear. The necessity to work, which is at the root of the misery of the human race, is responsible for economic systems, whose job is to organize production. Capitalism, the highest form of production, creates both wealth and the heightened misery of extreme alienation. At the same time, the dialectical process, the continuous evolution of the economic system toward communism, the point at which man and nature are reunited and alienation ends, goes on.

Marx's most complete statement of the nature, causes, and implications of alienation are found in his Economic and Philosophic Manuscripts of 1844. *Selections from this document make up the bulk of Chapter II.*

In the short section entitled "Commodity Fetishism" Marx shows how the products of human labor are objectified as "commodities," which the capitalist economic system separates from the human energy and intelligence that creates them. A commodity that is bought and sold on the market is in reality the alienated product of labor.

Finally, in the section entitled "Money Alienation" Marx argues that money stands between man and man and corrupts standards: ". . . money *transforms the* real essential powers of man and nature *into what are merely abstract conceits (and transforms) es-*

sential powers which are really impotent . . . into real powers and faculties" (infra *p. 106*).

●

Alienation and Political Economy

We have proceeded from the premises of political economy. We have accepted its language and its laws. We presupposed private property, the separation of labour, capital and land, and of wages, profit of capital and rent of land—likewise division of labour, competition, the concept of exchange-value, etc. On the basis of political economy itself, in its own words, we have shown that the worker sinks to the level of a commodity and becomes indeed the most wretched of commodities; that the wretchedness of the worker is in inverse proportion to the power and magnitude of his production; that the necessary result of competition is the accumulation of capital in a few hands, and thus the restoration of monopoly in a more terrible form; that finally the distinction between capitalist and land-rentier, like that between the tiller of the soil and the factory-worker, disappears and that the whole of society must fall apart into the two classes—the property-*owners* and the propertyless *workers*.

Political economy proceeds from the fact of private property, but it does not explain it to us. It expresses in general, abstract formulae the *material* process through which private property actually passes, and these formulae it then takes for *laws*. It does not *comprehend* these laws—i.e., it does not demonstrate how they arise from the very nature of private property. Political economy does not disclose the source of the division between labour and capital, and between capital and land. When, for example, it defines the relationship of wages to profit, it takes the interest of the capitalists to be the ultimate cause; i.e., it takes for granted what it is supposed to evolve. Similarly, competition comes in everywhere. It is explained from external circumstances. As to how far these external and apparently fortuitous circumstances are but the expression of a necessary course of development, political economy teaches us nothing. We have seen how, to it, exchange itself appears to be a fortuitous fact. The only wheels which political economy sets in motion are *avarice* and the *war amongst the avaricious—competition.*

Precisely because political economy does not grasp the connections within the movement, it was possible to counterpose, for instance, the doctrine of competition to the doctrine of monopoly, the doctrine of craft-liberty to the doctrine of the corporation, the doctrine of the division of landed property to the doctrine of the big estate—for competition, craft-liberty and the division of landed property were explained and comprehended only as fortuitous, premeditated and violent consequences of monopoly, the corporation, and feudal property, not as their necessary, inevitable and natural consequences.

Now, therefore, we have to grasp the essential connection between private property, avarice, and the separation of labour, capital and landed property; between exchange and competition, value and the devaluation of men, monopoly and competition, etc.; the connection between this whole estrangement and the *money*-system.

Do not let us go back to a fictitious primordial condition as the political economist does, when he tries to explain. Such a primordial condition explains nothing. He merely pushes the question away into a grey nebulous distance. He assumes in the form of fact, of an event, what he is supposed to deduce—namely, the necessary relationship between two things—between, for example, division of labour and exchange. Theology in the same way explains the origin of evil by the fall of man: that is, it assumes as a fact, in historical form, what has to be explained.

We proceed from an *actual* economic fact.

The worker becomes all the poorer the more wealth he produces, the more his production increases in power and range. The worker becomes an ever cheaper commodity the more commodities he creates. With the *increasing value* of the world of things proceeds in direct proportion the *devaluation* of the world of men. Labour produces not only commodities: it produces itself and the worker as a *commodity*—and does so in the proportion in which it produces commodities generally.

This fact expresses merely that the object which labour produces —labour's product—confronts it as *something alien,* as a *power independent* of the producer. The product of labour is labour which has been congealed in an object, which has become material: it is the *objectification* of labour. Labour's realisation is its objectification. In the conditions dealt with by political economy this realisation of labour appears as *loss of reality* for the workers; objectification as *loss of the object* and *object-bondage;* appropriation as *estrangement,* as *alienation.*

So much does labour's realisation appear as loss of reality that the worker loses reality to the point of starving to death. So much does objectification appear as loss of the object that the worker is robbed of the objects most necessary not only for his life but for his work. Indeed, labour itself becomes an object which he can get hold of only with the greatest effort and with the most irregular interruptions. So much does the appropriation of the object appear as estrangement that the more objects the worker produces the fewer can he possess and the more he falls under the dominion of his product, capital.

All these consequences are contained in the definition that the worker is related to the *product of his labour* as to an *alien* object. For on this premise it is clear that the more the worker spends himself, the more powerful the alien objective world becomes which he creates over-against himself, the poorer he himself—his inner world —becomes, the less belongs to him as his own. It is the same in religion. The more man puts into God, the less he retains in himself. The worker puts his life into the object; but now his life no longer belongs to him but to the object. Hence, the greater this activity, the greater is the worker's lack of objects. Whatever the product of his labour is, he is not. Therefore the greater this product, the less is he himself. The *alienation* of the worker in his product means not only that his labour becomes an object, an *external* existence, but that it exists *outside him,* independently, as something alien to him, and that it becomes a power on its own confronting him; it means that the life which he has conferred on the object confronts him as something hostile and alien.

Let us now look more closely at the *objectification,* at the production of the worker; and therein at the *estrangement,* the *loss* of the object, his product.

The worker can create nothing without *nature,* without the *sensuous external world.* It is the material on which his labour is manifested, in which it is active, from which and by means of which it produces.

But just as nature provides labour with the *means of life* in the sense that labour cannot *live* without objects on which to operate, on the other hand, it also provides the *means of life* in the more restricted sense—i.e., the means for the physical subsistence of the *worker* himself.

Thus the more the worker by his labour *appropriates* the external world, sensuous nature, the more he deprives himself of *means of life* in the double respect: first, that the sensuous external world more and more ceases to be an object belonging to his labour—to be his labour's *means of life;* and secondly, that it more and more ceases to be *means of life* in the immediate sense, means for the physical subsistence of the worker.

Thus in this double respect the worker becomes a slave of his object, first, in that he receives an *object of labour,* i.e., in that he receives *work;* and secondly, in that he receives *means of subsistence.* Therefore, it enables him to exist, first, as a *worker;* and, second, as a *physical subject.* The extremity of this bondage is that it is only as a *worker* that he continues to maintain himself as a *physical subject,* and that it is only as a *physical subject* that he is a *worker.*

(The laws of political economy express the estrangement of the worker in his object thus: the more the worker produces, the less he has to consume; the more values he creates, the more valueless, the more unworthy he becomes; the better formed his product, the more deformed becomes the worker; the more civilised his object, the more barbarous becomes the worker; the mightier labour becomes, the more powerless becomes the worker; the more ingenious labour becomes, the duller becomes the worker and the more he becomes nature's bondsman.)

Political economy conceals the estrangement inherent in the nature of labour by not considering the direct relationship between the worker (labour) *and production.* It is true that labour produces for the rich wonderful things—but for the worker it produces privation. It produces palaces—but for the worker, hovels. It produces beauty —but for the worker, deformity. It replaces labour by machines— but some of the workers it throws back to a barbarous type of labour, and the other workers it turns into machines. It produces intelligence—but for the worker idiocy, cretinism.

The direct relationship of labour to its produce is the relationship of the worker to the objects of his production. The relationship of the man of means to the objects of production and to production itself is only a *consequence* of this first relationship—and confirms it. We shall consider this other aspect later.

When we ask, then, what is the essential relationship of labour we are asking about the relationship of the *worker* to production.

Till now we have been considering the estrangement, the alienation of the worker only in one of its aspects, i.e., the worker's *relationship to the products of his labour*. But the estrangement is manifested not only in the result but in the *act of production*— within the *producing activity* itself. How would the worker come to face the product of his activity as a stranger, were it not that in the very act of production he was estranging himself from himself? The product is after all but the summary of the activity, of production. If then the product of labour is alienation, production itself must be active alienation, the alienation of activity, the activity of alienation. In the estrangement of the object of labour is merely summarised the estrangement, the alienation, in the activity of labour itself.

What, then, constitutes the alienation of labour?

First, the fact that labour is *external* to the worker, i.e., it does not belong to his essential being; that in his work, therefore, he does not affirm himself but denies himself, does not feel content but unhappy, does not develop freely his physical and mental energy but mortifies his body and ruins his mind. The worker therefore only feels himself outside his work, and in his work feels outside himself. He is at home when he is not working, and when he is working he is not at home. His labour is therefore not voluntary, but coerced; it is *forced labour*. It is therefore not the satisfaction of a need; it is merely a *means* to satisfy needs external to it. Its alien character emerges clearly in the fact that as soon as no physical or other compulsion exists, labour is shunned like the plague. External labour, labour in which man alienates himself, is a labour of self-sacrifice, of mortification. Lastly, the external character of labour for the worker appears in the fact that it is not his own, but someone else's, that it does not belong to him, that in it he belongs, not to himself, but to another. Just as in religion the spontaneous activity of the human imagination, of the human brain and the human heart, operates independently of the individual—that is, operates on him as an alien, divine or diabolical activity—in the same way the worker's activity is not his spontaneous activity. It belongs to another; it is the loss of his self.

As a result, therefore, man (the worker) no longer feels himself to be freely active in any but his animal functions—eating, drinking, procreating, or at most in his dwelling and in dressing-up, etc.; and in his human functions he no longer feels himself to be anything but an animal. What is animal becomes human and what is human becomes animal.

Certainly eating, drinking, procreating, etc., are also genuinely human functions. But in the abstraction which separates them from the sphere of all other human activity and turns them into sole and ultimate ends, they are animal.

We have considered the act of estranging practical human activity, labour, in two of its aspects. (1) The relation of the worker to the *product of labour* as an alien object exercising power over him. This relation is at the same time the relation to the sensuous external world, to the objects of nature as an alien world antagonistically opposed to him. (2) The relation of labour to the *act of production* within the *labour* process. This relation is the relation of the worker to his own activity as an alien activity not belonging to him; it is activity as suffering, strength as weakness, begetting as emasculating, the worker's *own* physical and mental energy, his personal life or what is life other than activity—as an activity which is turned against him, neither depends on nor belongs to him. Here we have *self-estrangement,* as we had previously the estrangement of the *thing*.

We have yet a third aspect of *estranged labour* to deduce from the two already considered.

Man is a species being, not only because in practice and in theory he adopts the species as his object (his own as well as those of other things), but—and this is only another way of expressing it—but also because he treats himself as the actual, living species; because he treats himself as a *universal* and therefore a free being.

The life of the species, both in man and in animals, consists physically in the fact that man (like the animal) lives on inorganic nature; and the more universal man is compared with an animal, the more universal is the sphere of inorganic nature on which he lives. Just as plants, animals, stones, the air, light, etc., constitute a part of human consciousness in the realm of theory, partly as objects of natural science, partly as objects of art—his spiritual inorganic nature, spiritual nourishment which he must first prepare to make it palatable and digestible—so too in the realm of practice they constitute a part of human life and human activity. Physically man lives only on these products of nature, whether they appear in the form of food, heating, clothes, a dwelling, or whatever it may be. The universality of man is in practice manifested precisely in the universality which makes all nature his *inorganic* body—both inasmuch as nature is (1) his direct means of life, and (2) the material, the object, and the instrument of his life-activity. Nature is man's *inorganic body*—nature, that is, in so far as it is not itself the human body. Man *lives* on nature—means that nature is his *body*, with which he must remain in continuous intercourse if he is not to die. That man's physical and spiritual life is linked to nature means simply that nature is linked to itself, for man is a part of nature.

In estranging from man (1) nature, and (2) himself, his own active functions, his life-activity, estranged labour estranges the *species* from man. It turns for him the *life of the species* into a means of individual life. First it estranges the life of the species and individual life, and secondly it makes individual life in its abstract form the purpose of the life of the species, likewise in its abstract and estranged form.

For in the first place labour, *life-activity, productive life* itself, appears to man merely as a *means* of satisfying a need—the need to maintain the physical existence. Yet the productive life is the life of the species. It is life-engendering life. The whole character of a species—its species character—is contained in the character of its life-activity; and free, conscious activity is man's species character. Life itself appears only as a *means to life.*

The animal is immediately identical with its life-activity. It does not distinguish itself from it. It is its *life-activity.* Man makes his life-activity itself the object of his will and of his consciousness. He has conscious life-activity. It is not a determination with which he directly merges. Conscious life-activity directly distinguishes man from animal life-activity. It is just because of this that he is a species being. Or it is only because he is a species being that he is a Conscious Being, i.e., that his own life is an object for him. Only because of that is his activity free activity. Estranged labour reverses this relationship, so that it is just because man is a conscious being that he makes his life-activity, his *essential* being, a mere means to his *existence.*

In creating an *objective world* by his practical activity, in *working-up* inorganic nature, man proves himself a conscious species being, i.e., as a being that treats the species as its own essential being, or that treats itself as a species being. Admittedly animals also produce. They build themselves nests, dwellings, like the bees, beavers, ants, etc. But an animal only produces what it immediately needs for itself or its young. It produces one-sidedly, whilst man produces universally. It produces only under the dominion of immediate physical need, whilst man produces even when he is free from physical need and only truly produces in freedom therefrom. An animal produces only itself, whilst man reproduces the whole of nature. An animal's product belongs immediately to its physical body, whilst man freely confronts his product. An animal forms things in accordance with the standard and the need of the species to which it belongs, whilst man knows how to produce in accordance with the standard of every species, and knows how to apply everywhere the inherent standard to the object. Man therefore also forms things in accordance with the laws of beauty.

It is just in the working-up of the objective world, therefore, that man first really proves himself to be a *species being.* This production is his active species life. Through and because of this production, nature appears as *his* work and his reality. The object of labour is, therefore, the *objectification of man's species life:* for he duplicates himself not only, as in consciousness, intellectually, but also actively, in reality, and therefore he contemplates himself in a world that he has created. In tearing away from man the object of his production, therefore, estranged labour tears from his *species life,* his real species objectivity, and transforms his advantage over animals into the disadvantage that his inorganic body, nature, is taken from him.

Similarly, in degrading spontaneous activity, free activity, to a means, estranged labour makes man's species life a means to his physical existence.

The consciousness which man has of his species is thus transformed by estrangement in such a way that the species life becomes for him a means.

Estranged labour turns thus:

(3) *Man's species being,* both nature and his spiritual species property, into a being *alien* to him, into a *means* to his *individual existence.* It estranges man's own body from him, as it does external nature and his spiritual essence, his *human* being.

(4) An immediate consequence of the fact that man is estranged from the product of his labour, from his life-activity, from his species being is the *estrangement of man* from *man.* If a man is confronted by himself, he is confronted by the *other* man. What applies to a man's relation to his work, to the product of his labour and to himself, also holds of a man's relation to the other man, and to the other man's labour and object of labour.

In fact, the proposition that man's species nature is estranged from him means that one man is estranged from the other, as each of them is from man's essential nature.

The estrangement of man, and in fact every relationship in which man stands to himself, is first realised and expressed in the relationship in which a man stands to other men.

Hence within the relationship of estranged labour each man

views the other in accordance with the standard and the position in which he finds himself as a worker.

We took our departure from a fact of political economy—the estrangement of the worker and his production. We have formulated the concept of this fact—*estranged, alienated* labour. We have analysed this concept—hence analysing merely a fact of political economy.

Let us now see, further, how in real life the concept of estranged, alienated labour must express and present itself.

If the product of labour is alien to me, if it confronts me as an alien power, to whom, then, does it belong?

If my own activity does not belong to me, if it is an alien, a coerced activity, to whom, then, does it belong?

To a being *other* than me.

Who is this being?

The *gods?* To be sure, in the earliest times the principal production (for example, the building of temples, etc., in Egypt, India and Mexico) appears to be in the service of the gods, and the product belongs to the gods. However, the gods on their own were never the lords of labour. No more was *nature*. And what a contradiction it would be if, the more man subjugated nature by his labour and the more the miracles of the gods were rendered superfluous by the miracles of industry, the more man were to renounce the joy of production and the enjoyment of the produce in favour of these powers.

The *alien* being, to whom labour and the produce of labour belongs, in whose service labour is done and for whose benefit the produce of labour is provided, can only be *man* himself.

If the product of labour does not belong to the worker, if it confronts him as an alien power, this can only be because it belongs to some *other man than the worker*. If the worker's activity is a torment to him, to another it must be *delight* and his life's joy. Not the gods, not nature, but only man himself can be this alien power over man.

We must bear in mind the above-stated proposition that man's relation to himself only becomes *objective* and *real* for him through his relation to the other man. Thus, if the product of his labour, his labour *objectified,* is for him an *alien,* hostile, powerful object independent of him, then his position towards it is such that someone else is master of this object, someone who is alien, hostile, powerful, and independent of him. If his own activity is to him an unfree activity, then he is treating it as activity performed in the service, under the dominion, the coercion and the yoke of another man.

Every self-estrangement of man from himself and from nature appears in the relation in which he places himself and nature to men other than and differentiated from himself. For this reason religious self-estrangement necessarily appears in the relationship of the layman to the priest, or again to a mediator, etc., since we are here dealing with the intellectual world. In the real practical world self-estrangement can only become manifest through the real practical relationship to other men. The medium through which estrangement takes place is itself *practical.* Thus through estranged labour man not only engenders his relationship to the object and to the act of production as to powers that are alien and hostile to him; he also engenders the relationship in which other men stand to his production and to his product, and the relationship in which he stands to these other men. Just as he begets his own production as the loss of his reality, as his punishment; just as he begets his own product as a loss, as a product not belonging to him; so he begets the dominion of the one who does not produce over production and over the product. Just as he estranges from himself his own activity, so he confers to the stranger activity which is not his own.

Till now we have only considered this relationship from the standpoint of the worker and later we shall be considering it also from the standpoint of the non-worker.

Through *estranged, alienated labour,* then, the worker produces the relationship to this labour of a man alien to labour and standing outside it. The relationship of the worker to labour engenders the relation to it of the capitalist, or whatever one chooses to call the master of labour. *Private property* is thus the product, the result, the necessary consequence, of *alienated labour,* of the external relation of the worker to nature and to himself.

Private property thus results by analysis from the concept of *alienated labour*—i.e., of *alienated man,* of estranged labour, of estranged life, of *estranged* man.

True, it is as a result of the *movement of private property* that we have obtained the concept of *alienated labour* (*of alienated life*) from political economy. But on analysis of this concept it becomes clear that though private property appears to be the source, the cause of alienated labour, it is really its consequence, just as the gods *in the beginning* are not the cause but the effect of man's intellectual confusion. Later this relationship becomes reciprocal.

Only at the very culmination of the development of private property does this, its secret, re-emerge, namely, that on the one hand it is the *product* of alienated labour, and that secondly it is the *means* by which labour alienates itself, the *realisation of this alienation.*

This exposition immediately sheds light on various hitherto unsolved conflicts.

(1) Political economy starts from labour as the real soul of production; yet to labour it gives nothing, and to private property everything. From this contradiction Proudhon has concluded in favour of labour and against private property. We understand, however, that this apparent contradiction is the contradiction of *estranged labour* with itself, and that political economy has merely formulated the laws of estranged labour.

We also understand, therefore, that *wages* and *private property* are identical: where the product, the object of labour pays for labour itself, the wage is but a necessary consequence of labour's estrangement, for after all in the wage of labour, labour does not appear as an end in itself but as the servant of the wage. We shall develop this point later, and meanwhile will only deduce some conclusions.

A *forcing-up of wages* (disregarding all other difficulties, including the fact that it would only be by force, too, that the higher wages, being an anomaly, could be maintained) would therefore be nothing but *better payment for the slave,* and would not conquer either for the worker or for labour their human status and dignity.

Indeed, even the *equality of wages* demanded by Proudhon only transforms the relationship of the present-day worker to his labour into the relationship of all men to labour. Society is then conceived as an abstract capitalist.

Wages are a direct consequence of estranged labour, and estranged labour is the direct cause of private property. The downfall of the one aspect must therefore mean the downfall of the other.

(2) From the relationship of estranged labour to private property it further follows that the emancipation of society from private property, etc., from servitude, is expressed in the *political* form of the *emancipation of the workers;* not that *their* emancipation alone was at stake but because the emancipation of the workers contains universal human emancipation—and it contains this, because the whole of human servitude is involved in the relation of the worker to production, and every relation of servitude is but a modification and consequence of this relation.

Just as we have found the concept of *private property* from the concept of *estranged, alienated labour by analysis,* in the same way every *category* of political economy can be evolved with the help of these two factors; and we shall find again in each category, e.g., trade, competition, capital, money, only a *definite* and *developed expression* of the first foundations.

Before considering this configuration, however, let us try to solve two problems.

(1) To define the general *nature of private property,* as it has arisen as a result of estranged labour, in its relation to *truly human, social property.*

(2) We have accepted the *estrangement of labour,* its *alienation* as a fact, and we have analysed this fact. How, we now ask, does *man* come to *alienate,* to estrange, *his labour?* How is this estrangement rooted in the nature of human development? We have already gone a long way to the solution of this problem by *transforming* the question as to the *origin of private property* into the question as to the relation of *alienated labour* to the course of humanity's development. For when one speaks of *private property,* one thinks of being concerned with something external to man.

When one speaks of labour, one is directly concerned with man himself. This new formulation of the question already contains its solution.

As to (1): The general nature of private property and its relation to truly human property.

Alienated labour has resolved itself for us into two elements which mutually condition one another, or which are but different expressions of one and the same relationship. *Appropriation* appears as *estrangement,* as *alienation;* and *alienation* appears as *appropriation, estrangement* as true *enfranchisement.*

We have considered the one side—*alienated* labour—in relation to the *worker* himself, i.e., the *relation of alienated labour to itself.* The *property-relation of the non-worker to the worker and to labour* we have found as the product, the necessary outcome of this relation of alienated labour. *Private property,* as the material, summary expression of alienated labour, embraces both relations —*the relation of the worker to work, to the product of his labour and to the non-worker,* and the relation of the *non-worker to the worker and to the product of his labour.*

Having seen that in relation to the worker who *appropriates* nature by means of his labour, this appropriation appears as estrangement, his own spontaneous activity as activity for another and as activity of another, vitality as a sacrifice of life, production of the object as loss of the object to an alien power, to an *alien* person—we shall now consider the relation to the worker, to labour and its object of this person who is *alien* to labour and the worker.

First it has to be noticed, that everything which appears in the worker as an *activity of alienation, of estrangement,* appears in the non-worker as a *state of alienation, of estrangement.*

Secondly, that the worker's *real, practical attitude* in production and to the product (as a state of mind) appears in the non-worker confronting him as a *theoretical* attitude.

Thirdly, the non-worker does everything against the worker which the worker does against himself; but he does not do against himself what he does against the worker.

Let us look more closely at these three relations.

[ANTITHESIS OF CAPITAL AND LABOUR. LANDED PROPERTY AND CAPITAL]

. . . forms the interest on his capital. The worker is the subjective manifestation of the fact that capital is man wholly lost to himself, just as capital is the objective manifestation of the fact that labour is man lost to himself. But the *worker* has the misfortune to be a *living* capital, and therefore a capital *with needs*—one which loses its interest, and hence its livelihood, every moment it is not working. The *value* of the worker as capital rises according to demand and supply, and even *physically* his *existence, his life,* was and is looked upon as a supply of a *commodity* like any other. The worker produces capital, capital produces him—hence he produces himself, and man as *worker,* as a *commodity,* is the product of this entire cycle. To the man who is nothing more than a *worker*—and to him as a worker—his human qualities only exist in so far as they exist for capital *alien* to him. Because man and capital are foreign to each other, however, and thus stand in an indifferent, external and fortuitous relationship to each other, it is inevitable that this foreignness should also appear as something *real.* As soon, therefore, as it occurs to capital (whether from necessity or caprice) no longer to be for the worker, he himself is no longer for himself: he has *no* work, hence *no* wages, and as he has no existence as a *human being* but only as a *worker,* he can go and bury himself, starve to death, etc. The worker exists as a worker only when he exists *for himself* as capital; and he exists as capital only when some *capital* exists *for him.* The existence of capital is *his* existence, his *life;* as it determines the tenor of his life in a manner indifferent to him.

Political economy, therefore, does not recognise the unoccupied worker, the workman, in so far as he happens to be outside this labour-relationship. The cheat-thief, swindler, beggar, and unemployed man; the starving, wretched and criminal working-man—these are *figures* who do not exist for *political economy* but only for other eyes, those of the doctor, the judge, the grave-digger and bum-bailiff, etc.; such figures are spectres outside the domain of political economy. For it, therefore, the worker's needs are but the one *need*—to maintain him *whilst he is working* in so far as may be necessary to *prevent the race of labourers from dying out.* The wages of labour have thus exactly the same significance as the *maintenance* and *servicing* of any other productive instrument, or as the *consumption of a capital,* required for its reproduction with interest; or as the oil which is applied to wheels to keep them turning. Wages, therefore, belong to capital's and the capitalist's necessary *costs,* and must not exceed the bounds of this necessity. It was therefore quite logical for the English factory-owners to deduct from the wages of the worker the public charity which he was receiving out of the Poor Rate before the Amendment Bill of 1834, and to consider this to be an integral part of the wage.

Production does not simply produce man as a *commodity,* the *commodity-man,* man in the role of *commodity;* it produces him in keeping with this role as a *spiritually* and physically *dehumanised* being.—Immorality, deformity, and hebetation of the workers and the capitalists.—Its product is the *self-conscious and self-acting commodity.* . . . The commodity-*man.* . . . Great advance of Ricardo, Mill, etc., on Smith and Say, to declare the *existence* of the human being—the greater or lesser human productivity of the commodity—to be a matter of *indifference* and even *harmful.* Not how many workers are maintained by a given capital, but rather how much interest it brings in, the sum-total of the annual *saving,* is said to be the true purpose of production.

It was likewise a great and logical advance of modern English political economy, that, whilst elevating *labour* to the position of its *sole* principle, it should at the same time expound with complete clarity the *inverse* relation between wages and interest on capital, and the fact that the capitalist could normally *only* gain by pressing down wages, and vice versa. Not the doing-down of the consumer, but the capitalist and the worker doing-down each other, is shown to be the *normal* relationship.

The relations of private property contain latent within them the relations of private property as *labour,* the same relations as *capital,* and the *mutual* relation of these two to one another. There is the production of human activity as *labour*—that is, as an activity quite alien to itself, to man and to nature, and therefore to consciousness and the flow of life—the *abstract* existence of man as a mere *workman* who may therefore daily fall from his filled void into the absolute void—into his social, and therefore actual, non-existence. On the other hand there is the production of the object of human activity as *capital*—in which all the natural and social determinateness of the object is *extinguished;* in which private property has lost its natural and social quality (and therefore every political and social illusion, and is unmixed with any *seemingly* human relationships); in which the *selfsame* capital remains the *same* in the most diverse social and natural manifestations, totally indifferent to its *real* content. This contradiction, driven to the limit, is of necessity the limit, the culmination, and the downfall of the whole private-property relationship.

It is therefore another great achievement of modern English political economy to have declared rent to be the difference in the interest yielded by the worst and the best land under cultivation; to have exposed the landowner's romantic illusions—his alleged social importance and identity of his interest with the interest of society, still maintained by *Adam Smith* after the physiocrats; and to have anticipated and prepared the movement of the real world which will transform the landowner into an ordinary, prosaic capitalist, and thus simplify and sharpen the antithesis between labour and capital and hasten its resolution. *Land as land,* and *rent as rent,* have lost their *distinction of rank* and become dumb *capital* and *interest*—or rather, become capital and interest that only talk money.

The *distinction* between capital and land, between profit and rent, and between both and wages, and *industry,* and *agriculture,* and *immovable* and *movable* private property—this distinction is not an inherently essential one, but a *historical* distinction, a *fixed* moment in the formation and development of the antithesis between capital and labour. Industry, etc., as opposed to immovable landed property, is only the expression of the way industry came into being and of the contradiction to agriculture in which industry developed. This distinction of industry only continues to exist as a *special* sort of work—as an *essential, important* and *life-embracing* distinction

—so long as industry (town life) develops *over-against* landed property (aristocratic feudal life) and itself continues to bear the feudal character of its opposite in the form of monopoly, craft, guild, corporation, etc., within which labour still has a *seemingly social* significance, still the significance of *real community-life,* and has not yet reached the stage of *indifference* to its content, of complete being-for-self, i.e., of abstraction from all other being, and hence has not yet become *liberated* capital.

But liberated industry, *industry* constituted for itself as such, and *liberated capital,* are a necessary *development* of labour. The power of industry over its opposite is at once revealed in the emergence of *agriculture* as a real industry, most of the work having previously been left to the soil and to the *slave* of the soil, through whom the land cultivated itself. With the transformation of the slave into a *free* worker—i.e., into a *hireling*—the landlord himself is transformed into a captain of industry, into a capitalist—a transformation which takes place at first through the intermediacy of the *tenant farmer*. The *farmer,* however, is the landowner's representative—the landowner's revealed *secret:* it is only through him that the landowner has his *economic* existence—his existence as a private proprietor—for the rent of his land only exists due to the competition between the farmers. Thus, in the person of the *tenant farmer* the landlord has already become in essence a *common* capitalist. And thus must work itself out, too, in actual fact: the capitalist engaged in agriculture—the farmer—must become a landlord, or vice versa. The farmer's *industrial trade* is the *landowner's* trade, for the being of the former postulates the being of the latter.

But mindful of their contrasting origin—of their line of descent—the landowner knows the capitalist as his insolent, liberated slave of yesterday now become rich, and sees himself as a *capitalist* who is threatened by him. The capitalist knows the landowner as the idle, cruel and egotistical master of yesterday; he knows that he injures him as a capitalist, and yet that it is to industry that he, the landowner, owes all his present social significance, his possessions and his pleasures; he sees in him an antithesis to *free* industry and to *free* capital—to capital independent of every natural determination. This contradiction between landowner and capitalist is extremely bitter, and each side gives the truth about the other. One need only read the attacks of immovable on movable property and vice versa to obtain a clear picture of their respective worthlessness. The landowner lays stress on the noble lineage of his property, on feudal mementoes, reminiscences, the poetry of recollections, on his romantic disposition, on his political importance, etc.; and when he talks economics, it is *only* agriculture that he holds to be productive. At the same time he depicts his adversary as a sly, haggling, deceitful, greedy, mercenary, rebellious, heart- and soul-less cheapjack—extorting, pimping, servile, smooth, flattering, fleecing, dried-up twister without honour, principles, poetry, substance, or anything else—a person estranged from the community who freely trades it away and who breeds, nourishes and cherishes competition, and with it pauperism, crime, and the dissolution of all social bonds.

. . .

Movable property for its part points to the miracles of industry and progress. It is the child of the modern time and its legitimate, native-born son. It pities its adversary as a simpleton, *unenlightened* about his own nature (and in this it is completely right), who wants to replace moral capital and free labour by brute, immoral force and serfdom. It depicts him as a Don Quixote who under the guise of *bluntness, decency, the general interest, and stability,* conceals incapacity for progress, greedy self-indulgence, selfishness, sectional interest and evil intent. It declares him for an artful *monopolist;* it pours cold water on his reminiscences, his poetry, and his romanticism by a historical and sarcastic enumeration of the baseness, cruelty, degradation, prostitution, infamy, anarchy and rebellion, of which romantic castles were the workshops.

It claims to have obtained political freedom for the people; to have loosed the chains binding civil society; to have linked together different worlds; to have created trade promoting friendship between the peoples; to have created pure morality and an agreeable degree of culture; to have given the people civilised [*sic*] in place of their crude needs, and the means of satisfying them. Meanwhile, it claims, the land-owner—this idle, troublesome, parasitic grain-jobber—puts up the price of the people's basic necessities and so forces the capitalist to raise wages without being able to increase productivity, thus impeding and eventually cancelling the nation's annual income, the accumulation of capital, and therefore the possibility of providing work for the people and wealth for the country, and producing in consequence a general decline—whilst he parasitically exploits *every* advantage of modern civilisation without doing the least thing for it, and without even abating in the slightest his feudal prejudices. Finally, let him—for whom the cultivation of the land and the land itself exist only as a source of money, which comes to him as a present—let him just take a look at his *tenant farmer* and say whether he himself is not a *"decent," deluded sly* scoundrel who in his heart and in actual fact has for a long time belonged to *free* industry and to *beloved* trade, however much he may protest and prattle about historical memories and ethical or political goals. Everything which he can really advance to justify himself is true only of the *cultivator of the land* (the capitalist and the labourers), of whom the *landowner* is rather the *enemy*. Thus he gives evidence against himself. *Without* capital landed property is dead, worthless matter. Movable property's civilised victory has precisely been to discover and make human labour the source of wealth in place of the dead thing. (See Paul Louis Courier, Saint-Simon, Ganilh, Ricardo, Mill, MacCulloch and Destutt de Tracy and Michel Chevalier.)

The *real* course of development (to be inserted at this point) results in the necessary victory of the *capitalist* over the *landowner*—that is to say, of developed over undeveloped immature private property—just as generally movement must triumph over immobility—open, self-conscious baseness over hidden, unconscious baseness; *avarice* over *self-indulgence;* the avowedly restless, adroit self-interest of *enlightenment* over the parochial, world-wise, naive, idle and deluded *self-interest of superstition;* and *money* over the other forms of private property.

Those states which divine something of the danger attaching to fully-developed free industry, to fully-developed pure morality and to the full development of trade promoting friendship between the peoples, try, but in vain, to hold in check the capitalisation of landed property.

Landed property in its distinction from capital is private property—capital—still afflicted with *local* and political prejudices; it is capital which has not yet regained itself from its entanglement with the world—capital not yet *fully-developed.* It must in the course of its *world-wide development* achieve its abstract, that is, its *pure,* expression.

The relations of *private property* are labour, capital, and the relations between these two.

The movement through which these constituents have to pass is:

[*First*] *Unmediated or mediated unity of the two.*

Capital and labour at first still united. Then, though separated and estranged, they reciprocally develop and foster each other as *positive* conditions.

[*Second*] *The two in opposition,* mutually excluding each other. The worker knows the capitalist as his non-existence, and vice versa: each tries to rob the other of his existence.

[*Third*] *Opposition* of each *to* itself. Capital—stored-up labour—labour. Capital as such—splitting into capital *itself* and into its *interest,* and this latter again into *interest* and *profit.* The capitalist completely sacrificed. He falls into the working class, whilst the worker (but only exceptionally) becomes a capitalist. Labour as a moment of capital—its *costs.* Thus the wages of labour—a sacrifice of capital.

Splitting of labour into *labour itself* and the *wages of labour.* The worker himself a capital, a commodity.

Inimical mutual opposition.

[THE MEANING OF HUMAN REQUIREMENTS WHERE THERE IS PRIVATE PROPERTY AND UNDER SOCIALISM. THE DIFFERENCE BETWEEN EXTRAVAGANT WEALTH AND INDUSTRIAL WEALTH. DIVISION OF LABOUR IN BOURGEOIS SOCIETY]

(7) We have seen what significance, given socialism, the *wealth* of human needs has, and what significance, therefore, both a *new mode of production* and a new *object* of production have: a new

manifestation of the forces of *human* nature and a new enrichment of *human* nature. Under private property their significance is reversed: every person speculates on creating a *new* need in another, so as to drive him to a fresh sacrifice, to place him in a new dependence and to seduce him into a new mode of *gratification* and therefore economic ruin. Each tries to establish over the other an *alien* power, so as thereby to find satisfaction of his own selfish need. The increase in the quantity of objects is accompanied by an extension of the realm of the alien powers to which man is subjected, and every new product represents a new *potency* of mutual swindling and mutual plundering. Man becomes ever poorer as man; his need for *money* becomes ever greater if he wants to overpower hostile being; and the power of his *money* declines exactly in inverse proportion to the increase in the volume of production: that is, his neediness grows as the *power* of money increases.

The need for money is therefore the true need produced by the modern economic system, and it is the only need which the latter produces. The *quantity* of money becomes to an ever greater degree its sole *effective* attribute: just as it reduces everything to its abstract form, so it reduces itself in the course of its own movement to something merely *quantitative*. *Excess* and *intemperance* come to be its true norm. Subjectively, this is even partly manifested in that the extension of products and needs falls into *contriving* and ever-*calculating* subservience to inhuman, refined, unnatural and *imaginary* appetites. Private property does not know how to change crude need into *human* need. Its *idealism* is *fantasy, caprice* and *whim;* and no eunuch flatters his despot more basely or uses more despicable means to stimulate his dulled capacity for pleasure in order to sneak a favour for himself than does the industrial eunuch —the producer—in order to sneak for himself a few pennies—in order to charm the golden birds out of the pockets of his Christianly beloved neighbours. He puts himself at the service of the other's most depraved fancies, plays the pimp between him and his need, excites in him morbid appetites, lies in wait for each of his weaknesses—all so that he can then demand the cash for this service of love. (Every product is a bait with which to seduce away the other's very being, his money; every real and possible need is a weakness which will lead the fly to the gluepot. General exploitation of communal human nature, just as every imperfection in man, is a bond with heaven—an avenue giving the priest access to his heart; every need is an opportunity to approach one's neighbour under the guise of the utmost amiability and to say to him: Dear friend, I give you what you need, but you know the *conditio sine qua non;* you know the ink in which you have to sign yourself over to me; in providing for your pleasure, I fleece you.)

And partly, this estrangement manifests itself in that it produces refinement of needs and of their means on the one hand, and a bestial barbarisation, a complete, unrefined, abstract simplicity of need, on the other; or rather in that it merely resurrects itself in its opposite. Even the need for fresh air ceases for the worker. Man returns to living in a cave, which is now, however, contaminated with the mephitic breath of plague given off by civilisation, and which he continues to occupy only *precariously,* it being for him an alien habitation which can be withdrawn from him any day —a place from which, if he does not pay, he can be thrown out any day. For this mortuary he has to *pay*. A dwelling in the *light,* which Prometheus in Aeschylus designated as one of the greatest boons, by means of which he made the savage into a human being, ceases to exist for the worker. Light, air, etc.—the simplest *animal* cleanliness—ceases to be a need for man. *Dirt*—this stagnation and putrefaction of man—the *sewage* of civilisation (speaking quite literally)—comes to be the *element of life* for him. Utter, *unnatural* neglect, putrefied nature, comes to be his life-element. None of his senses exist any longer, and not only in his human fashion, but in an *inhuman* fashion, and therefore not even in an animal fashion. The crudest *modes* (and *instruments*) of human labour are coming back: the *tread-mill* of the Roman slaves, for instance, is the means of production, the means of existence, of many English workers. It is not only that man has no human needs—even his *animal* needs are ceasing to exist. The Irishman no longer knows any need now but the need to *eat,* and indeed only the need to eat *potatoes*— and *scabby potatoes* at that, the worst kind of potatoes. But in each of their industrial towns England and France have already a *little* Ireland. The savage and the animal have at least the need to hunt, to roam, etc.—the need of companionship. Machine labour is simplified in order to make a worker out of the human being still in the making, the completely immature human being, the *child* —whilst the worker has become a neglected child. The machine accommodates itself to the *weakness* of the human being in order to make the *weak* human being into a machine.

How the multiplication of needs and of the means of their satisfaction breeds the absence of needs and of means is demonstrated by the political economist (and the capitalist: it should be noted that it is always *empirical* business men we are talking about when we refer to political economists—their *scientific* confession and mode of being). This he shows:

(1) By reducing the worker's need to the barest and most miserable level of physical subsistence, and by reducing his activity to the most abstract mechanical movement. Hence, he says: Man has no other need either of activity or of enjoyment. For he calls *even* this life *human* life and existence.

(2) By *counting* the *lowest* possible level of life (existence) as the standard, indeed as the general standard—general because it is applicable to the mass of men. He changes the worker into an insensible being lacking all needs, just as he changes his activity into a pure abstraction from all activity. To him, therefore, every *luxury* of the worker seems to be reprehensible, and everything that goes beyond the most abstract need—be it in the realm of passive enjoyment, or a manifestation of activity—seems to him a luxury. Political economy, this science of *wealth,* is therefore simultaneously the science of denial, of want, of *thrift, of saving*—and it actually reaches the point where it *spares* man the *need* of either fresh *air* or physical *exercise.* This science of marvellous industry is simultaneously the science of *asceticism,* and its true ideal is the *ascetic* but *extortionate* miser and the *ascetic* but *productive* slave. Its moral ideal is the *worker* who takes part of his wages to the savings-bank, and it has even found ready-made an abject *art* in which to clothe this its pet idea: they have presented it, bathed in sentimentality, on the stage. Thus political economy—despite its

worldly and wanton appearance—is a true moral science, the most moral of all the sciences. Self-denial, the denial of life and of all human needs, is its cardinal doctrine. The less you eat, drink and read books; the less you go to the theatre, the dance hall, the public-house; the less you think, love, theorise, sing, paint, fence, etc., the more you *save*—the *greater* becomes your treasure which neither moths nor dust will devour—your *capital*. The less you *are*, the more you *have;* the less you express your own life, the greater is your alienated life—the greater is the store of your estranged being. Everything which the political economist takes from you in life and in humanity, he replaces for you in *money* and in *wealth;* and all the things which you cannot do, your money can do. It can eat and drink, go to the dance hall and the theatre; it can travel, it can appropriate art, learning, the treasures of the past, political power—all this it *can* appropriate for you—it can buy all this for you: it is the true *endowment.* Yet being all this, it is *inclined* to do nothing but create itself, buy itself; for everything else is after all its servant. And when I have the master I have the servant and do not need his servant. All passions and all activity must therefore be submerged in *avarice.* The worker may only have enough for him to want to live, and may only want to live in order to have [enough].

Of course a controversy now arises in the field of political economy. The one side (Lauderdale, Malthus, etc.) recommends *luxury* and execrates thrift. The other (Say, Ricardo, etc.) recommends thrift and execrates luxury. But the former admits that it wants luxury in order to produce *labour* (i.e., absolute thrift); and the latter admits that it recommends thrift in order to produce *wealth* (i.e., luxury). The Lauderdale-Malthus school has the *romantic* notion that avarice alone ought not to determine the consumption of the rich, and it contradicts its own laws in advancing *extravagance* as a direct means of enrichment. Against it, therefore, the other side very earnestly and circumstantially proves that I do not increase but reduce my *possessions* by being extravagant. The Say-Ricardo school, however, is hypocritical in not admitting that it is precisely whim and caprice which determine production. It forgets the "refined needs"; it forgets that there would be no production without consumption; it forgets that as a result of competition production can only become more extensive and luxurious. It forgets that it is use that determines a thing's value, and that fashion determines use. It wishes to see only "useful things" produced, but it forgets that production of too many useful things produces too large a *useless* population. Both sides forget that extravagance and thrift, luxury and privation, wealth and poverty are equal.

And you must not only stint the immediate gratification of your senses, as by stinting yourself of food, etc.: you must also spare yourself all sharing of general interest, all sympathy, all trust, etc.; if you want to be economical, if you do not want to be ruined by illusions.

You must make everything that is yours *saleable*, i.e., useful. If I ask the political economist: Do I obey economic laws if I extract money by offering my body for sale, by surrendering it to another's lust? (The factory workers in France call the prostitution of their wives and daughters the xth working hour, which is literally correct.)—Or am I not acting in keeping with political economy if I sell my friend to the Moroccans? (And the direct sale of men in the form of a trade in conscripts, etc., takes place in all civilised countries.)—Then the political economist replies to me: You do not transgress my laws; but see what Cousin Ethics and Cousin Religion have to say about it. My *political economic* ethics and religion have nothing to reproach you with, but— But whom am I now to believe, political economy or ethics? The ethics of political economy is *acquisition*, work, thrift, sobriety—but political economy promises to satisfy my needs. The political economy of ethics is the opulence of a good conscience, of virtue, etc.; but how can I live virtuously if I do not live? And how can I have a good conscience if I am not conscious of anything? It stems from the very nature of estrangement that each sphere applies to me a different and opposite yardstick—ethics one and political economy another; for each is a specific estrangement of man and focuses attention on a particular round of estranged essential activity, and each stands in an estranged relation to the other. Thus M. *Michel Chevalier* reproaches Ricardo with having abstracted from ethics. But Ricardo is allowing political economy to speak its own language, and if it does not speak ethically, this is not Ricardo's fault. M. Chevalier abstracts from political economy in so far as he moralises, but he really and necessarily abstracts from ethics in so far as he practises political economy. The reference of political economy to ethics, if it is other than an arbitarary, contingent and therefore unfounded and unscientific reference, if it is not being put up as a *sham* but is meant to be *essential,* can only be the reference of the laws of political economy to ethics. If there is no such connection, or if the contrary is rather the case, can Ricardo help it? Besides, the opposition between political economy and ethics is only a *sham* opposition and just as much no opposition as it is an opposition. All that happens is that political economy expresses moral laws *in its own way*.

Needlessness as the principle of political economy is *most brilliantly* shown in its *theory of population.* There are *too many* people. Even the existence of men is a pure luxury; and if the worker is *"ethical,"* he will be *sparing* in procreation. (Mill suggests public acclaim for those who prove themselves continent in their sexual relations, and public rebuke for those who sin against such barrenness of marriage. . . . Is not this the ethics, the teaching of asceticism?) The production of people appears in the form of public misery.

The meaning which production has in relation to the rich is seen *revealed* in the meaning which it has for the poor. At the top the manifestation is always refined, veiled, ambiguous—a sham; lower, it is rough, straightforward, frank—the real thing. The worker's *crude* need is a far greater source of gain than the *refined* need of the rich. The cellar-dwellings in London bring more to those who let them than do the palaces; that is to say, with reference to the landlord they constitute *greater wealth,* and thus (to speak the language of political economy) greater *social* wealth.

Industry speculates on the refinement of needs, but it speculates just as much on their *crudeness,* but on their artificially produced crudeness, whose true enjoyment, therefore, is *self-stupefaction*—this *seeming* satisfaction of need—this civilisation contained *within* the crude barbarism of need; the English gin-shops are therefore the *symbolical embodiments* of private property. Their *luxury* reveals the true relation of industrial luxury and wealth to man. They are therefore rightly the only Sunday pleasures of the people, dealt with at least mildly by the English police.

We have already seen how the political economist establishes the unity of labour and capital in a variety of ways:—(1) *Capital is accumulated labour.* (2) The purpose of capital within production—partly, reproduction of capital with profit, partly, capital as raw material (material of labour), and partly, as itself a *working instrument* (the machine is capital directly equated with labour)—is *productive labour*. (3) The worker is a capital. (4) Wages belong to costs of capital. (5) In relation to the worker, labour is the reproduction of his life-capital. (6) In relation to the capitalist, labour is an aspect of his capital's activity.

Finally, (7) the political economist postulates the original unity of capital and labour in the form of the unity of the capitalist and the worker; this is the original state of paradise. The way in which these two aspects in the form of two persons leap at each other's throats is for the political economist a *contingent* event, and hence only to be explained by reference to external factors. (See Mill.)

The nations which are still dazzled by the sensuous splendour of precious metals, and are therefore still fetish-worshippers of metal money, are not yet fully developed money-nations. Contrast of France and England. The extent to which the solution of theoretical riddles is the task of practice and effected through practice, just as true practice is the condition of a real and positive theory, is shown, for example, in *fetishism.* The sensuous consciousness of the fetish-worshipper is different from that of the Greek, because his sensuous existence is still different. The abstract enmity between sense and spirit is necessary so long as the human feeling for nature, the human sense of nature, and therefore also the *natural* sense of *man,* are not yet produced by man's own labour.

Equality is nothing but a translation of the German "Ich = Ich" into the French, i.e., political form. Equality as the *groundwork* of communism is its *political* justification, and it is the same as when the German justifies it by conceiving man as *universal self-consciousness*. Naturally, the transcendence of the estrangement always proceeds from that form of the estrangement which is the *dominant* power: in Germany, *self-consciousness;* in France, *equality,* because politics; in England, real, material, *practical* need taking only itself as its standard. It is from this standpoint that Proudhon is to be criticised and appreciated.

If we characterise *communism* itself because of its character as negation of the negation, as the appropriation of the human essence which mediates itself with itself through the negation of private property—as being not yet the *true,* self-originating position but rather a position originating from private property, [. . . .]

Since in that case the real estrangement of the life of man remains, and remains all the more, the more one is conscious of it as such, it may be accomplished solely by putting communism into operation.

In order to abolish the *idea* of private property, the *idea* of communism is completely sufficient. It takes *actual* communist action to abolish actual private property. History will come to it; and this movement, which in *theory* we already know to be a self-transcending movement, will constitute *in actual fact* a very severe and protracted process. But we must regard it as a real advance to have gained beforehand a consciousness of the limited charactor as well as of the goal of this historical movement—and a consciousness which reaches out beyond it.

When communist *workmen* associate with one another, theory, propaganda, etc., is their first end. But at the same time, as a result of this association, they acquire a new need—the need for society—and what appears as a means becomes an end. You can observe this practical process in its most splendid results whenever you see French socialist workers together. Such things as smoking, drinking, eating, etc., are no longer means of contact or means that bring together. Company, association, and conversation, which again has society as its end, are enough for them; the brotherhood of man is no mere phrase with them, but a fact of life, and the nobility of man shines upon us from their work-hardened bodies.

When political economy claims that demand and supply always balance each other, it immediately forgets that according to its own claim (theory of population) the supply of *people* always exceeds the demand, and that, therefore, in the essential result of the whole production process—the existence of man—the disparity between demand and supply gets its most striking expression.

The extent to which money, which appears as a means, constitutes true *power* and the sole *end*—the extent to which in general that means which gives me substance, which gives me possession of the objective substance of others, is an *end in itself*—can be clearly seen from the facts that landed property wherever land is the source of life, and *horse* and *sword* wherever these are the *true means of life,* are also acknowledged as the true political powers in life. In the Middle Ages a social class is emancipated as soon as it is allowed to carry the *sword*. Amongst nomadic people it is the *horse* which makes me a free man and a participant in the life of the community.

We have said above that man is regressing to the *cave dwelling*, etc.—but that he is regressing to it in an estranged, malignant form. The savage in his cave—a natural element which freely offers itself for his use and protection—feels himself no more a stranger, or rather feels himself to be just as much at home as a *fish* in water. But the cellar-dwelling of the poor man is a hostile dwelling, "an alien, restraining power which only gives itself up to him in so far as he gives up to it his blood and sweat"—a dwelling which he cannot look upon as his own home where he might at last exclaim, "Here I am at home," but where instead he finds himself in *someone else's* house, in the house of a *stranger* who daily lies in wait for him and throws him out if he does not pay his rent. Similarly, he is also aware of the contrast in quality between his dwelling and a human dwelling—a residence in that *other* world, the heaven of wealth.

Estrangement is manifested not only in the fact that *my* means of life belong to *someone else,* that *my* desire is the inaccessible possession of *another*, but also in the fact that everything is in itself something *different* from itself—that my activity is *something else* and that, finally (and this applies also to the capitalist), all is under the sway of *inhuman* power. There is a form of inactive, extravagant wealth given over wholly to pleasure, the enjoyer of which on the one hand *behaves* as a mere *ephemeral* individual frantically spending himself to no purpose, knows the slave-labour of others (human *sweat and blood*) as the prey of his cupidity, and therefore knows man himself, and hence also his own self, as a sacrificed and empty being. With such wealth the contempt of man makes its appearance, partly as arrogance and as the throwing-away of what can give sustenance to a hundred human lives, and partly as the infamous illusion that his own unbridled extravagance and ceaseless, unproductive consumption is the condition of the other's *labour* and therefore of his *subsistence*. He knows the realisation of the *essential powers* of man only as the realisation of his own excesses, his whims and capricious, bizarre notions. This wealth which, on the other hand, again knows wealth as a mere means, as something that is good for nothing but to be annihilated and which is therefore at once slave and master, at once generous and mean, capricious, presumptuous, conceited, refined, cultured and witty—this wealth has not yet experienced *wealth* as an utterly *alien power* over itself: it sees in it, rather, only its own power, and not wealth but *gratification* [is its] final aim and end.

. . .

Society, as it appears to the political economist, is *civil society,* in which every individual is a totality of needs and only exists for the other person, as the other exists for him, in so far as each becomes a means for the other. The political economist reduces everything (just as does politics in its *Rights of Man*) to man, i.e., to the individual whom he strips of all determinateness so as to class him as capitalist or worker.

The *division of labour* is the expression in political economy of the *social character of labour* within the estrangement. Or, since *labour* is only an expression of human activity within alienation, of the living of life as the alienating of life, the *division of labour,* too, is therefore nothing else but the *estranged, alienated* positing of human activity as a *real activity of the species* or as *activity of man as a species being.*

As for *the essence of the division of labour*—and of course the division of labour had to be conceived as a major driving force in the production of wealth as soon as *labour* was recognised as *the essence of private property*—i.e., about *the estranged and alienated form of human activity as an activity of the species*—the political economists are very unclear and self-contradictory about it.

. . .

The whole of modern political economy agrees, however, that division of labour and wealth of production, division of labour and accumulation of capital, are mutually interrelated; just as it agrees that *liberated* private property alone—private property left to itself—can produce the most useful and comprehensive division of labour.

Adam Smith's argument can be summed up as follows: Division of labour bestows on labour infinite production capacity. It stems from the *propensity to exchange* and *barter,* a specifically human propensity which is probably not fortuitous but is conditioned by the use of reason and speech. The motive of those who engage in exchange is not *humanity* but *egoism.* The diversity of human talents is more the effect than the cause of the division of labour—i.e., of exchange. Besides, it is only the latter which makes such diversity useful. The differences between the particular attributes to which nature gives rise within a species of animal are much more marked than the degrees of difference in human aptitude and activity. But because animals are unable to engage in *exchange,* no individual animal benefits from the difference in the attributes of animals of the same species but of different breeds. Animals are unable to combine the different attributes of their species, and are unable to contribute anything to the *common* advantage and comfort of the species. It is otherwise with *men,* amongst whom the most dissimilar talents and forms of activity are of use to one another, *because* they can bring their *different* products together into a common stock, from which each can purchase. As the division of labour springs from the propensity to *exchange* it grows and is limited by the *extent of exchange*—by the *extent of the market.* In advanced conditions, every man is a *merchant,* and society is a *commercial society.*

. . .

The examination of *division of labour* and *exchange* is of extreme interest, because these are *perceptibly alienated* expressions of human *activity* and of *essential human power* as a *species* activity and power.

To assert that *division of labour* and *exchange* rest on *private property* is nothing short of asserting that *labour* is the essence of private property—an assertion which the political economist cannot prove and which we wish to prove for him. Precisely in the fact that *division of labour* and *exchange* are embodiments of private property lies the twofold proof, on the one hand that *human* life required *private property* for its realisation, and on the other hand that it now requires the supersession of private property.

Division of labour and *exchange* are the two *phenomena* in connection with which the political economist boasts of the social character of his science and in the same breath gives expression to the contradiction in his science—the establishment of society through unsocial, particular interests.

—Marx, *Economic and Philosophic Manuscripts of 1844,* pp. 67–92, 115–26, 129–30, 133, 134–35

To work at a machine, the workman should be taught from childhood, in order that he may learn to adapt his own movements to the uniform and unceasing motion of an automaton. When the machinery, as a whole, forms a system of manifold machines, working simultaneously and in concert, the co-operation based upon it, requires the distribution of various groups of workmen among the different kinds of machines. But the employment of machinery does away with the necessity of crystallizing this distribution after the manner of Manufacture, by the constant annexation of a particular man to a particular function. Since the motion of the whole system does not proceed from the workman, but from the machinery, a change of persons can take place at any time without an interruption of the work. The most striking proof of this is afforded by the *relays system,* put into operation by the manufacturers during their revolt from 1848–1850. Lastly, the quickness with which machine work is learnt by young people, does away with the necessity of bringing up for exclusive employment by machinery, a special class of operatives. With regard to the work of the mere attendants, it can, to some extent, be replaced in the mill by machines, and owing to its extreme simplicity, it allows of a rapid and constant change of the individuals burdened with this drudgery.

Although then, technically speaking, the old system of division of labour is thrown overboard by machinery, it hangs on in the factory, as a traditional habit handed down from Manufacture, and is afterwards systematically re-moulded and established in a more hideous form by capital, as a means of exploiting labour-power. The life-long specialty of handling one and the same tool, now becomes the life-long specialty of serving one and the same machine. Machinery is put to a wrong use, with the object of transforming the workman, from his very childhood, into a part of a detail-machine.[1] In this way, not only are the expenses of his re-production considerably lessened, but at the same time his helpless dependence upon the factory as a whole, and therefore upon the capitalist, is rendered complete. Here as everywhere else, we must distinguish between the increased productiveness due to the development of the social process of production, and that due to the capitalist exploitation of that process. In handicrafts and manufacture, the workman makes use of a tool, in the factory, the machine makes use of him. There the movements of the instrument of labour proceed from him, here it is the movements of the machine that he must follow. In manufacture the workmen are parts of a living mechanism. In the factory we have a lifeless mechanism independent of the workman, who becomes its mere living appendage.

. . .

. . . within the capitalist system all methods for raising the social productiveness of labour are brought about at the cost of the individual labourer; all means for the development of production transform themselves into means of domination over, and exploitation of, the producers; they mutilate the labourer into a fragment of a man, degrade him to the level of an appendage of a machine, destroy every remnant of charm in his work and turn

[1] So much then for Proudhon's wonderful idea: he "construes" machinery not as a synthesis of instruments of labour, but as a synthesis of detail operations for the benefit of the labourer himself.

it into a hated toil; they estrange from him the intellectual potentialities of the labour-process in the same proportion as science is incorporated in it as an independent power; they distort the conditions under which he works, subject him during the labour-process to a despotism the more hateful for its meanness; they transform his life-time into working-time, and drag his wife and child beneath the wheels of the Juggernaut of capital . . .

—Marx, *Capital:* Vol. I, pp. 460–62, 708

Commodity Fetishism

A commodity appears, at first sight, a very trivial thing, and easily understood. Its analysis shows that it is, in reality, a very queer thing, abounding in metaphysical subtleties and theological niceties. So far as it is a value in use, there is nothing mysterious about it, whether we consider it from the point of view that by its properties it is capable of satisfying human wants, or from the point that those properties are the product of human labour. It is as clear as noon-day, that man, by his industry, changes the forms of the materials furnished by nature, in such a way as to make them useful to him. The form of wood, for instance, is altered, by making a table out of it. Yet, for all that the table continues to be that common, every-day thing, wood. But, so soon as it steps forth as a commodity, it is changed into something transcendent. It not only stands with its feet on the ground, but, in relation to all other commodities, it stands on its head, and evolves out of its wooden brain grotesque ideas, far more wonderful than "table-turning" ever was.

The mystical character of commodities does not originate, therefore, in their use-value. Just as little does it proceed from the nature of the determining factors of value. For, in the first place, however varied the useful kinds of labour, or productive activities, may be, it is a physiological fact, that they are functions of the human organism, and that each such function, whatever may be its nature or form, is essentially the expenditure of human brain, nerves, muscles, &c. Secondly, with regard to that which forms the groundwork for the quantitative determination of value, namely, the duration of that expenditure, or the quantity of labour, it is quite clear that there is a palpable difference between its quantity and quality. In all states of society, the labour-time that it costs to produce the means of subsistence must necessarily be an object of interest to mankind, though not of equal interest in different stages of development. And lastly, from the moment that men in any way work for one another, their labour assumes a social form.

Whence, then, arises the enigmatical character of the product of labour, so soon as it assumes the form of commodities? Clearly from this form itself. The equality of all sorts of human labour is expressed objectively by their products all being equally values; the measure of the expenditure of labour-power by the duration of that expenditure, takes the form of the quantity of value of the products of labour; and finally, the mutual relations of the producers, within which the social character of their labour affirms itself, take the form of a social relation between the products.

A commodity is therefore a mysterious thing, simply because in it the social character of men's labour appears to them as an objective character stamped upon the product of that labour; because the relation of the producers to the sum total of their own labour is presented to them as a social relation, existing not between themselves, but between the products of their labour. This is the reason why the products of labour become commodities, social things whose qualities are at the same time perceptible and imperceptible by the senses. In the same way the light from an object is perceived by us not as the subjective excitation of our optic nerve, but as the objective form of something outside the eye itself. But, in the act of seeing, there is at all events, an actual passage of light from one thing to another, from the external object to the eye. There is a physical relation between physical things. But it is different with commodities. There, the existence of the things *qua* commodities, and the value relation between the products of labour which stamps them as commodities, have absolutely no connection with their physical properties and with the material relations arising therefrom. There it is a definite social relation between men, that assumes, in their eyes, the fantastic form of a relation between things. In order, therefore, to find an analogy, we must have recourse to the mist-enveloped regions of the religious world. In that world the productions of the human brain appear as independent beings endowed with life, and entering into relation both with one another and the human race. So it is in the world of commodities with the products of men's hands. This I call the Fetishism which attaches itself to the products of labour, so soon as they are produced as commodities, and which is therefore inseparable from the production of commodities.

This Fetishism of commodities has its origin, as the foregoing analysis has already shown, in the peculiar social character of the labour that produces them.

As a general rule, articles of utility become commodities, only because they are products of the labour of private individuals or groups of individuals who carry on their work independently of each other. The sum total of the labour of all these private individuals forms the aggregate labour of society. Since the producers do not come into social contact with each other until they exchange their products, the specific social character of each producer's labour does not show itself except in the act of exchange. In other words, the labour of the individual asserts itself as a part of the labour of society, only by means of the relations which the act of exchange establishes directly between the products, and indirectly, through them, between the producers. To the latter, therefore, the relations connecting the labour of one individual with that of the rest appear, not as direct social relations between individuals at work, but as what they really are, material relations between persons and social relations between things.

—Marx, *Capital:* Vol. I, pp. 81–84

Money Alienation

[THE POWER OF MONEY IN BOURGEOIS SOCIETY]

If man's *feelings*, passions, etc., are not merely anthropological phenomena in the [narrower] sense, but truly *ontological* affirmations of essential being (of nature), and if they are only really affirmed because their *object* exists for them as an object of *sense,* then it is clear:

(1) That they have by no means merely one mode of affirmation, but rather that the distinctive character of their existence, of their life, is constituted by the distinctive mode of their affirmation. In what manner the object exists for them, is the characteristic mode of their *gratification.*

(2) Wherever the sensuous affirmation is the direct annulment of the object in its independent form (as in eating, drinking, working up of the object, etc.), this is the affirmation of the object.

(3) In so far as man, and hence also his feeling, etc., are *human,* the affirmation of the object by another is likewise his own enjoyment.

(4) Only through developed industry—i.e., through the medium of private property—does the ontological essence of human passion come to be both in its totality and in its humanity; the science of man is therefore itself a product of man's establishment of himself by practical activity.

(5) The meaning of private property—liberated from its estrangement—is the *existence of essential objects* for man, both as objects of enjoyment and as objects of activity.

By possessing the *property* of buying everything, by possessing the property of appropriating all objects, *money* is thus the *object* of eminent possession. The universality of its *property* is the omnipotence of its being. It therefore functions as the almighty being. Money is the *pimp* between man's need and the object, between his life and his means of life. But *that which* mediates *my* life for me, also *mediates* the existence of other people *for me.* For me it is the *other* person.

. . .

That which is for me through the medium of *money*—that for which I can pay (i.e., which money can buy)—that am *I,* the possessor of the money. The extent of the power of money is the extent of my power. Money's properties are my properties and essential powers—the properties and powers of its possessor. Thus, what I *am* and *am capable* of is by no means determined by my individuality. I am ugly, but I can buy for myself the most *beauti-*

ful of women. Therefore I am not *ugly,* for the effect of *ugliness*—its deterrent power—is nullified by money. I, in my character as an individual, am *lame,* but money furnishes me with twenty-four feet. Therefore I am not lame. I am bad, dishonest, unscrupulous, stupid; but money is honoured, and therefore so is its possessor. Money is the supreme good, therefore its possessor is good. Money, besides, saves me the trouble of being dishonest: I am therefore presumed honest. I am *stupid,* but money is the *real mind* of all things and how then should its possessor be stupid? Besides, he can buy talented people for himself, and is he who has power over the talented not more talented than the talented? Do not I, who thanks to money am capable of *all* that the human heart longs for, possess all human capacities? Does not my money therefore transform all my incapacities into their contrary?

If *money* is the bond binding me to *human* life, binding society to me, binding me and nature and man, is not money the bond of all *bonds*? Can it not dissolve and bind all ties? Is it not, therefore, the universal *agent of divorce*? It is the true *agent of divorce* as well as the true *binding agent*—the [universal] *galvano-chemical* power of Society.

Shakespeare stresses especially two properties of money:

(1) It is the visible divinity—the transformation of all human and natural properties into their contraries, the universal confounding and overturning of things: it makes brothers of impossibilities. (2) It is the common whore, the common pimp of people and nations.

The overturning and confounding of all human and natural qualities, the fraternisation of impossibilities—the *divine* power of money—lies in its *character* as men's estranged, alienating and self-disposing *species-nature*. Money is the alienated *ability of mankind*.

That which I am unable to do as a *man,* and of which therefore all my individual essential powers are incapable, I am able to do by means of *money*. Money thus turns each of these powers into something which in itself it is not—turns it, that is, into its *contrary*.

If I long for a particular dish or want to take the mail-coach because I am not strong enough to go by foot, money fetches me the dish and the mail-coach: that is, it converts my wishes from something in the realm of imagination, translates them from their meditated, imagined or willed existence into their *sensuous, actual* existence—from imagination to life, from imagined being into real being. In effecting this mediation, money is the *truly creative* power.

No doubt *demand* also exists for him who has no money, but his demand is a mere thing of the imagination without effect or existence for me, for a third party, for the others, and which therefore remains for me *unreal* and *objectless*. The difference between effective demand based on money and ineffective demand based on my need, my passion, my wish, etc., is the difference between *being* and *thinking,* between the imagined which *exists* merely within me and the imagined as it is for me outside me as a *real object.*

If I have no money for travel, I have no *need*—that is, no real and self-realising need—to travel. If I have the *vocation* for study but no money for it, I have *no* vocation for study—that is, no *effective,* no *true* vocation. On the other hand, if I have really *no* vocation for study but have the will *and* the money for it, I have an *effective* vocation for it. Being the external, common *medium* and *faculty* for turning an *image* into *reality* and *reality* into a mere *image* (a faculty not springing from man as man or from human society as society), *money* transforms the *real essential powers of man and nature* into what are merely abstract conceits and therefore *imperfections*—into tormenting chimeras—just as it transforms *real imperfections and chimeras*—essential powers which are really impotent, which exist only in the imagination of the individual—into *real powers* and *faculties.*

In the light of this characteristic alone, money is thus the general overturning of *individualities* which turns them into their contrary and adds contradictory attributes to their attributes.

Money, then, appears as this *overturning* power both against the individual and against the bonds of society, etc., which claim to be essences in themselves. It transforms fidelity into infidelity, love into hate, hate into love, virtue into vice, vice into virtue, servant into master, master into servant, idiocy into intelligence and intelligence into idiocy.

Since money, as the existing and active concept of value, confounds and exchanges all things, it is the general *confounding* and *compounding* of all things—the world upside-down—the confounding and compounding of all natural and human qualities.

He who can buy bravery is brave, though a coward. As money is not exchanged for any one specific quality, for any one specific thing, or for any particular human essential power, but for the entire objective world of man and nature, from the standpoint of its possessor it therefore serves to exchange every property for every other, even contradictory, property and object: it is the fraternisation of impossibilities. It makes contradictions embrace.

Assume *man* to be *man* and his relationship to the world to be a human one: then you can exchange love only for love, trust for trust, etc. If you want to enjoy art, you must be an artistically-cultivated person; if you want to exercise influence over other people, you must be a person with a stimulating and encouraging effect on other people. Every one of your relations to man and to nature must be a *specific expression,* corresponding to the object of your will, of your *real individual* life. If you love without evoking love in return—that is, if your loving as loving does not produce reciprocal love; if through a *living expression* of yourself as a loving person you do not make yourself a *loved person,* then your love is impotent—a misfortune.

—Marx, *Economic and Philosophic Manuscripts of 1844,* pp. 136–41

III

The Materialist Conception of History

Introduction

The materialist conception of history rests upon the assumption that the world exists independently of our senses and that it is made up of matter. While Hegel did not deny the existence of an objective world, he believed that all history was the unfolding of the rational idea. Institutions were simply manifestations of the progress of the rational idea toward perfection.

For Marx ideas are impotent in the sense that by themselves *they cannot lead to social change. The materialist conception states only that economic relationships are ultimately determining. It does not deny that ideas are part of the material world. Ideas seen as part of, rather than independent of, the real world also have consequences, according to Marx.*

The role which Marx assigns man in making history is limited, basically, only by the underlying economic reality—the state of technology. The property system, the methods of production and exchange, are derived from the tools man has available to him in a particular historic epoch. The super-structure, the institutions under which men live—the state, family, law, and religion—are, in turn, derivative of these economic relations.

The opening selection of Chapter III, entitled "The Material Basis of Human History," is written by Engels and represents Marx's most fully developed position regarding the relationship of the substructure (economic factors) to the superstructure (social institutions). He shows that freedom is circumscribed by the economic and social order, not determined by it.

In short, Marx's theory makes economics the single most important independent variable in his system. Ideas and institutions, (other than economic institutions) as dependent variables, play influential though basically supportive roles. These elements of the real world place constraints on the capacity of human will to do as it pleases.

> Man makes his own history, but he does not make it out of whole cloth, he does not make it out of conditions chosen by himself, but out of such as he finds close at hand.[1]

Behind Marx's theory rest three assumptions: (1) the inevitability of progress; (2) the validity of the dialectical method; (3) the goodness of human nature. The first two Marx derived from Hegel, the third from the Enlightenment. For Marx, history had a purpose—to bring man in his world to perfection. The dialectical process was thought by Marx to be much superior to Darwinism (which influenced Marx profoundly) with its implication of the inevitability and desirability of competitive struggles to the death.

This chapter may be seen as completing the framework for the operation of Marx's model. Chapters I and II developed his philosophic preconceptions. In this chapter, Chapter III, philosophy is translated into social science. In Chapters IV, V, and VI the social science model works itself out in the world of men.

[1]*Infra* p. 188.

The Material Base of Human History

Men make their own history, whatever its outcome may be, in that each person follows his own consciously desired end, and it is precisely the resultant of these many wills operating in different directions and of their manifold effects upon the outer world that constitutes history. Thus it is also a question of what the many individuals desire. The will is determined by passion or deliberation. But the levers which immediately determine passion or deliberation are of very different kinds. Partly they may be external objects, partly ideal motives, ambition, "enthusiasm for truth and justice," personal hatred or even purely individual whims of all kinds. But, on the one hand, we have seen that the many individual wills active in history for the most part produce results quite other than those intended—often quite the opposite; that their motives, therefore, in relation to the total result are likewise of only secondary importance. On the other hand, the further question arises: What driving forces in turn stand behind these motives? What are the historical causes which transform themselves into these motives in the brains of the actors?

. . .

When, therefore, it is a question of investigating the driving powers which—consciously or unconsciously, and indeed very often unconsciously—lie behind the motives of men who act in history and which constitute the real ultimate driving forces of history, then it is not a question so much of the motives of single individuals, however eminent, as of those motives which set in motion great masses, whole peoples, and again whole classes of the people in each people; and this, too, not momentarily, for the transient flaring up of a straw-fire which quickly dies down, but for a lasting action resulting in a great historical transformation. To ascertain the driving causes which here in the minds of acting masses and their leaders—the so-called great men—are reflected as conscious motives, clearly or unclearly, directly or in ideological, even glorified, form—that is the only path which can put us on the track of the laws holding sway both in history as a whole, and at particular periods and in particular lands. Everything which sets men in motion must go through their minds; but what form it will take in the mind will depend very much upon the circumstances. The workers have by no means become reconciled to capitalist machine industry, even though they no longer simply break the machines to pieces as they still did in 1848 on the Rhine.

But while in all earlier periods the investigation of these driving causes of history was almost impossible—on account of the complicated and concealed interconnections between them and their effects—our present period has so far simplified these interconnections that the riddle could be solved. Since the establishment of large-scale industry, that is, at least since the European peace of 1815, it has been no longer a secret to any man in England that the whole political struggle there turned on the claims to supremacy of two classes: the landed aristocracy and the bourgeoisie (middle class). In France, with the return of the Bourbons, the same fact was perceived, the historians of the Restoration period, from Thierry to Guizot, Mignet and Thiers, speak of it everywhere as the key to the understanding of all French history since the Middle Ages. And since 1830 the working class, the proletariat, has been recognized in both countries as a third competitor for power. Conditions had become so simplified that one would have had to close one's eyes deliberately not to see in the fight of these three great classes and in the conflict of their interests the driving force of modern history—at least in the two most advanced countries.

But how did these classes come into existence? If it was possible at first glance still to ascribe the origin of the great, formerly feudal landed property—at least in the first instance—to political causes, to taking possession by force, this could not be done in regard to the bourgeoisie and the proletariat. Here the origin and development of two great classes was seen to lie clearly and palpably in purely economic causes. And it was just as clear that in the struggle between landed property and the bourgeoisie, no less than in the struggle between the bourgeoisie and the proletariat, it was a question, first and foremost, of economic interests, to the furtherance of which political power was intended to serve merely as a means. Bourgeoisie and proletariat both arose in consequence of a transformation of the economic conditions, more precisely, of the mode of production. The transition, first from guild handicrafts to manufacture, and then from manufacture to large-scale industry, with steam and mechanical power, had caused the development of these two classes. At a certain stage the new productive forces set in motion by the bourgeoisie—in the first place the division of labour and the combination of many detail labourers [*Teilarbeiter*] in one general manufactory—and the conditions and requirements of exchange, developed through these productive forces, became incompatible with the existing order of production handed down by history and sanctified by law, that is to say, incompatible with the privileges of the guild and the numerous other personal and local privileges (which were only so many fetters to the unprivileged estates) of the feudal order of society. The productive forces represented by the bourgeoisie rebelled against the order of production represented by the feudal landlords and the guild-masters. The result is known: the feudal fetters were smashed, gradually in England, at one blow in France. In Germany the process is not yet finished. But just as, at a definite stage of its development, manufacture came into conflict with the feudal order of production, so now large-scale industry has already come into conflict with the bourgeois order of production established in its place. Tied down by this order, by the narrow limits of the capitalist mode of production, this industry produces, on the one hand, an ever-increasing proletarianization of the great mass of the people, and on the other hand, an ever greater mass of unsaleable products. Over-production and mass misery, each the cause of the other—that is the absurd contradiction which is its outcome, and which of necessity calls for the liberation of the productive forces by means of a change in the mode of production.

In modern history at least it is, therefore, proved that all political struggles are class struggles, and all class struggles for emancipation, despite their necessarily political form—for every class struggle is a political struggle—turn ultimately on the question of *economic* emancipation. Therefore, here at least, the state—the political order—is the subordinate, and civil society—the realm of economic relations—the decisive element. The traditional conception, to which Hegel, too, pays homage, saw in the state the determining element, and in civil society the element determined by it. Appearances correspond to this. As all the driving forces of the actions of any individual person must pass through his brain, and transform themselves into motives of his will in order to set him into action, so also all the needs of civil society—no matter which class happens to be the ruling one—must pass through the will of the state in order to secure general validity in the form of laws. That is the formal aspect of the matter—the one which is self-evident. The question arises, however, what is the content of this merely formal will—of the individual as well as of the state—and whence is this content derived? Why is just this willed and not something else? If we enquire into this we discover that in modern history the will of the state is, on the whole, determined by the changing needs of civil society, by the supremacy of this or that class, in the last resort, by the development of the productive forces and relations of exchange.

But if even in our modern era, with its gigantic means of production and communication, the state is not an independent domain with an independent development, but one whose existence as well as development is to be explained in the last resort by the economic conditions of life of society, then this must be still more true of all earlier times when the production of the material life of man was not yet carried on with these abundant auxiliary means, and when, therefore, the necessity of such production must have exercised a still greater mastery over men. If the state even today, in the era of big industry and of railways, is on the whole only a reflection, in concentrated form, of the economic needs of the class controlling production, then this must have been much more so in an epoch when each generation of men was forced to spend a far greater part of its aggregate lifetime in satisfying material needs, and was therefore much more dependent on them than we are today. An examination of the history of earlier periods, as soon as it is seriously undertaken from this angle, most abundantly confirms this. But, of course, this cannot be gone into here.

If the state and public law are determined by economic relations, so, too, of course is private law, which indeed in essence only sanctions the existing economic relations between individuals which are normal in the given circumstances. The form in which this happens can, however, vary considerably. It is possible, as happened in England, in harmony with the whole national development, to retain in the main the forms of the old feudal laws while giving them a bourgeois content; in fact, directly reading a bourgeois meaning into the feudal name. But, also, as happened in western continental Europe, Roman Law, the first world law of a commodity-producing society, with its unsurpassably fine elaboration of all the essential legal relations of simple commodity owners (of buyers and sellers, debtors and creditors, contracts, obligations, etc.) can be taken as the foundation. In which case, for the benefit of a still petty-bourgeois and semi-feudal society, it can either be reduced to the level of such a society simply through judicial practice (common law) or, with the help of allegedly enlightened, moralizing jurists it can be worked into a special code of law to correspond with such social level—a code which in these circumstances will be a bad one also from the legal standpoint (for instance, Prussian *Landrecht*). In which case, however, after a great bourgeois revolution, it is also possible for such a classic law code of bourgeois society as the French *Code Civil* to be worked out upon the basis of this same Roman Law. If, therefore, bourgeois legal rules merely express the economic life conditions of society in legal form, then they can do so well or ill according to circumstances.

—Engels, "Ludwig Feuerbach and the End of Classical German Philosophy," *MESW II*, pp. 391–96

The premises from which we begin are not arbitrary ones, not dogmas, but real premises from which abstraction can only be made in the imagination. They are the real individuals, their activity and the material conditions under which they live, both those which they find already existing and those produced by their activity. These premises can thus be verified in a purely empirical way.

The first premise of all human history is, of course, the existence of living human individuals. Thus the first fact to be established is the physical organization of these individuals and their consequent relation to the rest of nature. Of course, we cannot here go either into the actual physical nature of man, or into the natural conditions in which man finds himself—geological, orohydrographical, climatic and so on. The writing of history must always set out from these natural bases and their modification in the course of history through the action of man.

Men can be distinguished from animals by consciousness, by religion or anything else you like. They themselves begin to distinguish themselves from animals as soon as they begin to *produce* their means of subsistence, a step which is conditioned by their physical organization. By producing their means of subsistence men are indirectly producing their actual material life.

The way in which men produce their means of subsistence depends first of all on the nature of the actual means they find in existence and have to reproduce. This mode of production must not be considered simply as being the reproduction of the physical existence of the individuals. Rather it is a definite form of activity of these individuals, a definite form of expressing their life, a definite *mode of life* on their part. As individuals express their life, so they are. What they are, therefore, coincides with their production, both with *what* they produce and with *how* they produce. The nature of individuals thus depends on the material conditions determining their production.

This production only makes its appearance with the increase of population. In its turn this presupposes the intercourse of individuals with one another. The form of this intercourse is again determined by production.

The relations of different nations among themselves depend upon the extent to which each has developed its productive forces, the division of labour and internal intercourse. This statement is generally recognized. But not only the relation of one nation to others, but also the whole internal structure of the nation itself depends on the stage of development reached by its production and its internal and external intercourse. How far the productive forces of a nation are developed is shown most manifestly by the degree to which the division of labour has been carried. Each new productive force, in so far as it is not merely a quantitative extension of productive forces already known (for instance the bringing into cultivation of fresh land), brings about a further development of the division of labour.

The division of labour inside a nation leads at first to the separation of industrial and commercial from agricultural labour, and hence to the separation of town and country and a clash of interests between them. Its further development leads to the separation of commercial from industrial labour. At the same time through the division of labour there develop further, inside these various branches, various divisions among the individuals co-operating in definite kinds of labour. The relative position of these individual groups is determined by the methods employed in agriculture, industry and commerce (patriarchalism, slavery, estates, classes). These same conditions are to be seen (given a more developed intercourse) in the relations of different nations to one another.

The various stages of development in the division of labour are just so many different forms of ownership; i.e. the existing stage in the division of labour determines also the relations of individuals to one another with reference to the material, instrument, and product of labour.

The first form of ownership is tribal ownership. It corresponds to the undeveloped stage of production, at which a people lives by hunting and fishing, by the rearing of beasts or, in the highest stage, agriculture. In the latter case it presupposes a great mass of uncultivated stretches of land. The division of labour is at this stage still very elementary and is confined to a further extension of the natural division of labour imposed by the family. The social structure is therefore limited to an extension of the family; patriarchal family chieftains; below them the members of the tribe; finally slaves. The slavery latent in the family only develops gradually with the increase of population, the growth of wants, and with the extension of external relations, of war or of trade.

The second form is the ancient communal and State ownership which proceeds especially from the union of several tribes into a city by agreement or by conquest, and which is still accompanied by slavery. Beside communal ownership we already find movable, and later also immovable, private property developing, but as an abnormal form subordinate to communal ownership. It is only as a community that the citizens hold power over their labouring slaves, and on this account alone, therefore, they are bound to the form of communal ownership. It is the communal private property which compels the active citizens to remain in this natural form of association over against their slaves. For this reason the whole structure of society based on this communal ownership, and with it the power of the people, decays in the same measure as immovable private property evolves. The division of labour is already more developed. We already find the antagonism of town and country; later the antagonism between those states which represent town interests and those which represent country, and inside the towns themselves the antagonism between industry and maritime commerce. The class relation between citizens and slaves is now completely developed.

. . .

The third form of ownership is feudal or estate-property. If antiquity started out from the town and its little territory, the Middle Ages started out from the country. This different starting-point was determined by the sparseness of the population at that time, which was scattered over a large area and which received no large increase from the conquerors. In contrast to Greece and Rome, feudal development therefore extends over a much wider field, prepared by the Roman conquests and the spread of agriculture at first associated with it. The last centuries of the declining Roman Empire and its conquest by the barbarians destroyed a number of productive forces; agriculture had declined, industry had decayed for want of a market, trade had died out or been violently suspended, the rural and urban population had decreased. From these conditions and the mode of organization of the conquest determined by them, feudal property developed under the influence of the Germanic military constitution. Like tribal and communal ownership, it is based again on a community; but the directly producing class standing over against it is not, as in the case of the ancient community, the slaves, but the enserfed small peasantry. As soon as feudalism is fully developed, there also arises antagonism to the towns. The hierarchical system of land ownership, and the armed bodies of retainers associated with it, gave the nobility power over the serfs. This feudal organization was, just as much as the ancient communal ownership, an association against a subjected producing class; but the form of association and the relation to the direct producers were different because of the different conditions of production.

This feudal organization of land-ownership had its counterpart in the towns in the shape of corporative property, the feudal organization of trades. Here property consisted chiefly in the labour of each individual person. The necessity for association against the organized robber-nobility, the need for communal covered markets in an age when the industrialist was at the same time a merchant, the growing competition of the escaped serfs swarming into the rising towns, the feudal structure of the whole country: these combined to bring about the guilds. Further, the gradually accumulated capital of individual craftsmen and their stable numbers, as against the growing population, evolved the relation of journeyman and apprentice, which brought into being in the towns a hierarchy similar to that in the country.

Thus the chief form of property during the feudal epoch consisted on the one hand of landed property with serf-labour chained to it, and on the other of individual labour with small capital commanding the labour of journeymen. The organization of both was determined by the restricted conditions of production—the small-scale and primitive cultivation of the land, and the craft type of industry. There was little division of labour in the heyday of feudalism. Each land bore in itself the conflict of town and country and the division into estates was certainly strongly marked; but apart from the differentiation of princes, nobility, clergy and peasants in the country, and masters, journeymen, apprentices and soon also the rabble of casual labourers in the towns, no division of importance took place. In agriculture it was rendered difficult by the strip-system, beside which the cottage industry of the peasants themselves emerged as another factor. In industry there was no division of labour at all in the individual trades themselves, and very little between them. The separation of industry and commerce was found already in existence in older towns; in the newer it only developed later, when the towns entered into mutual relations.

The grouping of larger territories into feudal kingdoms was a necessity for the landed nobility as for the towns. The organization of the ruling class, the nobility, had, therefore, everywhere a monarch at its head.

The fact is, therefore, that definite individuals who are productively active in a definite way enter into these definite social and political relations. Empirical observation must in each separate instance bring out empirically, and without any mystification and speculation, the connection of the social and political structure with production. The social structure and the State are continually evolving out of the life-process of definite individuals, but of individuals, not as they may appear in their own or other people's imagination, but as they really are; i.e. as they are effective, produce materially, and are active under definite material limits, presuppositions and conditions independent of their will.

The production of ideas, of conceptions, of consciousness, is at first directly interwoven with the material activity and the material intercourse of men, the language of real life. Conceiving, thinking, the mental intercourse of men, appear at this stage as the direct efflux of their material behaviour. The same applies to mental production as expressed in the language of the politics, laws, morality, religion, metaphysics of a people. Men are the producers of their conceptions, ideas, etc.—real, active men, as they are conditioned by a definite development of their productive forces and of the intercourse corresponding to these, up to its furthest forms. Consciousness can never be anything else than conscious existence, and the existence of men is their actual life-process. If in all ideology men and their circumstances appear upside down as in a *camera obscura,* this phenomenon arises just as much from their historical life-process as the inversion of objects on the retina does from their physical life-process.

In direct contrast to German philosophy which descends from heaven to earth, here we ascend from earth to heaven. That is to say, we do not set out from what men say, imagine, conceive, nor from men as narrated, thought of, imagined, conceived, in order to arrive at men in the flesh. We set out from real, active men, and on the basis of their real life-process we demonstrate the development of the ideological reflexes and echoes of this life-process. The phantoms formed in the human brain are also, necessarily, sublimates of their material life-process, which is empirically verifiable and bound to material premises. Morality, religion, metaphysics, all the rest of ideology and their corresponding forms of consciousness, thus no longer retain the semblance of independence. They have no history, no development; but men, developing their material production and their material intercourse, alter, along with this their real existence, their thinking and the products of their thinking. Life is not determined by consciousness, but consciousness by life. In the first method of approach the starting-point is consciousness taken as the living individual; in the second it is the real living individuals themselves, as they are in actual life, and consciousness is considered solely as *their* consciousness.

This method of approach is not devoid of premises. It starts out from the real premises and does not abandon them for a moment. Its premises are men, not in any fantastic isolation or abstract definition, but in their actual, empirically perceptible process of development under definite conditions. As soon as this active life-process is described, history ceases to be a collection of dead facts as it is with the empiricists (themselves still abstract), or an imagined activity of imagined subjects, as with the idealists.

Where speculation ends—in real life—there real, positive science begins: the representation of the practical activity, of the practical process of development of men. Empty talk about consciousness ceases, and real knowledge has to take its place. When reality is depicted, philosophy as an independent branch of activity loses its medium of existence. At the best its place can only be taken by a summing-up of the most general results, abstractions which arise from the observation of the historical development of men. Viewed apart from real history, these abstractions have in themselves no value whatsoever. They can only serve to facilitate the arrangement of historical material, to indicate the sequence of its separate strata. But they by no means afford a recipe or schema, as does philosophy, for neatly trimming the epochs of history. On the contrary, our difficulties begin only when we set about the observation and the arrangement—the real depiction—of our historical material, whether of a past epoch or of the present. The removal of these difficulties is governed by premises which it is quite impossible to state here, but which only the study of the actual life-process and the activity of the individuals of each epoch will make evident. We shall select here some of these abstractions, which we use to refute the ideologists, and shall illustrate them by historical examples.

(*a*) *History*

Since we are dealing with the Germans, who do not postulate anything, we must begin by stating the first premise of all human existence, and therefore of all history, the premise namely that men must be in a position to live in order to be able to "make history." But life involves before everything else eating and drinking, a habitation, clothing and many other things. The first historical act is thus the production of the means to satisfy these needs, the production of material life itself. And indeed this is an historical act, a fundamental condition of all history, which to-day, as thousands of years ago, must daily and hourly be fulfilled merely in order to sustain human life.

. . .

The second fundamental point is that as soon as a need is satisfied (which implies the action of satisfying, and the acquisition of an instrument), new needs are made; and this production of new needs is the first historical act. Here we recognize immediately the spiritual ancestry of the great historical wisdom of the Germans who, when they run out of positive material and when they can serve up neither theological nor political nor literary rubbish, do not write history at all, but invent the "prehistoric era." They do not, however, enlighten us as to how we proceed from this nonsensical "prehistory" to history proper; although, on the other hand, in their historical speculation they seize upon this "prehistory" with especial eagerness because they imagine themselves safe there from interference on the part of "crude facts," and, at the same time, because there they can give full rein to their speculative impulse and set up and knock down hypotheses by the thousand.

The third circumstance which, from the very first, enters into historical development, is that men, who daily remake their own life, begin to make other men, to propagate their kind: the relation between man and wife, parents and children, the FAMILY. The family which to begin with is the only social relationship, becomes later, when increased needs create new social relations and the increased population new needs, a subordinate one (except in Germany), and must then be treated and analysed according to the existing empirical data,* not according to "the concept of the family," as is the custom in Germany. These three aspects of social activity are not of course to be taken as three different stages, but just, as I have said, as three aspects or, to make it clear to the Germans, three "moments," which have existed simultaneously

* The building of houses. With savages each family has of course its own cave or hut like the separate family tent of the nomads. This separate domestic economy is made only the more necessary by the further development of private property. With the agricultural peoples a communal domestic economy is just as impossible as a communal cultivation of the soil. A great advance was the building of towns. In all previous periods, however, the abolition of individual economy, which is inseparable from the abolition of private property, was impossible for the simple reason that the material conditions governing it were not present. The setting-up of a communal domestic economy presupposes the development of machinery, of the use of natural forces and of many other productive forces—e.g. of water-supplies, of gas-lighting, steam-heating, etc., the removal of the antagonism of town and country. Without these conditions a communal economy would not in itself form a new productive force; lacking any material basis and resting on a purely theoretical foundation, it would be a mere freak and would end in nothing more than a monastic economy.—What was possible can be seen in the formation of towns and the erection of communal buildings for various definite purposes (prisons, barracks, etc.). That the abolition of individual economy is inseparable from the abolition of the family is self-evident.

since the dawn of history and the first men, and still assert themselves in history to-day.

The production of life, both of one's own in labour and of fresh life in procreation, now appears as a double relationship: on the one hand as a natural, on the other as a social relationship. By social we understand the co-operation of several individuals, no matter under what conditions, in what manner and to what end. It follows from this that a certain mode of production, or industrial stage, is always combined with a certain mode of co-operation, or social stage, and this mode of co-operation is itself a "productive force." Further, that the multitude of productive forces accessible to men determines the nature of society, hence that the "history of humanity" must always be studied and treated in relation to the history of industry and exchange.

. . .

Our conception of history depends on our ability to expound the real process of production, starting out from the simple material production of life, and to comprehend the form of intercourse connected with this and created by this (i.e. civil society in its various stages), as the basis of all history; further, to show it in its action as State; and so, from this starting-point, to explain the whole mass of different theoretical products and forms of consciousness, religion, philosophy, ethics etc., etc., and trace their origins and growth, by which means, of course, the whole thing can be shown in its totality (and therefore, too, the reciprocal action of these various sides on one another). It has not, like the idealistic view of history, in every period to look for a category, but remains constantly on the real ground of history; it does not explain practice from the idea but explains the formation of ideas from material practice; and accordingly it comes to the conclusion that all forms and products of consciousness cannot be dissolved by mental criticism, by resolution into "self-consciousness" or transformation into "apparitions," "spectres," "fancies," etc., but only by the practical overthrow of the actual social relations which gave rise to this idealistic humbug; that not criticism but revolution is the driving force of history, also of religion, of philosophy and all other types of theory. It shows that history does not end by being resolved into "self-consciousness" as "spirit of the spirit," but that in it at each stage there is found a material result: a sum of productive forces, a historically created relation of individuals to nature and to one another, which is handed down to each generation from its predecessor; a mass of productive forces, different forms of capital, and conditions, which, indeed, is modified by the new generation on the one hand, but also on the other prescribes for it its conditions of life and gives it a definite development, a special character. It shows that circumstances make men just as much as men make circumstances.

This sum of productive forces, forms of capital and social forms of intercourse, which every individual and generation finds in existence as something given, is the real basis of what the philosophers have conceived as "substance" and "essence of man," and what they have deified and attacked: a real basis which is not in the least disturbed, in its effect and influence on the development of men, by the fact that these philosophers revolt against it as "self-consciousness" and "the unique." These conditions of life, which different generations find in existence, decide also whether or not the periodically recurring revolutionary convulsion will be strong enough to overthrow the basis of all existing forms. And if these material elements of a complete revolution are not present (namely, on the one hand the existence of productive forces, on the other the formulation of a revolutionary mass, which revolts not only against separate conditions of society up till then, but against the very "production of life" till then, the "total activity" on which it was based), then, as far as practical development is concerned, it is absolutely immaterial whether the "idea" of this revolution has been expressed a hundred times already; as the history of communism proves.

In the whole conception of history up to the present this real basis of history has either been totally neglected or else considered as a minor matter quite irrelevant to the course of history. History must therefore always be written according to an extraneous standard; the real production of life seems to be beyond history, while the truly historical appears to be separated from ordinary life, something extra-superterrestrial. With this the relation of man to nature is excluded from history and hence the antithesis of nature and history is created. The exponents of this conception of history have consequently only been able to see in history the political actions of princes and States, religious and all sorts of theoretical struggles, and in particular in each historical epoch have had to share the *illusion of that epoch*. For instance, if an epoch imagines itself to be actuated by purely "political" or "religious" motives, although "religion" and "politics" are only forms of its true motives, the historian accepts this opinion. The "idea," the "conception" of these conditioned men about their real practice, is transformed into the sole determining, active force, which controls and determines their practice. When the crude form in which the division of labour appears with the Indians and Egyptians calls forth the caste-system in their State and religion, the historian believes that the caste-system is the power which has produced this crude social form. While the French and the English at least hold by the political illusion, which is moderately close to reality, the Germans move in the realm of the "pure spirit," and make religious illusion the driving force of history.

· · ·

History is nothing but the succession of the separate generations, each of which exploits the materials, the forms of capital, the productive forces handed down to it by all preceding ones, and thus on the one hand continues the traditional activity in completely changed circumstances and, on the other, modifies the old circumstances with a completely changed activity. This can be speculatively distorted so that later history is made the goal of earlier history, e.g. the goal ascribed to the discovery of America is to further the eruption of the French Revolution. Thereby history receives its own special aims and becomes "a person ranking with other persons" (to wit: "self-consciousness, criticism, the Unique," etc.), while what is designated with the words "destiny," "goal," "germ," or "idea" of earlier history is nothing more than an abstraction formed from later history, from the active influence which earlier history exercises on later history. The further the separate spheres, which interact on one another, extend in the course of this development, the more the original isolation of the separate nationalities is destroyed by the developed mode of production and intercourse and the division of labour naturally brought forth by these, the more history becomes world-history. Thus, for instance, if in England a machine is invented, which in India or China deprives countless workers of bread, and overturns the whole form of existence of these empires, this invention becomes a world-historical fact. Or again, take the case of sugar and coffee which have proved their world-historical importance in the nineteenth century by the fact that the lack of these products, occasioned by the Napoleonic Continental system, caused the Germans to rise against Napoleon, and thus became the real basis of the glorious Wars of Liberation of 1813. From this it follows that this transformation of history into world-history is not indeed a mere abstract act on the part of the "self-consciousness," the world-spirit, or of any other metaphysical spectre, but a quite material, empirically verifiable act, an act the proof of which every individual furnishes as he comes and goes, eats, drinks and clothes himself.

—Marx and Engels, *The German Ideology,* pp. 6–18, 28–30, 38–39

In the social production of their life, men enter into definite relations that are indispensable and independent of their will, relations of production which correspond to a definite stage of development of their material productive forces. The sum total of these relations of production constitutes the economic structure of society, the real foundation, on which rises a legal and political superstructure and to which correspond definite forms of social consciousness. The mode of production of material life conditions the social, political and intellectual life process in general. It is not the consciousness of men that determines their being, but, on the contrary, their social being that determines their consciousness. At a certain stage of their development, the material productive forces of society come in conflict with the existing relations of production, or—what is but a legal expression for the same thing—with the property relations within which they have been at work hitherto. From forms of development of the productive forces these relations turn into their fetters. Then begins an epoch of social revolution. With the change of the economic foundation the entire immense superstructure is more or less rapidly transformed. In considering such transformations a distinction should always be made between the material transformation of the economic conditions of production, which can be determined with the precision of natural science, and the legal, political, religious, aesthetic or philosophic—in short, ideological forms in which men become conscious of this conflict and fight it out. Just as our opinion of an individual is not based on what he thinks of himself, so can we not judge of such a period of transformation by its own consciousness; on the contrary, this consciousness must be explained rather from the contradictions of material life, from the existing conflict between the social productive forces and the relations of production. No social order ever perishes before all the productive forces for which there is room in it have developed; and new, higher relations of production never appear before the material conditions of their existence have matured in the womb of the old society itself. Therefore mankind always sets itself only such tasks as it can solve; since, looking at the matter more closely, it will always be found that the task itself arises only when the material conditions for its solution already exist or are at least in the process of formation. In broad outlines Asiatic, ancient, feudal, and modern bourgeois modes of production can be designated as progressive epochs in the economic formation of society. The bourgeois relations of production are the last antagonistic form of the social process of production—antagonistic not in the sense of individual antagonism, but of one arising from the social conditions of life of the individuals; at the same time the productive forces developing in the womb of bourgeois society create the material conditions for the solution of that antagonism. This social formation brings, therefore, the prehistory of human society to a close.

—Marx, Preface to "A Contribution to the Critique of Political Economy," *MESW I*, pp. 362–64

With man we enter *history*. Animals also have a history, that of their derivation and gradual evolution to their present state. This history, however, is made for them, and in so far as they themselves take part in it, this occurs without their knowledge or desire. On the other hand, the further human beings become removed from animals in the narrower sense of the word, the more they make their history themselves, consciously, the less becomes the influence of unforeseen effects and uncontrolled forces on this history, and the more accurately does the historical result correspond to the aim laid down in advance. If, however, we apply this measure to human history, to that of even the most developed peoples of the present day, we find that there still exists here a colossal discrepancy between the proposed aims and the results arrived at, that unforeseen effects predominate, and that the uncontrolled forces are far more powerful than those set into motion according to plan. And this cannot be otherwise as long as the most essential historical activity of men, the one which has raised them from bestiality to humanity and which forms the material foundation of all their other activities, namely, the production of their means of subsistence, that is, today, social production, is particularly subject to the interplay of unintended effects of uncontrolled forces and achieves its desired end only by way of exception and, much more frequently, the exact opposite. In the most advanced industrial countries we have subdued the forces of nature and pressed them into the service of mankind; we have thereby infinitely multiplied production, so that a child now produces more than a hundred adults previously. And what is the consequence? Increasing overwork and increasing misery of the masses, and every ten years a great crash. Darwin did not know what a bitter satire he wrote on mankind, and especially on his countrymen, when he showed that free competition, the struggle for existence, which the economists celebrate as the highest historical achievement, is the normal state of the *animal kingdom*. Only conscious organization of social production, in which production and distribution are carried on in a planned way, can elevate mankind above the rest of the animal world socially in the same way that production in general has done this for men specifically. Historical development makes such an organization daily more indispensable, but also with every day more possible. From it will date a new epoch of history, in which mankind itself, and with mankind all branches of its activity, and especially natural science, will experience an advance before which everything preceding it will pale into insignificance.

—Engels, Introduction to "The Dialectics of Nature," *MESW II*, pp. 75–76

. . . According to the materialist conception of history, the *ultimately* determining element in history is the production and reproduction of real life. More than this neither Marx nor I have ever asserted. Hence if somebody twists this into saying that the economic element is the *only* determining one, he transforms that proposition into a meaningless, abstract, senseless phrase. The economic situation is the basis, but the various elements of the superstructure—political forms of the class struggle and its results, to wit: constitutions established by the victorious class after a successful battle, etc., juridical forms, and even the reflexes of all these actual struggles in the brains of the participants, political, juristic, philosophical theories, religious views and their further development into systems of dogmas—also exercise their influence upon the course of the historical struggles and in many cases preponderate in determining their *form*. There is an interaction of all these elements in which, amid all the endless host of accidents (that is, of things and events whose inner interconnection is so remote or so impossible of proof that we can regard it as non-existent, as negligible) the economic movement finally asserts itself as necessary. Otherwise the application of the theory to any period of history would be easier than the solution of a simple equation of the first degree.

We make our history ourselves, but, in the first place, under very definite assumptions and conditions. Among these the economic ones are ultimately decisive. But the political ones, etc., and indeed even the traditions which haunt human minds also play a part, although not the decisive one. The Prussian state also arose and developed from historical, ultimately economic, causes. But it could scarcely be maintained without pedantry that among the many small states of North Germany, Brandenburg was specifically determined by economic necessity to become the great power embodying the economic, linguistic and, after the Reformation, also the religious difference between North and South, and not by other elements as well (above all by its entanglement with Poland, owing to the possession of Prussia, and hence with international political relations—which were indeed also decisive in the formation of the Austrian dynastic power). Without making oneself ridiculous it would be a difficult thing to explain in terms of economics the existence of every small state in Germany, past and present, or the origin of the High German consonant permutations, which widened the geographic partition wall formed by the mountains from the Sudetic range to the Taunus to form a regular fissure across all Germany.

In the second place, however, history is made in such a way that the final result always arises from conflicts between many individual wills, of which each in turn has been made what it is by a host of particular conditions of life. Thus there are innumerable intersecting forces, an infinite series of parallelograms of forces which give rise to one resultant—the historical event. This may again itself be viewed as the product of a power which works as a whole *unconsciously* and without volition. For what each individual wills is obstructed by everyone else, and what emerges is something that no one willed. Thus history has proceeded hitherto in the manner of a natural process and is essentially subject to the same laws of motion. But from the fact that the wills of individuals—each of whom desires what he is impelled to by his physical constitution and external, in the last resort economic, circumstances (either his own personal circumstances or those of society in general)—do not attain what they want, but are merged into an aggregate mean, a common resultant, it must not be concluded that they are equal to zero. On the contrary, each contributes to the resultant and is to this extent included in it.

I would furthermore ask you to study this theory from its original sources and not at second-hand; it is really much easier. Marx hardly wrote anything in which it did not play a part. But especially

*The Eighteenth Brumaire of Louis Bonaparte** is a most excellent example of its application. There are also many allusions to it in *Capital.* Then may I also direct you to my writings: *Herr Eugen Dühring's Revolution in Science* and *Ludwig Feuerbach and the End of Classical German Philosophy,* in which I have given the most detailed account of historical materialism which, as far as I know, exists.

Marx and I are ourselves partly to blame for the fact that the younger people sometimes lay more stress on the economic side than is due to it. We had to emphasize the main principle *vis-a-vis* our adversaries, who denied it, and we had not always the time, the place or the opportunity to give their due to the other elements involved in the interaction. But when it came to presenting a section of history, that is, to making a practical application, it was a different matter and there no error was permissible. Unfortunately, however, it happens only too often that people think they have fully understood a new theory and can apply it without more ado from the moment they have assimilated its main principles, and even those not always correctly. And I cannot exempt many of the more recent "Marxists" from this reproach, for the most amazing rubbish has been produced in this quarter, too. . . .

—Engels to J. Bloch (September 21–22, 1890), *Selected Correspondence,* pp. 498–500

Here is the answer to your questions:

1. What we understand by the economic relations, which we regard as the determining basis of the history of society, is the manner and method by which men in a given society produce their means of subsistence and exchange the products among themselves (in so far as division of labour exists). Thus the *entire technique* of production and transport is here included. According to our conception this technique also determines the manner and method of exchange and, further, of the distribution of products and with it, after the dissolution of gentile society, also the division into classes,

* See the Appendix to Chapter IV [*note by R. Freedman*].

and hence the relations of lordship and servitude and with them the state, politics, law, etc. Further included in economic relations are the *geographical basis* on which they operate and those remnants of earlier stages of economic development which have actually been transmitted and have survived—often only through tradition or by force of inertia; also of course the external environment which surrounds this form of society.

If, as you say, technique largely depends on the state of science, science depends far more still on the *state* and the *requirements* of technique. If society has a technical need, that helps science forward more than ten universities. The whole of hydrostatics (Torricelli, etc.) was called forth by the necessity for regulating the mountain streams of Italy in the sixteenth and seventeenth centuries. We have known anything reasonable about electricity only since its technical applicability was discovered. But unfortunately it has become the custom in Germany to write the history of the sciences as if they had fallen from the skies.

2. We regard economic conditions as that which ultimately conditions historical development. But race is itself an economic factor. Here, however, two points must not be overlooked:

a) Political, juridical, philosophical, religious, literary, artistic, etc., development is based on economic development. But all these react upon one another and also upon the economic basis. It is not that the economic situation is *cause, solely active,* while everything else is only passive effect. There is, rather, interaction on the basis of economic necessity, which *ultimately* always asserts itself. The state, for instance, exercises an influence by protective tariffs, free trade, good or bad fiscal system; and even the deadly inanition and impotence of the German philistine, arising from the miserable economic condition of Germany from 1648 to 1830 and expressing themselves at first in pietism, then in sentimentality and cringing servility to princes and nobles, were not without economic effect. That was one of the greatest hindrances to recovery and was not shaken until the revolutionary and Napoleonic wars made the chronic misery an acute one. So it is not, as people try here and there conveniently to imagine, that the economic situation produces an automatic effect. No. Men make their history themselves, only they do so in a given environment, which conditions it, and on the basis of actual relations already existing, among which the economic relations, however much they may be influenced by the other—the political and ideological relations, are still ultimately the decisive ones, forming the keynote which runs through them and alone leads to understanding.

b) Men make their history themselves, but not as yet with a collective will according to a collective plan or even in a definite, delimited given society. Their aspirations clash, and for that very reason all such societies are governed by *necessity,* the complement and form of appearance of which is *accident.* The necessity which here asserts itself athwart all accident is again ultimately economic necessity. This is where the so-called great men come in for treatment. That such and such a man and precisely that man arises at a particular time in a particular country is, of course, pure chance. But cut him out and there will be a demand for a substitute, and this substitute will be found, good or bad, but in the long run he will be found. That Napoleon, just that particular Corsican, should have been the military dictator whom the French Republic, exhausted by its own warfare, had rendered necessary, was chance; but that, if a Napoleon had been lacking, another would have filled the place is proved by the fact that the man was always found as soon as he became necessary: Caesar, Augustus, Cromwell, etc. While Marx discovered the materialist conception of history, Thierry, Mignet, Guizot and all the English historians up to 1850 are evidence that it was being striven for, and the discovery of the same conception by Morgan proves that the time was ripe for it and that it simply *had* to be discovered.

So with all the other accidents, and apparent accidents, of history. The further the particular sphere which we are investigating is removed from the economic sphere and approaches that of pure abstract ideology, the more shall we find it exhibiting accidents in its development, the more will its curve run zigzag. But if you plot the average axis of the curve, you will find that this axis will run more and more nearly parallel to the axis of economic development the longer the period considered and the wider the field dealt with.

In Germany the greatest hindrance to correct understanding is the irresponsible neglect by literature of economic history. It is so hard not only to disaccustom oneself to the ideas of history drilled into one at school but still more to rake up the necessary material for doing so. Who, for instance, has read at least old G. von Gülich, whose dry collection of material nevertheless contains so much stuff for the clarification of innumerable political facts!

For the rest, the fine example which Marx has given in *The Eighteenth Brumaire* should, I think, provide you fairly well with information on your questions, just because it is a practical example. I have also, I believe, already touched on most of the points in *Anti-Dühring* I, chs. 9–11, and II, 2–4, as well as in III, 1, or Introduction, and also in the last section of Feuerbach.

Please do not weigh each word in the above too scrupulously, but keep the general connection in mind; I regret that I have not the time to word what I am writing to you as exactly as I should be obliged to do for publication. . . .

—Engels to H. Starkenburg (January 25, 1894), *Selected Correspondence,* pp. 548–51

. . . Otherwise only one more point is lacking, which, however, Marx and I always failed to stress enough in our writings and in regard to which we are all equally guilty. That is to say, we all laid, and *were bound* to lay, the main emphasis, in the first place, on the *derivation* of political, juridical and other ideological notions, and of actions arising through the medium of these notions, from basic economic facts. But in so doing we neglected the formal side —the ways and means by which these notions, etc., come about— for the sake of the content. This has given our adversaries a welcome opportunity for misunderstandings and distortions, of which Paul Barth is a striking example.

Ideology is a process accomplished by the so-called thinker consciously, it is true, but with a false consciousness. The real motive forces impelling him remain unknown to him; otherwise it simply would not be an ideological process. Hence he imagines false or seeming motive forces. Because it is a process of thought he derives its form as well as its content from pure thought, either his own or that of his predecessors. He works with mere thought material, which he accepts without examination as the product of thought, and does not investigate further for a more remote source independent of thought; indeed this is a matter of course to him, because, as all action is *mediated* by thought, it appears to him to be ultimately *based* upon thought.

The historical ideologist (historical is here simply meant to comprise the political, juridical, philosophical, theological—in short, all the spheres belonging to *society* and not only to nature) thus possesses in every sphere of science material which has formed itself independently out of the thought of previous generations and has gone through its own independent course of development in the brains of these successive generations. True, external facts belonging to one or another sphere may have exercised a codetermining influence on this development, but the tacit presupposition is that these facts themselves are also only the fruits of a process of thought, and so we still remain within that realm of mere thought, which apparently has successfully digested even the hardest facts.

It is above all this semblance of an independent history of state constitutions, of systems of law, of ideological conceptions in every separate domain that dazzles most people. If Luther and Calvin "overcome" the official Catholic religion or Hegel "overcomes" Fichte and Kant or Rousseau with his republican *Contrat social* indirectly "overcomes" the constitutional Montesquieu, this is a process which remains within theology, philosophy or political science, represents a stage in the history of these particular spheres of thought and never passes beyond the sphere of thought. And since the bourgeois illusion of the eternity and finality of capitalist production has been added as well, even the overcoming of the mercantilists by the physiocrats and Adam Smith is accounted as a sheer victory of thought; not as the reflection in thought of changed economic facts but as the finally achieved correct understanding of actual conditions subsisting always and everywhere—in fact, if Richard Coeur-de-Lion and Philip Augustus had introduced free trade instead of getting mixed up in the crusades we should have been spared five hundred years of misery and stupidity.

This aspect of the matter, which I can only indicate here, we have all, I think, neglected more than it deserves. It is the old story: form is always neglected at first for content. As I say, I have done that too and the mistake has always struck me only later. So I am not only far from reproaching you with this in any way—as the older of the guilty parties I certainly have no right to do so; on the contrary. But I would like all the same to draw your attention to this point for the future.

Hanging together with this is the fatuous notion of the ideologists that because we deny an independent historical development to the various ideological spheres which play a part in history we also deny them any *effect upon history*. The basis of this is the common undialectical conception of cause and effect as rigidly opposite poles, the total disregarding of interaction. These gentlemen often almost deliberately forget that once an historic element has been brought into the world by other, ultimately economic causes, it reacts, can react on its environment and even on the causes that have given rise to it. . . .

—Engels to F. Mehring (July 14, 1893), *Selected Correspondence*, pp. 540–42.

Relics of by-gone instruments of labour possess the same importance for the investigation of extinct economical forms of society, as do fossil bones for the determination of extinct species of animals. It is not the articles made, but how they are made, and by what instruments, that enables us to distinguish different economical epochs.[1] Instruments of labour not only supply a standard of the degree of development to which human labour has attained,

[1]. . . However little our written histories up to this time notice the development of material production, which is the basis of all social life, and therefore of all real history, yet prehistoric times have been classified in accordance with the results, not of so called historical, but of materialistic investigations. These periods have been divided, to correspond with the materials from which their implements and weapons are made, viz., into the stone, the bronze, and the iron ages.

but they are also indicators of the social conditions under which that labour is carried on.

. . .

Technology discloses man's mode of dealing with Nature, the process of production by which he sustains his life, and thereby also lays bare the mode of formation of his social relations, and of the mental conceptions that flow from them. Every history of religion even, that fails to take account of this material basis, is uncritical. It is, in reality, much easier to discover by analysis the earthly core of the misty creations of religion, than, conversely, it is, to develop from the actual relations of life the corresponding celestialised forms of those relations. The latter method is the only materialistic, and therefore the only scientific one. The weak points in the abstract materialism of natural science, a materialism that excludes history and its process, are at once evident from the abstract and ideological conceptions of its spokesmen, whenever they venture beyond the bounds of their own speciality.

—Marx, *Capital:* Vol. I, pp. 200, 406–407 (Footnote 2)

IV

Economic Interpretation of History— Classes

Introduction

Social classes are variously defined in Marx's writings. The central determining factor of class position is the individual's relationship to property. An owner has the power to dictate the conditions under which labor uses his property. Without working, the capitalist can expropriate the product of labor. Property, then, confers monopoly power on owners, defining social and political relationships within society.

The property system is an aspect of the economic structure. The economic structure can be understood as a reflection of its technological base. The economic system, including the methods of production, exchange, and property, is dependent on the stage of economic progress of that society, which, in turn, is related to the tools available for production in a particular historic time. The property system and social classes are, therefore, a consequence of the division of labor necessitated by the economic system.

Therefore Marx always saw economics not merely as a method of production and distribution but as a social system. For Marx the cardinal sin of bourgeois economists was the reification of social relations. Marx refused to acknowledge economics as an impersonal science with objective classifications and laws separate from the human relationships that lay behind these laws. He was never willing to divorce economic and social affairs. The economic interpretation of history is a critical examination of the economics of capitalism and the social system it creates.

In the section entitled "The Economic Base of the Class Struggle," Marx and Engels explain the relationship between economic organization and the class system. In the section called "Capitalism and the Class Struggle," Marx shows how capitalism brings about the class struggle. Marx never accepted the doctrine of "harmony of interests" attributable to classical economics. Competition, which is seen by Marx as conflict between capitalists for markets, between workers for jobs, and between the two classes for survival, is the engine which drives the economy to enormous accomplishments in production as well as to its inevitable destruction.

The "Manifesto of the Communist Party" presents the social analogue of the theory of class struggle in the economy. Here is to be found the most graphic description in literature of history seen as class warfare. It is a celebration of the superiority of capitalism to all other systems in its capacity to create the material base of limitless well-being. At the same time it is a ferocious indictment of capitalism as a social system, which institutionalizes the division of labor, thereby creating the conditions for the most inhumane exploitation of man by man hitherto known.

The Appendix to Chapter IV provides, by means of its description of the events leading to the assumption of the French throne by Louis Bonaparte (nephew of Napoleon), an example of Marx's economic interpretation of history, which Engels thought was one of his finest achievements.

The Economic Base of the Class System

Political economy, in the widest sense, is the science of the laws governing the production and exchange of the material means of subsistence in human society. Production and exchange are two different functions. Production may occur without exchange, but exchange—being necessarily an exchange of products—cannot occur without production. Each of these two social functions is subject to the action of special external influences which to a great extent are peculiar to it and for this reason each has, also to a great extent, its own special laws. But on the other hand, they constantly determine and influence each other to such an extent that they might be termed the abscissa and ordinate of the economic curve.

The conditions under which men produce and exchange vary from country to country, and within each country again from generation to generation. Political economy, therefore, cannot be the same for all countries and for all historical epochs. A tremendous distance separates the bow and arrow, the stone knife and the acts of exchange among savages occurring only by way of exception, from the steam-engine of a thousand horse power, the mechanical loom, the railways and the Bank of England. The inhabitants of Tierra del Fuego have not got so far as mass production and world trade, any more than they have experience of bill-jobbing or a Stock Exchange crash. Anyone who attempted to bring the political economy of Tierra del Fuego under the same laws as are operative in present-day England would obviously produce nothing but the most banal commonplaces. Political economy is therefore essentially a *historical* science. It deals with material which is historical, that is, constantly changing; it must first investigate the special laws of each individual stage in the evolution of production and exchange, and only when it has completed this investigation will it be able to establish the few quite general laws which hold good for production and exchange in general. At the same time it goes without saying that the laws which are valid for definite modes of production and forms of exchange hold good for all historical periods in which these modes of production and forms of exchange prevail. Thus, for example, the introduction of metallic money brought into operation a series of laws which remain valid for all countries and historical epochs in which metallic money is a medium of exchange.

The mode of production and exchange in a definite historical society, and the historical conditions which have given birth to this society, determine the mode of distribution of its products. In the tribal or village community with common ownership of land—with which, or with the easily recognizable survivals of which, all civilized peoples enter history—a fairly equal distribution of products is a matter of course; where considerable inequality of distribution among the members of the community sets in, this is an indication that the community is already beginning to break up.

Both large- and small-scale agriculture admit of very diverse forms of distribution, depending upon the historical conditions from which they developed. But it is obvious that large-scale farming always gives rise to a distribution which is quite different from that of small-scale farming; that large-scale agriculture presupposes or creates a class antagonism—slave owners and slaves, feudal lords and serfs, capitalists and wage-workers—while small-scale agriculture does not necessarily involve class differences between the individuals engaged in agricultural production, and that on the contrary the mere existence of such differences indicates the incipient dissolution of small-holding economy.

The introduction and extensive use of metallic money in a country in which hitherto natural economy was universal or predominant is always associated with a more or less rapid revolutionization of the former mode of distribution, and this takes place in such a way that the inequality of distribution among the individuals and therefore the opposition between rich and poor becomes more and more pronounced.

The local guild-controlled handicraft production of the Middle Ages precluded the existence of big capitalists and lifelong wage-workers just as these are inevitably brought into existence by modern large-scale industry, the credit system of the present day, and the form of exchange corresponding to the development of both of them—free competition.

But with the differences in distribution, *class differences* emerge. Society divides into classes: the privileged and the dispossessed, the exploiters and the exploited, the rulers and the ruled; and the state, which the primitive groups of communities of the same tribe had at first arrived at only in order to safeguard their common interests (e.g., irrigation in the East) and for protection against external enemies, from this stage onwards acquires just as much the function of maintaining by force the conditions of existence and domination of the ruling class against the subject class.

Distribution, however, is not a merely passive result of production and exchange; it in its turn reacts upon both of these. Each new mode of production or form of exchange is at first retarded not only by the old forms and the political institutions which correspond to them, but also by the old mode of distribution; it can secure the distribution which is suitable to it only in the course of a long struggle. But the more mobile a given mode of production and exchange, the more capable it is of perfection and development, the more rapidly does distribution reach the stage at which it outgrows its progenitor, the hitherto prevailing mode of production and exchange, and comes into conflict with it. The old primitive communities which have already been mentioned could remain in existence for thousands of years—as in India and among the Slavs up to the present day—before intercourse with the outside world gave rise in their midst to the inequalities of property as a result of which they began to break up. On the contrary, modern capitalist production, which is hardly three hundred years old and has become predominant only since the introduction of modern industry, that is, only in the last hundred years, has in this short time brought about antitheses in distribution—concentration of capital in a few hands on the one side and concentration of the propertyless masses in the big towns on the other—which must of necessity bring about its downfall.

The connection between distribution and the material conditions of existence of society at any period lies so much in the nature of things that it is always reflected in popular instinct. So long as a mode of production still describes an ascending curve of development, it is enthusiastically welcomed even by those who come off worst from its corresponding mode of distribution. This was the case with the English workers in the beginnings of modern industry. And even while this mode of production remains normal for society, there is, in general, contentment with the distribution, and if objections to it begin to be raised, these come from within the ruling class itself (Saint-Simon, Fourier, Owen) and find no response whatever among the exploited masses. Only when the mode of production in question has already described a good part of its descending curve, when it has half outlived its day, when the conditions of its existence have to a large extent disappeared, and its successor is already knocking at the door—it is only at this stage that the constantly increasing inequality of distribution appears as unjust, it is only then that appeal is made from the facts which have had their day to so-called eternal justice. From a scientific standpoint, this appeal to morality and justice does not help us an inch further; moral indignation, however justifiable, cannot serve economic science as an argument, but only as a symptom. The task of economic science is rather to show that the social abuses which have recently been developing are necessary consequences of the existing mode of production, but at the same time also indications of its approaching dissolution; and to reveal, within the already dissolving economic form of motion, the elements of the future new organization of production and exchange which will put an end to those abuses. The wrath which creates the poet is absolutely in place in describing these abuses, and also in attacking those apostles of harmony in the service of the ruling class who either deny or palliate them; but how little it *proves* in any particular case is evident from the fact that in *every* epoch of past history there has been no lack of material for such wrath.

Political economy, however, as the science of the conditions and forms under which the various human societies have produced and exchanged and on this basis have distributed their products—political economy in this wider sense has still to be brought into being.

Such economic science as we possess up to the present is limited almost exclusively to the genesis and development of the capitalist mode of production: it begins with a critique of the survivals of the feudal forms of production and exchange, shows the necessity of their replacement by capitalist forms, then develops the laws of the capitalist mode of production and its corresponding forms of exchange in their positive aspects, that is, the aspects in which they further the general aims of society, and ends with a socialist critique of the capitalist mode of production, that is, with an exposition of its laws in their negative aspects, with a demonstration that this mode of production, by virtue of its own development, drives towards the point at which it makes itself impossible. This critique proves that the capitalist forms of production and exchange become more and more an intolerable fetter on production itself, that the mode of distribution necessarily determined by those forms has produced a situation among the classes which is daily becoming more intolerable—the antagonism, sharpening from day to day, between capitalists, constantly decreasing in number but constantly growing richer, and propertyless wage-workers, whose number is constantly increasing and whose conditions, taken as a whole, are steadily deteriorating; and finally, that the colossal productive forces created within the capitalist mode of production which the latter can no longer master, are only waiting to be taken possession of by a society organized for co-operative work on a planned basis to ensure to all members of society the means of existence and of the free development of their capacities, and indeed in constantly increasing measure.

—Engels, "Subject Matter and Method," *Anti-Dühring*, pp. 203–209

The owners of mere labor-power, the owners of capital, and the landlords, whose respective sources of income are wages, profit and ground-rent, in other words, wage laborers, capitalists and landlords, form the three great classes of modern society resting upon the capitalist mode of production.

In England, modern society is indisputably developed most highly and classically in its economic structure. Nevertheless the stratification of classes does not appear in its pure form, even there. Middle and transition stages obliterate even here all definite boundaries, although much less in the rural districts than in the cities. However, this is immaterial for our analysis. We have seen that the continual tendency and law of development of capitalist production is to separate the means of production more and more from labor, and to concentrate the scattered means of production more and more in large groups, thereby transforming labor into wage labor and the means of production into capital. In keeping with this tendency we have, on the other hand, the independent separation of private land from capital and labor, or the transformation of all property in land into a form of landed property corresponding to the capitalist mode of production.

The first question to be answered is this: What constitutes a class? And this follows naturally from another question, namely: What constitutes wage laborers, capitalists and landlords into three great social classes?

At first glance it might seem that the identity of their revenues and their sources of revenue does that. They are three great social groups, whose component elements, the individuals forming them, live on wages, profit and ground-rent, or by the utilization of their labor-power, their capital, and their private land.

However, from this point of view physicians and officials would also form two classes, for they belong to the two distinct social groups, and the revenues of their members flow from the same common source. The same would also be true of the infinite dissipation of interests and positions created by the social division of labor among laborers, capitalists and landlords. For instance, the landlords are divided into owners of vineyards, farms, forests, mines, fisheries.

[Here the manuscript ends.]

—Marx, *Capital,* Vol. III, pp. 1031–1032

But in order that our owner of money may be able to find labour-power offered for sale as a commodity, various conditions must first be fulfilled. The exchange of commodities of itself implies no other relations of dependence than those which result from its own nature. On this assumption, labour-power can appear upon the market as a commodity only if, and so far as, its possessor, the individual whose labour-power it is, offers it for sale, or sells it, as a commodity. In order that he may be able to do this, he must have it at his disposal, must be the untrammelled owner of his capacity for labour, *i.e.,* of his person.[1] He and the owner of money meet in the market, and deal with each other as on the basis of equal rights, with this difference alone, that one is buyer, the other seller; both, therefore, equal in the eyes of the law. The continuance of this relation demands that the owner of the labour-power should sell it only for a definite period, for if he were to sell it rump and stump, once for all, he would be selling himself, converting himself from a free man into a slave, from an owner of a commodity into a commodity.

. . .

Personal dependence here characterises the social relations of production just as much as it does the other spheres of life organized on the basis of that production.

. . .

The capitalist system presupposes the complete separation of the labourers from all property in the means by which they can realise their labour. As soon as capitalist production is once on its own legs, it not only maintains this separation, but reproduces it on a continually extending scale. The process, therefore, that clears the way for the capitalist system, can be none other than the process which takes away from the labourer the possession of his means of production; a process that transforms, on the one hand, the social means of subsistence and of production into capital, on the other, the immediate producers into wage-labourers.

—Marx, *Capital,* Vol. I, pp. 186, 89, 785–86

[1] In encyclopaedias of classical antiquities we find such nonsense as this —that in the ancient world capital was fully developed, "except that the free labourer and a system of credit was wanting." Mommsen also, in his "History of Rome," commits, in this respect, one blunder after another.

The economic conditions have in the first place transformed the mass of the people of a country into wage-workers. The domination of capital has created for this mass of people a common situation with common interests. Thus this mass is already a class, as opposed to capital, but not yet for itself. In the struggle, of which we have only noted some phases, this mass unites, it is constituted as a class for itself. The interests which it defends are the interests of its class. But the struggle between class and class is a political struggle.

In the bourgeoisie we have two phases to distinguish, that during which it is constituted as a class under the *régime* of feudalism and absolute monarchy, and that wherein, already constituted as a class, it overthrew feudalism and monarchy in order to make of society a bourgeois society. The first of these phases was the longest and necessitated the greatest efforts. That also commenced with partial combinations against the feudal lords.

Many researches have been made to trace the different historical phases through which the bourgeoisie has passed from the early commune to its constitution as a class.

. . .

As the economists are the scientific representatives of the bourgeois class, so the Socialists and Communists are the theorists of the proletarian class. So long as the proletariat is not sufficiently developed to constitute itself as a class, so long as, in consequence, the struggle between the proletariat and the bourgeoisie has not acquired a political character, and while the productive forces are not sufficiently developed in the bosom of the bourgeoisie itself to allow a perception of the material conditions necessary to the emancipation of the proletariat and the formation of a new society, so long these theorists are only utopians who, to obviate the distress of the oppressed classes, improvise systems and run after a regenerative science. But as history develops and with it the struggle of the proletariat becomes more clearly defined, they have no longer any need to seek for such a science in their own minds, they have only to give an account of what passes before their eyes and to make of that their medium. So long as they seek science and only make systems, so long as they are at the beginning of the struggle, they see in poverty only poverty, without seeing therein the revolutionary subversive side which will overturn the old society. From that moment science, produced by the historical movement and linking itself thereto in full knowledge of the facts of the case, has ceased to be doctrinaire and has become revolutionary.

—Marx, *The Poverty of Philosophy,* pp. 188–89, 136–67

Capitalism and the Class Struggle

I

From various quarters we have been reproached with not having presented the *economic relations* which constitute the material foundation of the present class struggles and national struggles. We have designedly touched upon these relations only where they directly forced themselves to the front in political conflicts.

The point was, above all, to trace the class struggle in current history, and to prove empirically by means of the historical material already at hand and which is being newly created daily, that, with the subjugation of the working class that February and March had wrought, its opponents were simultaneously defeated—the bourgeois republicans in France and the bourgeois and peasant classes which were fighting feudal absolutism throughout the continent of Europe; that the victory of the "honest republic" in France was at the same time the downfall of the nations that had responded to the February Revolution by heroic wars of independence; finally, that Europe, with the defeat of the revolutionary workers, had relapsed into its old double slavery, the *Anglo-Russian* slavery. The June struggle in Paris, the fall of Vienna, the tragicomedy of Berlin's November 1848, the desperate exertions of Poland, Italy and Hungary, the starving of Ireland into submission —these were the chief factors which characterized the European class struggle between bourgeoisie and working class and by means of which we proved that every revolutionary upheaval, however remote from the class struggle its goal may appear to be, must fail until the revolutionary working class is victorious, that every social reform remains a utopia until the proletarian revolution and the feudalistic counter-revolution measure swords in a *world war.* In our presentation, as in reality, *Belgium* and *Switzerland* were tragicomic genre-pictures akin to caricature in the great historical tableau, the one being the model state of the bourgeois monarchy, the other the model state of the bourgeois republic, both of them states which imagine themselves to be as independent of the class struggle as of the European revolution.

Now, after our readers have seen the class struggle develop in colossal political forms in 1848, the time has come to deal more closely with the economic relations themselves on which the existence of the bourgeoisie and its class rule, as well as the slavery of the workers, are founded.

We shall present in three large sections: 1) the relation of *wage labour to capital,* the slavery of the worker, the domination of the capitalist; 2) *the inevitable destruction of the middle bourgeois classes and of the so-called peasant estate under the present system;* 3) *the commercial subjugation and exploitation of the bourgeois classes of the various European nations* by the despot of the world market—*England.*

We shall try to make our presentation as simple and popular as possible and shall not presuppose even the most elementary notions of political economy. We wish to be understood by the workers. Moreover, the most remarkable ignorance and confusion of ideas prevails in Germany in regard to the simplest economic relations, from the accredited defenders of the existing state of things down to the *socialist miracle workers* and the *unrecognized political geniuses* in which fragmented Germany is even richer than in sovereign princes.

Now, therefore, for the first question: *What are wages? How are they determined?*

If workers were asked: "How much are your wages?" one would reply: "I get a mark a day from my employer"; another, "I get two marks," and so on. According to the different trades to which they belong, they would mention different sums of money which they receive from their respective employers for the performance of a particular piece of work, for example, weaving a yard of linen or type-setting a printed sheet. In spite of the variety of their statements, they would all agree on one point: wages are the sum of money paid by the capitalist for a particular labour time or for a particular output of labour.

The capitalist, it seems, therefore, *buys* their labour with money. They *sell* him their labour for money. But this is merely the appearance. In reality what they sell to the capitalist for money is their labour *power*. The capitalist buys this labour power for a day, a week, a month, etc. And after he has bought it, he uses it by having the workers work for the stipulated time. For the same sum with which the capitalist has bought their labour power, for example, two marks, he could have bought two pounds of sugar or a definite amount of any other commodity. The two marks, with which he bought two pounds of sugar, are the *price* of the two pounds of sugar. The two marks, with which he bought twelve hours' use of labour power, are the price of twelve hours' labour. Labour power, therefore, is a commodity, neither more nor less than sugar. The former is measured by the clock, the latter by the scales.

The workers exchange their commodity, labour power, for the commodity of the capitalist, for money, and this exchange takes place in a definite ratio. So much money for so long a use of labour power. For twelve hours' weaving, two marks. And do not the two marks represent all the other commodities which I can buy for two marks? In fact, therefore, the worker has exchanged his commodity, labour power, for other commodities of all kinds and that in a definite ratio. By giving him two marks, the capitalist has given him so much meat, so much clothing, so much fuel, light, etc., in exchange for his day's labour. Accordingly, the two marks express the ratio in which labour power is exchanged for other commodities, the *exchange value* of his labour power. The exchange value of a commodity, reckoned in *money,* is what is called its *price*. *Wages* are only a special name for the price of labour power, commonly called the *price of labour,* for the price of this peculiar commodity which has no other repository than human flesh and blood.

Let us take any worker, say, a weaver. The capitalist supplies him with the loom and yarn. The weaver sets to work and the yarn is converted into linen. The capitalist takes possession of the linen and sells it, say, for twenty marks. Now are the wages of the weaver a *share* in the linen, in the twenty marks, in the product of his labour? By no means. Long before the linen is sold, perhaps long before its weaving is finished, the weaver has received his wages. The capitalist, therefore, does not pay these wages with the money which he will obtain from the linen, but with money already in reserve. Just as the loom and the yarn are not the product of the weaver to whom they are supplied by his employer, so likewise with the commodities which the weaver receives in exchange for his commodity, labour power. It was possible that his employer found no purchaser at all for his linen. It was possible that he did not get even the amount of the wages by its sale. It is possible that he sells it very profitably in comparison with the weaver's wages. All that has nothing to do with the weaver. The capitalist buys the labour power of the weaver with a part of his available wealth, of his capital, just as he has bought the raw material—the yarn—and the instrument of labour—the loom—with another part of his wealth. After he has made these purchases, and these purchases include the labour power necessary for the production of linen, he produces only with the *raw materials and instruments of labour belonging to him.* For the latter include now, true enough, our good weaver as well, who has as little share in the product or the price of the product as the loom has.

Wages are, therefore, not the worker's share in the commodity produced by him. Wages are the part of already existing commodities with which the capitalist buys for himself a definite amount of productive labour power.

Labour power is, therefore, a commodity which its possessor, the wage-worker, sells to capital. Why does he sell it? In order to live.

But the exercise of labour power, labour, is the worker's own life-activity, the manifestation of his own life. And this *life-activity* he sells to another person in order to secure the necessary *means of subsistence*. Thus his life-activity is for him only a means to enable him to exist. He works in order to live. He does not even reckon labour as part of his life, it is rather a sacrifice of his life. It is a commodity which he has made over to another. Hence, also, the product of his activity is not the object of his activity. What he produces for himself is not the silk that he weaves, not the gold that he draws from the mine, not the palace that he builds. What he produces for himself is *wages,* and silk, gold, palace resolve themselves for him into a definite quantity of the means of subsistence, perhaps into a cotton jacket, some copper coins and a lodging in a cellar. And the worker, who for twelve hours weaves, spins, drills, turns, builds, shovels, breaks stones, carries loads, etc.—does he consider this twelve hours' weaving, spinning, drilling, turning, building, shovelling, stone breaking as a manifestation of his life, as life? On the contrary, life begins for him where this activity ceases, at table, in the public house, in bed. The twelve hours' labour, on the other hand, has no meaning for him as weaving, spinning, drilling, etc., but as *earnings,* which bring him to the table, to the public house, into bed. If the silk worm were to spin in order to continue its existence as a caterpillar, it would be a complete wage-worker. Labour power was not always a *commodity*. Labour was not always wage labour, that is, *free labour*. The *slave* did not sell his labour power to the slave owner, any more than the ox sells its services to the peasant. The slave, together with his labour power, is sold once and for all to his owner. He is a commodity which can pass from the hand of one owner to that of another. He is *himself* a commodity, but the labour power is not *his* commodity. The *serf* sells only a part of his labour power. He does not receive a wage from the owner of the land; rather the owner of the land receives a tribute from him.

The serf belongs to the land and turns over to the owner of the land the fruits thereof. The *free labourer,* on the other hand, sells himself and, indeed, sells himself piecemeal. He sells at auction eight, ten, twelve, fifteen hours of his life, day after day, to the highest bidder, to the owner of the raw materials, instruments of labour and means of subsistence, that is, to the capitalist. The worker belongs neither to an owner nor to the land, but eight, ten, twelve, fifteen hours of his daily life belong to him who buys them. The worker leaves the capitalist to whom he hires himself whenever he likes, and the capitalist discharges him whenever he thinks fit, as soon as he no longer gets any profit out of him, or not the anticipated profit. But the worker, whose sole source of livelihood is the sale of his labour power, cannot leave the *whole class of purchasers, that is, the capitalist class,* without renouncing his existence. He belongs not to this or that capitalist but to the *capitalist class,* and, moreover, it is his business to dispose of himself, that is, to find a purchaser within this capitalist class.

Now, before going more closely into the relation between capital and wage labour, we shall present briefly the most general relations which come into consideration in the determination of wages.

Wages, as we have seen, are the *price* of a definite commodity, of labour power. Wages are, therefore, determined by the same laws that determine the price of every other commodity. The question, therefore, is, *how is the price of a commodity determined?*

II

By what is the *price* of a commodity determined?

By competition between buyers and sellers, by the relation of inquiry to delivery, of demand to supply. Competition, by which the price of a commodity is determined, is *three-sided.*

The same commodity is offered by various sellers. With goods of the same quality, the one who sells most cheaply is certain of driving the others out of the field and securing the greatest sale for himself. Thus, the sellers mutually contend among themselves for sales, for the market. Each of them desires to sell, to sell as much as possible and, if possible, to sell alone, to the exclusion of the other sellers. Hence, one sells cheaper than another. Consequently, *competition* takes place *among the sellers,* which *depresses* the price of the *commodities* offered by them.

But *competition* also takes place *among the buyers,* which in its turn *causes* the commodities offered to *rise* in price.

Finally *competition* occurs *between buyers and sellers;* the former desire to buy as cheaply as possible, the latter to sell as dearly as possible. The result of this competition between buyers and sellers will depend upon how the two above-mentioned sides of the competition are related, that is, whether the competition is stronger in the army of buyers or in the army of sellers. Industry leads two armies into the field against each other, each of which again carries on a battle within its own ranks, among its own troops. The army whose troops beat each other up the least gains the victory over the opposing host.

Let us suppose there are 100 bales of cotton on the market and at the same time buyers for 1,000 bales of cotton. In this case, therefore, the demand is ten times as great as the supply. Competition will be very strong among the buyers, each of whom desires to get one, and if possible all, of the hundred bales for himself. This example is no arbitrary assumption. We have experienced periods of cotton crop failure in the history of the trade when a few capitalists in alliance have tried to buy, not one hundred bales, but all the cotton stocks of the world. Hence, in the example mentioned, one buyer will seek to drive the other from the field by offering a relatively higher price per bale of cotton. The cotton sellers, who see that the troops of the enemy army are engaged in the most violent struggle among themselves and that the sales of all their hundred bales is absolutely certain, will take good care not to fall out among themselves and depress the price of cotton at the moment when their adversaries are competing with one another to force it up. Thus, peace suddenly descends on the army of the sellers. They stand facing the buyers as one man, fold their arms philosophically, and there would be no bounds to their demands were it not that the offers of even the most persistent and eager buyers have very definite limits.

If, therefore, the supply of a commodity is lower than the demand for it, then only slight competition, or none at all, takes place among the sellers. In the same proportion as this competition decreases, competition increases among the buyers. The result is a more or less considerable rise in commodity prices.

It is well known that the reverse case with a reverse result occurs more frequently. Considerable surplus of supply over demand; desperate competition among the sellers; lack of buyers; disposal of goods at ridiculously low prices.

But what is the meaning of a rise, a fall in prices; what is the meaning of high price, low price? A grain of sand is high when examined through a microscope, and a tower is low when compared with a mountain. And if price is determined by the relation between supply and demand, what determines the relation between supply and demand?

Let us turn to the first bourgeois we meet. He will not reflect for an instant but, like another Alexander the Great, will cut this metaphysical knot with the multiplication table. If the production of the goods which I sell has cost me 100 marks, he will tell us, and if I get 110 marks from the sale of these goods, within the year of course—then that is sound, honest, legitimate profit. But if I get in exchange 120 or 130 marks, that is a high profit; and if I get as much as 200 marks, that would be an extraordinary, an enormous profit. What, therefore, serves the bourgeois as his *measure* of profit? The *cost of production* of his commodity. If he receives in exchange for this commodity an amount of other commodities which it has cost less to produce, he has lost. If he receives in exchange for his commodity an amount of other commodities the production of which has cost more, he has gained. And he calculates the rise or fall of the profit according to the degree in which the exchange value of his commodity stands above or below zero—the *cost of production.*

We have thus seen how the changing relation of supply and demand causes now a rise and now a fall of prices, now high, now low prices. If the price of a commodity rises considerably because of inadequate supply or disproportionate increase of the demand, the price of some other commodity must necessarily have fallen proportionately, for the price of a commodity only expressed in money the ratio in which other commodities are given in exchange for it. If, for example, the price of a yard of silk material rises from five marks to six marks, the price of silver in relation to silk material has fallen and likewise the prices of all other commodities that have remained at their old prices have fallen in relation to the silk. One has to give a larger amount of them in exchange to get the same amount of silks. What will be the consequence of the rising price of a commodity? A mass of capital will be thrown into that flourishing branch of industry and this influx of capital into the domain of the favoured industry will continue until it yields the ordinary profits or, rather, until the price of its products, through overproduction, sinks below the cost of production.

Conversely, if the price of a commodity falls below its cost of production, capital will be withdrawn from the production of this commodity. Except in the case of a branch of industry which has become obsolete and must, therefore, perish, the production of such a commodity, that is, its supply, will go on decreasing owing to this flight of capital until it corresponds to the demand, and consequently its price is again on a level with its cost of production or, rather, until the supply has sunk below the demand, that is, until its price rises again above its cost of production, *for the current price of a commodity is always either above or below its cost of production.*

We see how capital continually migrates in and out, out of the domain of one industry into that of another. High prices bring too great an immigration and low prices too great an emigration.

We could show from another point of view how not only supply but also demand is determined by the cost of production. But this would take us too far away from our subject.

We have just seen how the fluctuations of supply and demand continually bring the price of a commodity back to the cost of production. *The real price of a commodity, it is true, is always above or below its cost of production; but rise and fall reciprocally balance each other,* so that within a certain period of time, taking the ebb and flow of the industry together, commodities are exchanged for one another in accordance with their cost of production, their price, therefore, being determined by their cost of production.

This determination of price by cost of production is not to be understood in the sense of the economists. The economists say that the *average price* of commodities is equal to the cost of production; that this is a *law.* The anarchical movement, in which rise is compensated by fall and fall by rise, is regarded by them as chance. With just as much right one could regard the fluctuations as the law and the determination by the cost of production as chance, as has actually been done by other economists. But it is solely these fluctuations, which, looked at more closely, bring with them the most fearful devastations and, like earthquakes, cause bourgeois society to tremble to its foundations—it is solely in the course of these fluctuations that prices are determined by the cost of production. The total movement of this disorder is its order. In the course of this industrial anarchy, in this movement in a circle, competition compensates, so to speak, for one excess by means of another.

We see, therefore, that the price of a commodity is determined by its cost of production in such manner that the periods in which the price of this commodity rises above its cost of production, and vice versa. This does not hold good, of course, for separate, particular industrial products but only for the whole branch of industry. Consequently, it also does not hold good for the individual industrialist but only for the whole class of industrialists.

The determination of price by the cost of production is equivalent to the determination of price by the labour time necessary for the manufacture of a commodity, for the cost of production consists of 1) raw materials and depreciation of instruments, that is, of industrial products the production of which has cost a certain amount of labour days and which, therefore, represent a certain amount of labour time, and 2) of direct labour, the measure of which is, precisely, time.

Now, the same general laws that regulate the price of commodities in general of course also regulate *wages*, the *price of labour*.

Wages will rise and fall according to the relation of supply and demand, according to the turn taken by the competition between the buyers of labour power, the capitalists, and the sellers of labour power, the workers. The fluctuations in wages correspond in general to the fluctuations in prices of commodities. *Within these fluctuations, however, the price of labour will be determined by the cost of production, by the labour time necessary to produce this commodity—labour power.*

What, then, is the cost of production of labour power?

It is the cost required for maintaining the worker as a worker and of developing him into a worker.

The less the period of training, therefore, that any work requires the smaller is the cost of production of the worker and the lower is the price of his labour, his wages. In those branches of industry in which hardly any period of apprenticeship is required and where the mere bodily existence of the worker suffices, the cost necessary for his production is almost confined to the commodities necessary for keeping him alive and capable of working. The *price of his labour* will, therefore, be determined by the *price of the necessary means of subsistence.*

Another consideration, however, also comes in. The manufacturer in calculating his cost of production and, accordingly, the price of the products takes into account the wear and tear of the instruments of labour. If, for example, a machine costs him 1,000 marks and wears out in ten years, he adds 100 marks annually to the price of the commodities so as to be able to replace the worn-out machine by a new one at the end of ten years. In the same way, in calculating the cost of production of simple labour power, there must be included the cost of reproduction, whereby the race of workers is enabled to multiply and to replace worn-out workers by new ones. Thus the depreciation of the worker is taken into account in the same way as the depreciation of the machine.

The cost of production of simple labour power, therefore, amounts to the *cost of existence and reproduction of the worker.* The price of this cost of existence and reproduction constitutes wages. Wages so determined are called the *wage minimum.* This wage minimum, like the determination of the price of commodities by the cost of production in general, does not hold good for the *single individual* but for the *species.* Individual workers, millions of workers, do not get enough to be able to exist and reproduce themselves; *but the wages of the whole working class* level down, within their fluctuations, to this minimum.

Now that we have arrived at an understanding of the most general laws which regulate wages like the price of any other commodity, we can go into our subject more specifically.

III

Capital consists of raw materials, instruments of labour and means of subsistence of all kinds, which are utilized in order to produce new raw materials, new instruments of labour and new means of subsistence. All these component parts of capital are creations of labour, products of labour, *accumulated labour*. Accumulated labour which serves as a means of new production is capital.

So say the economists.

What is a Negro slave? A man of the black race. The one explanation is as good as the other.

A Negro is a Negro. He only becomes a slave in certain relations. A cotton-spinning jenny is a machine for spinning cotton. It becomes *capital* only in certain relations. Torn from these relationships it is no more capital than gold in itself is *money* or sugar the price of sugar.

In production, men not only act on nature but also on one another. They produce only by co-operating in a certain way and mutually exchanging their activities. In order to produce, they enter into definite connections and relations with one another and only within these social connections and relations does their action on nature, does production, take place.

These social relations into which the producers enter with one another, the conditions under which they exchange their activities and participate in the whole act of production, will naturally vary according to the character of the means of production. With the invention of a new instrument of warfare, firearms, the whole internal organization of the army necessarily changed; the relationships within which individuals can constitute an army and act as an army were transformed and the relations of different armies to one another also changed.

Thus the social relations within which individuals produce, *the social relations of production, change, are transformed, with the change and development of the material means of production, the productive forces. The relations of production in their totality constitute what are called the social relations, society, and, specifically, a society at a definite stage of historical development,* a society with a peculiar, distinctive character. *Ancient* society, *feudal* society, *bourgeois* society are such totalities of production relations, each of which at the same time denotes a special stage of development in the history of mankind.

Capital, also, is a social relation of production. *It is a bourgeois production relation,* a production relation of bourgeois society. Are not the means of subsistence, the instruments of labour, the raw materials of which capital consists, produced and accumulated under given social conditions, in definite social relations? Are they not utilized for new production under given social conditions, in definite social relations? And is it not just this definite social character which turns the products serving for new production into *capital?*

Capital consists not only of means of subsistence, instruments of labour and raw materials, not only of material products; it consists just as much of *exchange values.* All the products of which it consists are *commodities.* Capital is, therefore, not only a sum of material products; it is a sum of commodities, of exchange values, *of social magnitudes.*

Capital remains the same, whether we put cotton in place of wool, rice in place of wheat or steamships in place of railways, provided only that the cotton, the rice, the steamships—the body of capital—have the same exchange value, the same price as the wool, the wheat, the railways in which it was previously incorporated. The body of capital can change continually without the capital suffering the slightest alteration.

But while all capital is a sum of commodities, that is, of exchange values, not every sum of commodities, of exchange values, is capital.

Every sum of exchange values is an exchange value. Every separate exchange value is a sum of exchange values. For instance, a house that is worth 1,000 marks is an exchange value of 1,000 marks. A piece of paper worth a pfennig is a sum of exchange values of one-hundred hundredths of a pfennig. Products which are exchangeable for others are *commodities.* The particular ratio in which they are exchangeable constitutes their *exchange value* or, expressed in money, their *price.* The quantity of these products can change nothing in their quality of being *commodities* or representing an *exchange value* or having a definite price. Whether a tree is large or small it is a tree. Whether we exchange iron for other products in ounces or in hundred-weights, does this make any difference in its character as commodity, as exchange value? It is a commodity of greater or lesser value, of higher or lower price, depending upon the quantity.

How, then, does any amount of commodities, of exchange value, become capital?

By maintaining and multiplying itself as an independent social *power,* that is, as the power *of a portion of society,* by means of its *exchange for direct, living labour power.* The existence of a class which possesses nothing but its capacity to labour is a necessary prerequisite of capital.

It is only the domination of accumulated, past, materialized labour over direct, living labour that turns accumulated labour into capital.

Capital does not consist in accumulated labour serving living labour as a means for new production. It consists in living labour serving accumulated labour as a means for maintaining and multiplying the exchange value of the latter.

What takes place in the exchange between capitalist and wage-worker?

The worker receives means of subsistence in exchange for his labour power, but the capitalist receives in exchange for his means of subsistence labour, the productive activity of the worker, the creative power whereby the worker not only replaces what he consumes but *gives to the accumulated labour a greater value than it previously possessed.* The worker receives a part of the available means of subsistence from the capitalist. For what purpose do these means of subsistence serve him? For immediate consumption. As soon, however, as I consume the means of subsistence, they are irretrievably lost to me unless I use the time during which I am kept alive by them in order to produce new means of subsistence, in order during consumption to create by my labour new values in place of the values which perish in being consumed. But it is just this noble reproductive power that the worker surrenders to the capitalist in exchange for means of subsistence received. He has, therefore, lost it for himself.

Let us take an example: a tenant farmer gives his day labourer five silver groschen a day. For these five silver groschen the labourer works all day on the farmer's field and thus secures him a return of ten silver groschen. The farmer not only gets the value replaced that he has to give the day labourer; he doubles it. He has therefore employed, consumed, the five silver groschen that he gave to the labourer in a fruitful, productive manner. He has bought with the five silver groschen just that labour and power of the labourer which produces agricultural products of double value and makes ten silver groschen out of five. The day labourer, on the other hand, receives in place of his productive power, the effect of which he has bargained away to the farmer, five silver groschen, which he exchanges for means of subsistence, and these he consumes with greater or less rapidity. The five silver groschen have, therefore, been consumed in a double way, *reproductively* for capital, for they have been exchanged for labour power which produced ten silver groschen, *unproductively* for the worker, for they have been exchanged for means of subsistence which have disappeared forever and the value of which he can only recover by repeating the same exchange with the farmer. *Thus capital presupposes wage labour; wage labour presupposes capital. They reciprocally condition the existence of each other; they reciprocally bring forth each other.*

Does a worker in a cotton factory produce merely cotton textiles? No, he produces capital. He produces values which serve afresh to command his labour and by means of it to create new values.

Capital can only increase by exchanging itself for labour power, by calling wage labour to life. The labour power of the wage-worker can only be exchanged for capital by increasing capital, by strengthening the power whose slave it is. *Hence, increase of capital is increase of the proletariat, that is, of the working class.*

The interests of the capitalist and those of the worker are, therefore, *one and the same,* assert the bourgeois and their economists. Indeed! The worker perishes if capital does not employ him. Capital perishes if it does not exploit labour power, and in order to exploit it, it must buy it. The faster capital intended for production, productive capital, increases, the more, therefore, industry prospers, the more the bourgeoisie enriches itself and the better business is, the more workers does the capitalist need, the more dearly does the worker sell himself.

The indispensable condition for a tolerable situation of the worker *is, therefore, the fastest possible growth of productive capital.*

But what is the growth of productive capital? Growth of the power of accumulated labour over living labour. Growth of the domination of the bourgeoisie over the working class. If wage labour produces the wealth of others that rules over it, the power that is hostile to it, capital, then the means of employment, that is, the means of subsistence, flow back to it from this hostile power, on condition that it makes itself afresh into a part of capital, into the lever which hurls capital anew into an accelerated movement of growth.

To say that the interests of capital and those of the workers are one and the same is only to say that capital and wage labour are two sides of one and the same relation. The one conditions the other, just as usurer and squanderer condition each other.

As long as the wage-worker is a wage-worker his lot depends upon capital. That is the much-vaunted community of interests between worker and capitalist.

IV

If capital grows, the mass of wage labour grows, the number of wage-workers grows; in a word, the domination of capital extends over a greater number of individuals. Let us assume the most favourable case: when productive capital grows, the demand for labour grows; consequently, the price of labour, wages, goes up.

A house may be large or small; as long as the surrounding houses are equally small it satisfies all social demands for a dwelling. But let a palace arise beside the little house, and it shrinks from a little house to a hut. The little house shows now that its owner has only very slight or no demands to make; and however high it may shoot up in the course of civilization, if the neighbouring palace grows to an equal or even greater extent, the occupant of the relatively small house will feel more and more uncomfortable, dissatisfied and cramped within its four walls.

A noticeable increase in wages presupposes a rapid growth of productive capital. The rapid growth of productive capital brings about an equally rapid growth of wealth, luxury, social wants, social enjoyments. Thus, although the enjoyments of the worker have risen, the social satisfaction that they give has fallen in comparison with the increased enjoyments of the capitalist, which are inaccessible to the worker, in comparison with the state of development of society in general. Our desires and pleasures spring from society; we measure them, therefore, by society and not by the objects which serve for their satisfaction. Because they are of a social nature, they are of a relative nature.

In general, wages are determined not only by the amount of commodities for which I can exchange them. They embody various relations.

What the workers receive for their labour power is, in the first place, a definite sum of money. Are wages determined only by this money price?

In the sixteenth century, the gold and silver circulating in Europe increased as a result of the discovery of richer and more easily worked mines in America. Hence, the value of gold and silver fell in relation to other commodities. The workers received the same amount of coined silver for their labour power as before. The money price of their labour remained the same, and yet their wages had fallen, for in exchange for the same quantity of silver they received a smaller amount of other commodities. This was one of the circumstances which furthered the growth of capital and the rise of the bourgeoisie in the sixteenth century.

Let us take another case. In the winter of 1847, as a result of a crop failure, the most indispensable means of subsistence, cereals, meat, butter, cheese, etc., rose considerably in price. Assume that the workers received the same sum of money for their labour power as before. Had not their wages fallen? Of course. For the same money they received less bread, meat, etc., in exchange. Their wages had fallen, not because the value of silver had diminished, but because the value of the means of subsistence had increased.

Assume, finally, that the money price of labour remains the same while all agricultural and manufactured goods have fallen in price owing to the employment of new machinery, a favourable season, etc. For the same money the workers can now buy more commodities of all kinds. Their wages, therefore, have risen, just because the money value of their wages has not changed.

Thus, the money price of labour, nominal wages, do not coincide with real wages, that is, with the sum of commodities which is actually given in exchange for the wages. If, therefore, we speak of a rise or fall of wages, we must keep in mind not only the money price of labour, the nominal wages.

But neither nominal wages, that is, the sum of money for which the worker sells himself to the capitalist, nor real wages, that is, the sum of commodities which he can buy for this money, exhaust the relations contained in wages.

Wages are, above all, also determined by their relation to the gain, to the profit of the capitalist—comparative, relative wages.

Real wages express the price of labour in relation to the price of other commodities; relative wages, on the other hand, express the share of direct labour in the new value it has created in relation to the share which falls to accumulated labour, to capital.

We said above, page 14: "Wages are not the worker's share in the commodity produced by him. Wages are the part of already existing commodities with which the capitalist buys for himself a definite amount of productive labour power." But the capitalist must replace these wages out of the price at which he sells the product produced by the worker; he must replace it in such a way that there remains to him, as a rule, a surplus over the cost of production expended by him, a profit. For the capitalist, the selling price of the commodities produced by the worker is divided into three parts: *first,* the replacement of the price of the raw materials advanced by him together with replacement of the depreciation of the tools, machinery and other means of labour also advanced by him; *secondly,* the replacement of the wages advanced by him, and *thirdly,* the surplus left over, the capitalist's profit. While the first part only replaces *previously existing values,* it is clear that both the replacement of the wages and also the surplus profit of the capitalist are, on the whole, taken from the *new value created by the worker's labour* and added to the raw materials. And *in this sense,* in order to compare them with one another, we can regard both wages and profit as shares in the product of the worker.

Real wages may remain the same, they may even rise, and yet relative wages may fall. Let us suppose, for example, that all means of subsistence have gone down in price by two-thirds while wages per day have only fallen by one-third, that is to say, for example, from three marks to two marks. Although the worker can command a greater amount of commodities with these two marks than he previously could with three marks, yet his wages have gone down in relation to the profit of the capitalist. The profit of the capitalist (for example, the manufacturer) has increased by one mark; that is, for a smaller sum of exchange values which he pays to the worker, the latter must produce a greater amount of exchange values than before. The share of capital relative to the share of labour has risen. The division of social wealth between capital and labour has become still more unequal. With the same capital, the capitalist commands a greater quantity of labour. The power of the capitalist class over the working class has grown, the social position of the worker has deteriorated, has been depressed one step further below that of the capitalist.

What, then, is the general law which determines the rise and fall of wages and profit in their reciprocal relation?

They stand in inverse ratio to each other. Capital's share, profit, rises in the same proportion as labour's share, wages, falls, and vice versa. Profit rises to the extent that wages fall; it falls to the extent that wages rise.

The objection will, perhaps, be made that the capitalist can profit by a favourable exchange of his products with other capitalists, by increase of the demand for his commodities, whether as a result of the opening of new markets, or as a result of a momentarily increased demand in the old markets, etc.; that the capitalist's profit can, therefore, increase by overreaching other capitalists, independently of the rise and fall of wages, of the exchange value of labour power; or that the capitalist's profit may also rise owing to the improvement of the instruments of labour, a new application of natural forces, etc.

First of all, it will have to be admitted that the result remains the same, although it is brought about in reverse fashion. True, the profit has not risen because wages have fallen, but wages have fallen because the profit has risen. With the same amount of other people's labour, the capitalist has acquired a greater amount of exchange values, without having paid more for the labour on that account; that is, therefore, labour is paid less in proportion to the net profit which it yields the capitalist.

In addition, we recall that, in spite of the fluctuations in prices of commodities, the average price of every commodity, the ratio in which it is exchanged for other commodities, is determined by its *cost of production.* Hence the overreachings within the capitalist class necessarily balance one another. The improvement of machinery, new application of natural forces in the service of production, enable a larger amount of products to be created in a given period of time with the same amount of labour and capital, but not by any means a larger amount of exchange values. If, by the use of the spinning jenny, I can turn out twice as much yarn in an hour as before its invention, say, one hundred pounds instead of fifty, then in the long run I will receive for these hundred pounds no more commodities in exchange than formerly for the fifty pounds, because the cost of production has fallen by one-half, or because I can deliver double the product at the same cost.

Finally, in whatever proportion the capitalist class, the bourgeoisie, whether of one country or of the whole world market, shares the net profit of production within itself, the total amount of this net profit always consists only of the amount by which, on the whole, accumulated labour has been increased by direct labour. This total amount grows, therefore, in the proportion in which labour augments capital, that is, in the proportion in which profit rises in comparison with wages.

We see, therefore, that even if we remain *within the relation of capital and wage labour, the interests of capital and the interests of wage labour are diametrically opposed.*

A rapid increase of capital is equivalent to a rapid increase of profit. Profit can only increase rapidly if the price of labour, if relative wages, decrease just as rapidly. Relative wages can fall although real wages rise simultaneously with nominal wages, with the money value of labour, if they do not rise, however, in the same proportion as profit. If, for instance, in times when business is good, wages rise by five percent, profit on the other hand by thirty per cent, then the comparative, the relative wages, have not *increased* but *decreased.*

Thus if the income of the worker increases with the rapid growth of capital, the social gulf that separates the worker from the capitalist increases at the same time, and the power of capital over labour, the dependence of labour on capital, likewise increases at the same time.

To say that the worker has an interest in the rapid growth of capital is only to say that the more rapidly the worker increases the wealth of others, the richer will be the crumbs that fall to him, the greater is the number of workers that can be employed and called into existence, the more can the mass of slaves dependent on capital be increased.

We have thus seen that:

Even the *most favourable situation* for the working class, the *most rapid possible growth of capital,* however much it may improve the material existence of the worker, does not remove the antagonism between his interests and the interests of the bourgeoisie, the interests of the capitalists. *Profit and wages* remain as before in *inverse proportion.*

If capital is growing rapidly, wages may rise; the profit of capital rises incomparably more rapidly. The material position of the worker has improved, but at the cost of his social position. The social gulf that divides him from the capitalist has widened.

Finally:

To say that the most favourable condition for wage labour is the most rapid possible growth of productive capital is only to say that the more rapidly the working class increases and enlarges the power that is hostile to it, the wealth that does not belong to it and that rules over it, the more favourable will be the conditions under which it is allowed to labour anew at increasing bourgeois wealth, at enlarging the power of capital, content with forging for itself the golden chains by which the bourgeoisie drags it in its train.

V

Are *growth of productive capital and rise of wages* really so inseparably connected as the bourgeois economists maintain? We must not take their word for it. We must not even believe them when they say that the fatter capital is, the better will its slave be fed. The bourgeoisie is too enlightened, it calculates too well, to share the prejudices of the feudal lord who makes a display by the brilliance of his retinue. The conditions of existence of the bourgeoisie compel it to calculate.

We must, therefore, examine more closely:

How does the growth of productive capital affect wages?

If, on the whole, the productive capital of bourgeois society grows, a *more manifold* accumulation of labour takes place. The capitals increase in number and extent. The *numerical increase* of the capitals increases the *competition between the capitalists.* The *increasing extent* of the capitals provides the means for *bringing more powerful labour armies with more gigantic instruments of war into the industrial battlefield.*

One capitalist can drive another from the field and capture his capital only by selling more cheaply. In order to be able to sell more cheaply without ruining himself, he must produce more cheaply, that is, raise the productive power of labour as much as possible. But the productive power of labour is raised, above all, by *a greater division of labour,* by a more universal introduction and continual improvement of *machinery.* The greater the labour army among whom labour is divided, the more gigantic the scale on which machinery is introduced, the more does the cost of production proportionately decrease, the more fruitful is labour. Hence, a general rivalry arises among the capitalists to increase the division of labour and machinery and to exploit them on the greatest possible scale.

If, now, by a greater division of labour, by the utilization of new machines and their improvement, by more profitable and extensive exploitation of natural forces, one capitalist has found the means of producing with the same amount of labour or of accumulated labour a greater amount of products, of commodities, than his competitors, if he can, for example, produce a whole yard of linen in the same labour time in which his competitors weave half a yard, how will this capitalist operate?

He could continue to sell half a yard of linen at the old market price; this would, however, be no means of driving his opponents from the field and of enlarging his own sales. But in the same measure in which his production has expanded, his need to sell has also increased. The more powerful and costly means of production that he has called into life *enable* him, indeed, to sell his commodities more cheaply, they *compel* him, however, at the same time *to sell more commodities,* to conquer a much *larger* market for his commodities; consequently, our capitalist will sell his half yard of linen more cheaply than his competitors.

The capitalist will not, however, sell a whole yard as cheaply as his competitors sell half a yard, although the production of the whole yard does not cost him more than the half yard costs the others. Otherwise he would not gain anything extra but only get back the cost of production by the exchange. His possibly greater income would be derived from the fact of having set a larger capital into motion, but not from having made more of his capital than the others. Moreover, he attains the object he wishes to attain, if he puts the price of his goods only a small percentage lower than that of his competitors. He drives them from the field, he wrests from them at least a part of their sales, by *underselling* them. And, finally, it will be remembered that the current price always stands *above or below the cost of production,* according to whether the sale of the commodity occurs in a favourable or unfavourable industrial season. The percentage at which the capitalist who has employed new and more fruitful means of production sells above his real cost of production will vary, depending upon whether the market price of a yard of linen stands below or above its hitherto customary cost of production.

However, the *privileged position* of our capitalist is not of long duration; other competing capitalists introduce the same machines, the same division of labour, introduce them on the same or on a larger scale, and this introduction will become so general that the price of linen *is reduced* not only *below its old,* but *below its new cost of production.*

The capitalists find themselves, therefore, in the same position relative to one another as *before* the introduction of the new means of production, and if they are able to supply by these means double the production at the same price, they are *now* forced to supply the double product *below* the old price. On the basis of this new cost of production, the same game begins again. More division of labour, more machinery, enlarged scale of exploitation of machinery and division of labour. And again competition brings the same counter-action against this result.

We see how in this way the mode of production and the means of production are continually transformed, revolutionized, *how the division of labour is necessarily followed by greater division of labour, the application of machinery by still greater application of machinery, work on a large scale by work on a still larger scale.*

That is the law which again and again throws bourgeois production out of its old course and which compels capital to intensify the productive forces of labour, *because* it has intensified them, it, the law which gives capital no rest and continually whispers in its ear: "Go on! Go on!"

This law is none other than that which, within the fluctuations of trade periods, necessarily *levels out* the price of a commodity to its *cost of production.*

However powerful the means of production which a capitalist brings into the field, competition will make these means of production universal and from the moment when it has made them universal, the only result of the greater fruitfulness of his capital is that he must now supply *for the same price* ten, twenty, a hundred times as much as before. But, as he must sell perhaps a thousand times as much as before in order to outweigh the lower selling price by the greater amount of the product sold, because a more extensive sale is now necessary, not only in order to make more profit but in order to replace the cost of production—the instrument of production itself, as we have seen, becomes more and more expensive—and because this mass sale becomes a question of life and death not only for him but also for his rivals, the old struggle begins again *all the more violently the more fruitful the already discovered means of production are. The division of labour and the application of machinery, therefore, will go on anew on an incomparably greater scale.*

Whatever the power of the means of production employed may be, competition seeks to rob capital of the golden fruits of this power by bringing the price of the commodities back to the cost of production, by thus making cheaper production—the supply of ever greater amounts of products for the same total price—an imperative law to the same extent as production can be cheapened, that is, as more can be produced with the same amount of labour. Thus the capitalist would have won nothing by his own exertions but the obligation to supply more in the same labour time, in a word, *more difficult conditions for the augmentation of the value of his capital.* While, therefore, competition continually pursues him with its law of the cost of production and every weapon that he forges against his rivals recoils against himself, the capitalist continually tries to get the better of competition by incessantly introducing new machines, more expensive, it is true, but producing more cheaply, and new division of labour in place of the old, and by not waiting until competition has rendered the new ones obsolete.

If now we picture to ourselves this feverish simultaneous agitation on the *whole world market,* it will be comprehensible how the growth, accumulation and concentration of capital results in an uninterrupted division of labour, and in the application of new and the perfecting of old machinery precipitately and on an ever more gigantic scale.

But how do these circumstances, which are inseparable from the growth of productive capital, affect the determination of wages?

The greater *division of labour* enables *one* worker to do the work of five, ten or twenty; it therefore multiplies competition among the workers fivefold, tenfold and twentyfold. The workers do not only compete by one selling himself cheaper than another; they compete by *one* doing the work of five, ten, twenty; and the *di-*

vision of labour, introduced by capital and continually increased, compels the workers to compete among themselves in this way.

Further, as the *division of labour* increases, labour *is simplified.* The special skill of the worker becomes worthless. He becomes transformed into a simple, monotonous productive force that does not have to use intense bodily or intellectual faculties. His labour becomes a labour that anyone can perform. Hence, competitors crowd upon him on all sides, and besides we remind the reader that the more simple and easily learned the labour is, the lower the cost of production needed to master it, the lower do wages sink, for, like the price of every other commodity, they are determined by the cost of production.

Therefore, as labour becomes more unsatisfying, more repulsive, competition increases and wages decrease. The worker tries to keep up the amount of his wages by working more, whether by working longer hours or by producing more in one hour. Driven by want, therefore, he still further increases the evil effects of the division of labour. The result is that *the more he works the less wages he receives,* and for the simple reason that he competes to that extent with his fellow workers, hence makes them into so many competitors who offer themselves on just the same bad terms as he does himself, and that, therefore, in the last resort he *competes with himself, with himself as a member of the working class.*

Machinery brings about the same results on a much greater scale, by replacing skilled workers by unskilled, men by women, adults by children. It brings about the same results, where it is newly introduced, by throwing the hand workers on to the streets in masses, and, where it is developed, improved and replaced by more productive machinery, by discharging workers in smaller batches. We have portrayed above, in a hasty sketch, the industrial war of the capitalists among themselves; *this war has the peculiarity that its battles are won less by recruiting than by discharging the army of labour. The generals, the capitalists, compete with one another as to who can discharge most soldiers of industry.*

The economists tell us, it is true, that the workers rendered superfluous by machinery find *new* branches of employment.

They dare not assert directly that the same workers who are discharged find places in the new branches of labour. The facts cry out too loudly against this lie. They really only assert that new means of employment will open up for *other component sections of the working class,* for instance, for the portion of the young generation of workers that was ready to enter the branch of industry which has gone under. That is, of course, a great consolation for the disinherited workers. The worshipful capitalists will never want for fresh exploitable flesh and blood, and will let the dead bury their dead. This is a consolation which the bourgeois give themselves rather than one which they give the workers. If the whole class of wage-workers were to be abolished owing to machinery, how dreadful that would be for capital which, without wage labour, ceases to be capital!

Let us suppose, however, that those directly driven out of their jobs by machinery, and the entire section of the new generation that was already on the watch for this employment, *find a new occupation.* Does any one imagine that it will be as highly paid as that which has been lost? *That would contradict all the laws of economics.* We have seen how modern industry always brings with it the substitution of a more simple, subordinate occupation for the more complex and higher one.

How, then, could a mass of workers who have been thrown out of one branch of industry owing to machinery find refuge in another, unless the latter *is lower, worse paid?*

The workers who work in the manufacture of machinery itself have been cited as an exception. As soon as more machinery is demanded and used in industry, it is said, there must necessarily be an increase of machines, consequently of the manufacture of machines, and consequently of the employment of workers in the manufacture of machines; and the workers engaged in this branch of industry are claimed to be skilled, even educated workers.

Since the year 1840 this assertion, which even before was only half true, has lost all semblance of truth because ever more versatile machines have been employed in the manufacture of machinery, no more and no less than in the manufacture of cotton yarn, and the workers employed in the machine factories, confronted by highly elaborate machines, can only play the part of highly unelaborate machines.

But in place of the man who has been discharged owing to the machine, the factory employs maybe *three* children and *one* woman. And did not the man's wages have to suffice for the three children and a woman? Did not the minimum of wages have to suffice to maintain and to propagate the race? What, then, does this favourite bourgeois phrase prove? Nothing more than that now four times as many workers' lives are used up in order to gain a livelihood for *one* worker's family.

Let us sum up: *The more productive capital grows, the more the division of labour and the application of machinery expands. The more the division of labour and the application of machinery expands, the more competition among the workers expands and the more their wages contract.*

In addition, the working class gains recruits from the *higher strata of society* also; a mass of petty industrialists and small rentiers are hurled down into its ranks and have nothing better to do than urgently stretch out their arms alongside those of the workers. Thus the forest of uplifted arms demanding work becomes ever thicker, while the arms themselves become ever thinner.

That the small industrialist cannot survive in a contest one of the first conditions of which is to produce on an ever greater scale, that is, precisely to be a large and not a small industrialist, is self-evident.

That the interest on capital decreases in the same measure as the mass and number of capitals increase, as capital grows; that, therefore, the small rentier can no longer live on his interest but must throw himself into industry, and, consequently, help to swell the ranks of the small industrialists and thereby of candidates for the proletariat—all this surely requires no further explanation.

Finally, as the capitalists are compelled, by the movement described above, to exploit the already existing gigantic means of production on a larger scale and to set in motion all the main-springs of credit to this end, there is a corresponding increase in industrial earthquakes, in which the trading world can only maintain itself by sacrificing a part of wealth, of products and even of productive forces to the gods of the nether world—in a word, *crises* increase. They become more frequent and more violent, if only because, as the mass of production, and consequently the need for extended markets, grows, the world market becomes more and more contracted, fewer and fewer new markets remain available for exploitation, since every preceding crisis has subjected to world trade a market hitherto unconquered or only superficially exploited. But capital does not *live* only on labour. A lord, at once aristocratic and barbarous, it drags with it into the grave the corpses of its slaves, whole hecatombs of workers who perish in the crises. Thus we see: *if capital grows rapidly, competition among the workers grows incomparably more rapidly, that is, the means of employment, the means of subsistence, of the working class decrease proportionately so much the more, and, nevertheless, the rapid growth of capital is the most favourable condition for wage labour.*

—Marx, "Wage Labour and Capital," *MESW I,* pp. 79–105

The Struggle of the Bourgeois and Proletarians

I

BOURGEOIS AND PROLETARIANS

The history of all hitherto existing society is the history of class struggles.

Freeman and slave, patrician and plebeian, lord and serf, guild-master and journeyman, in a word, oppressor and oppressed, stood in constant opposition to one another, carried on an uninterrupted, now hidden, now open fight, a fight that each time ended, either in a revolutionary re-constitution of society at large, or in the common ruin of the contending classes.

In the earlier epochs of history, we find almost everywhere a complicated arrangement of society into various orders, a manifold gradation of social rank. In ancient Rome we have patricians, knights, plebeians, slaves; in the Middle Ages, feudal lords, vassals, guild-masters, journeymen, apprentices, serfs; in almost all of these classes, again, subordinate gradations.

The modern bourgeois society that has sprouted from the ruins of feudal society has not done away with class antagonisms. It has but established new classes, new conditions of oppression, new forms of struggle in place of the old ones.

Our epoch, the epoch of the bourgeoisie, possesses, however, this distinctive feature: it has simplified the class antagonisms. Society as a whole is more and more splitting up into two great hostile camps, into two great classes directly facing each other: Bourgeoisie and Proletariat.

From the serfs of the Middle Ages sprang the chartered burghers of the earliest towns. From these burgesses the first elements of the bourgeoisie were developed.

The discovery of America, the rounding of the Cape, opened up fresh ground for the rising bourgeoisie. The East-Indian and Chinese markets, the colonisation of America, trade with the colonies, the increase in the means of exchange and in commodities generally, gave to commerce, to navigation, to industry, an impulse never before known, and thereby, to the revolutionary element in the tottering feudal society, a rapid development.

The feudal system of industry, under which industrial production was monopolised by closed guilds, now no longer sufficed for the growing wants of the new markets. The manufacturing system took its place. The guild-masters were pushed on one side by the manufacturing middle class; division of labour between the different corporate guilds vanished in the face of division of labour in each single workshop.

Meantime the markets kept ever growing, the demand ever rising. Even manufacture no longer sufficed. Thereupon, steam and machinery revolutionised industrial production. The place of manufacture was taken by the giant, Modern Industry, the place of the industrial middle class, by industrial millionaires, the leaders of whole industrial armies, the modern bourgeois.

Modern industry has established the world-market, for which the discovery of America paved the way. This market has given an immense development to commerce, to navigation, to communication by land. This development has, in its turn, reacted on the extension of industry; and in proportion as industry, commerce, navigation, railways extended, in the same proportion the bourgeoisie developed, increased its capital, and pushed into the background every class handed down from the Middle Ages.

We see, therefore, how the modern bourgeoisie is itself the product of a long course of development, of a series of revolutions in the modes of production and of exchange.

Each step in the development of the bourgeoisie was accompanied by a corresponding political advance of that class. An oppressed class under the sway of the feudal nobility, an armed and self-governing association in the mediaeval commune[1]; here independent urban republic (as in Italy and Germany), there taxable "third estate" of the monarchy (as in France), afterwards, in the period of manufacture proper, serving either the semi-feudal or the absolute monarchy as a counterpoise against the nobility, and, in fact, corner-stone of the great monarchies in general, the bourgeoisie has at last, since the establishment of Modern Industry and of the world-market, conquered for itself, in the modern representative State, exclusive political sway. The executive of the modern State is but a committee for managing the common affairs of the whole bourgeoisie.

The bourgeoisie, historically, has played a most revolutionary part.

The bourgeoisie, wherever it has got the upper hand, has put an end to all feudal, patriarchal, idyllic relations. It has pitilessly torn asunder the motley feudal ties that bound man to his "natural superiors," and has left remaining no other nexus between man and man than naked self-interest, than callous "cash payment." It has drowned the most heavenly ecstasies of religious fervour, of

[1] "Commune" was the name taken, in France, by the nascent towns even before they had conquered from their feudal lords and masters local self-government and political rights as the "Third Estate." Generally speaking, for the economical development of the bourgeoisie, England is here taken as the typical country; for its political development, France. [*Note by Engels to the English edition of 1888.*]

This was the name given their urban communities by the townsmen of Italy and France, after they had purchased or wrested their initial rights of self-government from their feudal lords. [*Note by Engels to the German edition of 1890.*]

chivalrous enthusiasm, of philistine sentimentalism, in the icy water of egotistical calculation. It has resolved personal worth into exchange value, and in place of the numberless indefeasible chartered freedoms, has set up that single, unconscionable freedom—Free Trade. In one word, for exploitation, veiled by religious and political illusions, it has substituted naked, shameless, direct, brutal exploitation.

The bourgeoisie has stripped of its halo every occupation hitherto honoured and looked up to with reverent awe. It has converted the physician, the lawyer, the priest, the poet, the man of science, into its paid wage-labourers.

The bourgeoisie has torn away from the family its sentimental veil, and has reduced the family relation to a mere money relation.

The bourgeoisie has disclosed how it came to pass that the brutal display of vigor in the Middle Ages, which Reactionists so much admire, found its fitting complement in the most slothful indolence. It has been the first to show what man's activity can bring about. It has accomplished wonders far surpassing Egyptian pyramids, Roman aqueducts, and Gothic cathedrals; it has conducted expeditions that put in the shade all former Exoduses of nations and crusades.

The bourgeoisie cannot exist without constantly revolutionising the instruments of production, and thereby the relations of production, and with them the whole relations of society. Conservation of the old modes of production in unaltered form, was, on the contrary, the first condition of existence for all earlier industrial classes. Constant revolutionising of production, uninterrupted disturbance of all social conditions, everlasting uncertainty and agitation distinguish the bourgeois epoch from all earlier ones. All fixed, fast-frozen relations, with their train of ancient and venerable prejudices and opinions, are swept away, all new-formed ones become antiquated before they can ossify. All that is solid melts into air, all that is holy is profaned, and man is at last compelled to face with sober senses, his real conditions of life, and his relations with his kind.

The need of a constantly expanding market for its products chases the bourgeoisie over the whole surface of the globe. It must nestle everywhere, settle everywhere, establish connexions everywhere.

The bourgeoisie has through its exploitation of the world-market given a cosmopolitan character to production and consumption in every country. To the great chagrin of Reactionists, it has drawn from under the feet of industry the national ground on which it stood. All old-established national industries have been destroyed or are daily being destroyed. They are dislodged by new industries, whose introduction becomes a life and death question for all civilised nations, by industries that no longer work up indigenous raw material, but raw material drawn from the remotest zones; industries whose products are consumed, not only at home, but in every quarter of the globe. In place of the old wants, satisfied by the productions of the country, we find new wants, requiring for their satisfaction the products of distant lands and climes. In place of the old local and national seclusion and self-sufficiency, we have intercourse in every direction, universal inter-dependence of nations. And as in material, so also in intellectual production. The intellectual creations of individual nations become common property. National one-sidedness and narrow-mindedness become more and more impossible, and from the numerous national and local literatures, there arises a world literature.

The bourgeoisie, by the rapid improvement of all instruments of production, by the immensely facilitated means of communication, draws all, even the most barbarian, nations into civilisation. The cheap prices of its commodities are the heavy artillery with which it batters down all Chinese walls, with which it forces the barbarians' intensely obstinate hatred of foreigners to capitulate. It compels all nations, on pain of extinction, to adopt the bourgeois mode of production; it compels them to introduce what it calls civilisation into their midst, *i.e.,* to become bourgeois themselves. In one word, it creates a world after its own image.

The bourgeoisie has subjected the country to the rule of the towns. It has created enormous cities, has greatly increased the urban population as compared with the rural, and has thus rescued a considerable part of the population from the idiocy of rural life. Just as it has made the country dependent on the towns, so it has made barbarian and semi-barbarian countries dependent on the civilised ones, nations of peasants on nations of bourgeois, the East on the West.

The bourgeoisie keeps more and more doing away with the scattered state of the population, of the means of production, and of property. It has agglomerated population, centralised means of production, and has concentrated property in a few hands. The necessary consequence of this was political centralisation. Independent, or but loosely connected provinces, with separate interests, laws, governments and systems of taxation, became lumped together into one nation, with one government, one code of laws, one national class-interest, one frontier and one customs-tariff.

The bourgeoisie, during its rule of scarce one hundred years, has created more massive and more colossal productive forces than have all preceding generations together. Subjection of Nature's forces to man, machinery, application of chemistry to industry and agriculture, steam-navigation, railways, electric telegraphs, clearing of whole continents for cultivation, canalisation of rivers, whole populations conjured out of the ground—what earlier century had even a presentiment that such productive forces slumbered in the lap of social labour?

We see then: the means of production and of exchange, on whose foundation the bourgeoisie built itself up, were generated in feudal society. At a certain stage in the development of these means of production and of exchange, the conditions under which feudal society produced and exchanged, the feudal organisation of agriculture and manufacturing industry, in one word, the feudal relations of property became no longer compatible with the already developed productive forces; they became so many fetters. They had to be burst asunder; they were burst asunder.

Into their place stepped free competition, accompanied by a social and political constitution adapted to it, and by the economical and political sway of the bourgeois class.

A similar movement is going on before our own eyes. Modern bourgeois society with its relations of production, of exchange and of property, a society that has conjured up such gigantic means of production and of exchange, is like the sorcerer, who is no longer able to control the powers of the nether world whom he has called up by his spells. For many a decade past the history of industry and commerce is but the history of the revolt of modern productive forces against modern conditions of production, against the property relations that are the conditions for the existence of the bourgeoisie and of its rule. It is enough to mention the commercial crises that by their periodical return put on its trial, each time more threateningly, the existence of the entire bourgeois society. In these crises a great part not only of the existing products, but also of the previously created productive forces, are periodically destroyed. In these crises there breaks out an epidemic that, in all earlier epochs, would have seemed an absurdity—the epidemic of over-production. Society suddenly finds itself put back into a state of momentary barbarism; it appears as if a famine, a universal war of devastation had cut off the supply of every means of subsistence; industry and commerce seem to be destroyed; and why? Because there is too much civilisation, too much means of subsistence, too much industry, too much commerce. The productive forces at the disposal of society no longer tend to further the development of the conditions of bourgeois property; on the contrary, they have become too powerful for these conditions, by which they are fettered, and so soon as they overcome these fetters, they bring disorder into the whole of bourgeois society, endanger the existence of bourgeois property. The conditions of bourgeois society are too narrow to comprise the wealth created by them. And how does the bourgeoisie get over these crises? On the one hand by enforced destruction of a mass of productive forces; on the other, by the conquest of new markets, and by the more thorough exploitation of the old ones. That is to say, by paving the way for more extensive and more destructive crises, and by diminishing the means whereby crises are prevented.

The weapons with which the bourgeoisie felled feudalism to the ground are now turned against the bourgeoisie itself.

But not only has the bourgeoisie forged the weapons that bring death to itself; it has also called into existence the men who are to wield those weapons—the modern working class—the proletarians.

In proportion as the bourgeoisie, *i.e.*, capital, is developed, in the same proportion is the proletariat, the modern working class, developed—a class of labourers, who live only so long as they find work, and who find work only so long as their labour increases capital. These labourers, who must sell themselves piecemeal, are a commodity, like every other article of commerce, and are consequently exposed to all the vicissitudes of competition, to all the fluctuations of the market.

Owing to the extensive use of machinery and to division of labour, the work of the proletarians has lost all individual character, and, consequently, all charm for the workman. He becomes an appendage of the machine, and it is only the most simple, most monotonous, and most easily acquired knack, that is required of him. Hence, the cost of production of a workman is restricted, almost entirely, to the means of subsistence that he requires for his maintenance, and for the propagation of his race. But the price of a commodity, and therefore also of labour, is equal to its cost of production. In proportion, therefore, as the repulsiveness of the work increases, the wage decreases. Nay more, in proportion as the use of machinery and division of labour increases, in the same proportion the burden of toil also increases, whether by prolongation of the working hours, by increase of the work exacted in a given time or by increased speed of the machinery, etc.

Modern industry has converted the little workshop of the patriarchal master into the great factory of the industrial capitalist. Masses of labourers, crowded into the factory, are organised like soldiers. As privates of the industrial army they are placed under the command of a perfect hierarchy of officers and sergeants. Not only are they slaves of the bourgeois class, and of the bourgeois State; they are daily and hourly enslaved by the machine, by the over-looker, and, above all, by the individual bourgeois manufacturer himself. The more openly this despotism proclaims gain to be its end and aim, the more petty, the more hateful and the more embittering it is.

The less the skill and exertion of strength implied in manual labour, in other words, the more modern industry becomes developed, the more is the labour of men superseded by that of women. Differences of age and sex have no longer any distinctive social validity for the working class. All are instruments of labour, more or less expensive to use, according to their age and sex.

No sooner is the exploitation of the labour by the manufacturer, so far, at an end, than he receives his wages in cash, than he is set upon by the other portions of the bourgeoisie, the landlord, the shopkeeper, the pawnbroker, etc.

The lower strata of the middle class—the small tradespeople, shopkeepers, and retired tradesmen generally, the handicraftsmen and peasants—all these sink gradually into the proletariat, partly because their diminutive capital does not suffice for the scale on which Modern Industry is carried on, and is swamped in the competition with the large capitalists, partly because their specialised skill is rendered worthless by new methods of production. Thus the proletariat is recruited from all classes of the population.

The proletariat goes through various stages of development. With its birth begins its struggle with the bourgeoisie. At first the contest is carried on by individual labourers, then by the workpeople of a factory, then by the operatives of one trade, in one locality, against the individual bourgeois who directly exploits them. They direct their attacks not against the bourgeois conditions of production, but against the instruments of production themselves; they destroy imported wares that compete with their labour, they smash to pieces machinery, they set factories ablaze, they seek to restore by force the vanished status of the workman of the Middle Ages.

At this stage the labourers still form an incoherent mass scattered over the whole country, and broken up by their mutual competition. If anywhere they unite to form more compact bodies, this is not yet the consequence of their own active union, but of the union of the bourgeoisie, which class, in order to attain its own political ends, is compelled to set the whole proletariat in motion, and is moreover yet, for a time, able to do so. At this stage, therefore, the proletarians do not fight their enemies, but the enemies of their enemies, the remnants of absolute monarchy, the landowners, the non-industrial bourgeois, the petty bourgeoisie. Thus the whole historical movement is concentrated in the hands of the bourgeoisie; every victory so obtained is a victory for the bourgeoisie.

But with the development of industry the proletariat not only increases in number; it becomes concentrated in greater masses, its strength grows, and it feels that strength more. The various interests and conditions of life within the ranks of the proletariat are more and more equalised, in proportion as machinery obliterates all distinctions of labour, and nearly everywhere reduces wages to the same low level. The growing competition among the bourgeois, and the resulting commercial crises, make the wages of the workers ever more fluctuating. The unceasing improvement of machinery, ever more rapidly developing, makes their livelihood more and more precarious; the collisions between individual workmen and individual bourgeois take more and more the character of collisions between two classes. Thereupon the workers begin to form combinations (Trades' Unions) against the bourgeois; they club together in order to keep up the rate of wages; they found permanent associations in order to make provision beforehand for these occasional revolts. Here and there the contest breaks out into riots.

Now and then the workers are victorious, but only for a time. The real fruit of their battles lies, not in the immediate result, but in the ever-expanding union of the workers. This union is helped on by the improved means of communication that are created by modern industry and that place the workers of different localities in contact with one another. It was just this contact that was needed to centralise the numerous local struggles, all of the same character, into one national struggle between classes. But every class struggle is a political struggle. And that union, to attain which the burghers of the Middle Ages, with their miserable highways, required centuries, the modern proletarians, thanks to railways, achieve in a few years.

This organisation of the proletarians into a class, and consequently into a political party, is continually being upset again by the competition between the workers themselves. But it ever rises up again, stronger, firmer, mightier. It compels legislative recognition of particular interests of the workers, by taking advantage of the divisions among the bourgeoisie itself. Thus the ten-hours' bill in England was carried.

Altogether collisions between the classes of the old society further, in many ways, the course of development of the proletariat. The bourgeoisie finds itself involved in a constant battle. At first with the aristocracy; later on, with those portions of the bourgeoisie itself, whose interests have become antagonistic to the progress of industry; at all times, with the bourgeoisie of foreign countries. In all these battles it sees itself compelled to appeal to the proletariat, to ask for its help, and thus, to drag it into the political arena. The bourgeoisie itself, therefore, supplies the proletariat with its own elements of political and general education, in other words, it furnishes the proletariat with weapons for fighting the bourgeoisie.

Further, as we have already seen, entire sections of the ruling classes are, by the advance of industry, precipitated into the proletariat, or are at least threatened in their conditions of existence. These also supply the proletariat with fresh elements of enlightenment and progress.

Finally, in times when the class struggle nears the decisive hour, the process of dissolution going on within the ruling class, in fact within the whole range of old society, assumes such a violent, glaring character, that a small section of the ruling class cuts itself adrift, and joins the revolutionary class, the class that holds the future in its hands. Just as, therefore, at an earlier period, a section of the nobility went over to the bourgeoisie, so now a portion of the bourgeoisie goes over to the proletariat, and in particular, a portion of the bourgeois ideologists, who have raised themselves to the level of comprehending theoretically the historical movement as a whole.

Of all the classes that stand face to face with the bourgeoisie today, the proletariat alone is a really revolutionary class. The other classes decay and finally disappear in the face of Modern Industry; the proletariat is its special and essential product.

The lower middle class, the small manufacturer, the shopkeeper, the artisan, the peasant, all these fight against the bourgeoisie, to save from extinction their existence as fractions of the middle class.

They are therefore not revolutionary, but conservative. Nay more, they are reactionary, for they try to roll back the wheel of history. If by chance they are revolutionary, they are so only in view of their impending transfer into the proletariat, they thus defend not their present, but their future interests, they desert their own standpoint to place themselves at that of the proletariat.

The "dangerous class," the social scum, that passively rotting mass thrown off by the lowest layers of old society, may, here and there, be swept into the movement by a proletarian revolution, its conditions of life, however, prepare it far more for the part of a bribed tool of reactionary intrigue.

. . .

Though not in substance, yet in form, the struggle of the proletariat with the bourgeoisie is at first a national struggle. The proletariat of each country must, of course, first of all settle matters with its own bourgeoisie.

In depicting the most general phases of the development of the proletariat, we traced the more or less veiled civil war, raging within existing society, up to the point where that war breaks out into open revolution, and where the violent overthrow of the bourgeoisie lays the foundation for the sway of the proletariat.

Hitherto, every form of society has been based, as we have already seen, on the antagonism of oppressing and oppressed classes. But in order to oppress a class, certain conditions must be assured to it under which it can, at least, continue its slavish existence. The serf, in the period of serfdom, raised himself to membership in the commune, just as the petty bourgeois, under the yoke of feudal absolutism, managed to develop into a bourgeois. The modern labourer, on the contrary, instead of rising with the progress of industry, sinks deeper and deeper below the conditions of existence of his own class. He becomes a pauper, and pauperism develops more rapidly than population and wealth. And here it becomes evident, that the bourgeoisie is unfit any longer to be the ruling class in society, and to impose its conditions of existence upon society as an over-riding law. It is unfit to rule because it is incompetent to assure an existence to its slave within his slavery, because it cannot help letting him sink into such a state, that it has to feed him, instead of being fed by him. Society can no longer live under this bourgeoisie, in other words, its existence is no longer compatible with society.

The essential condition for the existence, and for the sway of the bourgeois class, is the formation and augmentation of capital; the condition for capital is wage-labour. Wage-labour rests exclusively on competition between the labourers. The advance of industry, whose involuntary promoter is the bourgeoisie, replaces the isolation of the labourers, due to competition, by their revolutionary combination, due to association. The development of Modern Industry, therefore, cuts from under its feet the very foundation on which the bourgeoisie produces and appropriates products. What the bourgeoisie, therefore, produces, above all, is its own grave-diggers. Its fall and the victory of the proletariat are equally inevitable.

—Marx and Engels, "Manifesto of the Communist Party," *MESW I,* pp. 34–45

Appendix: An Application of the Economic Interpretation—The Eighteenth Brumaire

Hegel says somewhere that all great historic facts and personages recur twice. He forgot to add: "Once as tragedy, and again as farce." Caussidiere for Danton, Louis Blanc for Robespierre, the "Mountain" of 1848–51 for the "Mountain" of 1793–1805, the Nephew for the Uncle. The identical caricature marks also the conditions under which the second edition of the eighteenth Brumaire is issued.

Man makes his own history, but he does not make it out of whole cloth; he does not make it out of conditions chosen by himself, but out of such as he finds close at hand. The tradition of all past generations weighs like an alp upon the brain of the living. At the very time when men appear engaged in revolutionizing things and themselves, in bringing about what never was before, at such very epochs of revolutionary crisis do they anxiously conjure up into their service the spirits of the past, assume their names, their battle cries, their costumes to enact a new historic scene in such time-honored disguise and with such borrowed language. Thus did Luther masquerade as the Apostle Paul; thus did the revolution of 1789–1814 drape itself alternately as Roman Republic and as Roman Empire; nor did the revolution of 1848 know what better to do than to parody at one time the year 1789, at another the revolutionary traditions of 1793–95. Thus does the beginner, who has acquired a new language, keep on translating it back into his own mother tongue; only then has he grasped the spirit of the new language and is able freely to express himself therewith when he moves in it without recollections of the old, and has forgotten in its use his own hereditary tongue.

When these historic conjurations of the dead past are closely observed a striking difference is forthwith noticeable. Camille Desmoulins, Danton, Robespierre, St. Juste, Napoleon, the heroes as well as the parties and the masses of the old French revolution, achieved in Roman costumes and with Roman phrases the task of their time: the emancipation and the establishment of modern bourgeois society. One set knocked to pieces the old feudal groundwork and mowed down the feudal heads that had grown upon it; Napoleon brought about, within France, the conditions under which alone free competition could develop, the partitioned lands be exploited, the nation's unshackled powers of industrial production be utilized; while, beyond the French frontier, he swept away everywhere the establishments of feudality, so far as requisite, to furnish the bourgeois social system of France with fit surroundings of the European continent, and such as were in keeping with the times. Once the new social establishment was set on foot, the antediluvian giants vanished, and, along with them, the resuscitated Roman world—the Brutuses, Gracchi, Publicolas, the Tribunes, the Senators, and Caesar himself. In its sober reality, bourgeois society had produced its own true interpreters in the Says, Cousins, Royer-Collards, Benjamin Constants and Guizots; its real generals sat behind the office desks; and the mutton-head of Louis XVIII. was its political head. Wholly absorbed in the production of wealth and in the peaceful fight of competition, this society could no longer understand that the ghosts of the days of Rome had watched over its cradle. And yet, lacking in heroism as bourgeois society is, it nevertheless had stood in need of heroism, of self-sacrifice, of terror, of civil war, and of bloody battle fields to bring it into the world. Its gladiators found in the stern classic traditions of the Roman republic the ideals and the form, the self-deceptions, that they needed in order to conceal from themselves the narrow bourgeois substance of their own struggles, and to keep their passion up to the height of a great historic tragedy.

. . .

In 1848–51 only the ghost of the old revolution wandered about, from Marrast the *"Republicain en gaunts jaunes,"* [1] who disguised himself in old Bailly, down to the adventurer, who hid his repulsively trivial features under the iron death mask of Napoleon. A whole people, that imagines it has imparted to itself accelerated powers of motion through a revolution, suddenly finds itself transferred back to a dead epoch, and, lest there be any mistake possible on this head, the old dates turn up again; the old calendars; the old names; the old edicts, which long since had sunk to the level of the antiquarian's learning; even the old bailiffs, who had long seemed mouldering with decay. The nation takes on the appearance of that crazy Englishman in Bedlam, who imagines he is living in the days of the Pharaohs, and daily laments the hard work that he must do in the Ethiopian mines as gold digger, immured in a subterranean prison, with a dim lamp fastened on his head, behind him the slave overseer with a long whip, and, at the mouths of the mine a mob of barbarous camp servants who understand neither the convicts in the mines nor one another, because they do not speak a common language. "And all this," cries the crazy Englishman, "is demanded of me, the free-born Englishman, in order to make gold for old Pharaoh." "In order to pay off the debts of the Bonaparte family"—sobs the French nation. The Englishman, so long as he was in his senses, could not rid himself of the rooted thought of making gold. The Frenchmen, so long as they were busy with a revolution, could not rid themselves of the Napoleonic memory, as

[1] Silk-stocking republican.

the election of December 10th proved. They longed to escape from the dangers of revolution back to the flesh pots of Egypt; the 2d of December, 1851, was the answer. They have not merely the caricature of the old Napoleon, but the old Napoleon himself—caricatured as he needs must appear in the middle of the nineteenth century.

. . .

The February revolution was a surprisal; old society was taken unawares; and the people proclaimed this political stroke a great historic act whereby the new era was opened. On the 2d of December, the February revolution is jockeyed by the trick of a false player, and what is seen to be overthrown is no longer the monarchy, but the liberal concessions which had been wrung from it by centuries of struggles. Instead of society itself having conquered a new point, only the State appears to have returned to its oldest form, to the simply brazen rule of the sword and the club. Thus, upon the "coup de main" of February, 1848, comes the response of the "coup de tête" of December, 1851. So won, so lost. Meanwhile, the interval did not go by unutilized. During the years 1848–1851, French society retrieved in abbreviated, because revolutionary, method the lessons and teachings, which—if it was to be more than a disturbance of the surface—should have preceded the February revolution, had it developed in regular order, by rule, so to say. Now French society seems to have receded behind its point of departure; in fact, however, it was compelled to first produce its own revolutionary point of departure, the situation, circumstances, conditions, under which alone the modern revolution is in earnest.

Bourgeois revolutions, like those of the eighteenth century, rush onward rapidly from success to success, their stage effects outbid one another, men and things seem to be set in flaming brilliants, ecstasy is the prevailing spirit; but they are short-lived, they reach their climax speedily, then society relapses into a long fit of nervous reaction before it learns how to appropriate the fruits of its period of feverish excitement. Proletarian revolutions, on the contrary, such as those of the nineteenth century, criticize themselves constantly; constantly interrupt themselves in their own course; come back to what seems to have been accomplished, in order to start over anew; scorn with cruel thoroughness the half measures, weaknesses and meannesses of their first attempts; seem to throw down their adversary only in order to enable him to draw fresh strength from the earth, and again to rise up against them in more gigantic stature; constantly recoil in fear before the undefined monster magnitude of their own objects—until finally that situation is created which renders all retreat impossible, and the conditions themselves cry out:

"Hic Rhodus, hic salta!" [2]

Every observer of average intelligence, even if he failed to follow step by step the course of French development, must have anticipated that an unheard of fiasco was in store for the revolution. It was enough to hear the self-satisfied yelpings of victory wherewith the Messieurs Democrats mutually congratulated one another upon the pardons of May 2d, 1852. Indeed, May 2d had become a fixed idea in their heads; it had become a dogma with them—something like the day on which Christ was to reappear and the Millennium to begin had formed in the heads of the Chiliasts. Weakness had, as it ever does, taken refuge in the wonderful; it believed the enemy was overcome if, in its imagination, it hocus-pocused him away; and it lost all sense of the present in the imaginary apotheosis of the future, that was at hand, and of the deeds, that it had "in petto," but which it did not yet want to bring to the scratch. The heroes, who ever seek to refute their established incompetence by mutually bestowing their sympathy upon one another and by pulling together, had packed their satchels, taken their laurels in advance payments and were just engaged in the work of getting discounted "in partibus," on the stock exchange, the republics for which, in the silence of their unassuming dispositions, they had carefully organized the government personnel. The 2d of December struck them like a bolt from a clear sky; and the peoples, who, in periods of timid despondency, gladly allow their hidden fears to be drowned by the loudest screamers, will perhaps have become convinced that the

[2] Here is Rhodes, leap here! An allusion to Æsop's Fables.

days are gone by when the cackling of geese could save the Capitol.

The constitution, the national assembly, the dynastic parties, the blue and the red republicans, the heroes from Africa, the thunder from the tribune, the flash-lightnings from the daily press, the whole literature, the political names and the intellectual celebrities, the civil and the criminal law, the "liberté, egalité, fraternité," together with the 2d of May, 1852,—all vanished like a phantasmagoria before the ban of one man, whom his enemies themselves do not pronounce an adept at witchcraft. Universal suffrage seems to have survived only for a moment, to the end that, before the eyes of the whole world, it should make its own testament with its own hands, and, in the name of the people, declare: "All that exists deserves to perish."

It is not enough to say, as the Frenchmen do, that their nation was taken by surprise. A nation, no more than a woman, is excused for the unguarded hour when the first adventurer who comes along can do violence to her. The riddle is not solved by such shifts, it is only formulated in other words. There remains to be explained how a nation of thirty-six millions can be surprised by three swindlers, and taken to prison without resistance.

Let us recapitulate in general outlines the phases which the French revolution of February 24th, 1848, to December, 1851, ran through.

Three main periods are unmistakable:

First—The February period;

Second—The period of constituting the republic, or of the constitutive national assembly (May 4, 1848, to May 29th, 1849);

Third—The period of the constitutional republic, or of the legislative national assembly (May 29, 1849, to December 2, 1851).

The first period, from February 24, or the downfall of Louis Philippe, to May 4, 1848, the date of the assembling of the constitutive assembly—the February period proper—may be designated as the prologue of the revolution. It officially expressed its own character in this, that the government which it improvised declared itself "provisional;" and, like the government, everything that was broached, attempted or uttered, pronounced itself provisional. Nobody and nothing dared to assume the right of permanent existence and of an actual fact. All the elements that had prepared or determined the revolution—dynastic opposition, republican bourgeoisie, democratic-republican small traders' class, social-democratic labor element—all found "provisionally" their place in the February government.

It could not be otherwise. The February days contemplated originally a reform of the suffrage laws, whereby the area of the politically privileged among the property-holding class was to be extended, while the exclusive rule of the aristocracy of finance was to be overthrown. When, however, it came to a real conflict, when the people mounted the barricades, when the National Guard stood passive, when the army offered no serious resistance, and the kingdom ran away, then the republic seemed self-understood. Each party interpreted it in its own sense. Won, arms in hand, by the proletariat, they put upon it the stamp of their own class, and proclaimed the social republic. Thus the general purpose of modern revolutions was indicated, a purpose, however, that stood in most singular contradiction to every thing that, with the material at hand, with the stage of enlightenment that the masses had reached, and under existing circumstances and conditions, could be immediately used. On the other hand, the claims of all the other elements, that had co-operated in the revolution of February, were recognized by the lion's share that they received in the government. Hence, in no period do we find a more motley mixture of high-sounding phrases together with actual doubt and helplessness; of more enthusiastic reform aspirations, together with a more slavish adherence to the old routine; more seeming harmony permeating the whole of society together with a deeper alienation of its several elements. While the Parisian proletariat was still gloating over the sight of the great perspective that had disclosed itself to their view, and was indulging in seriously meant discussions over the social problems, the old powers of society had groomed themselves, had gathered together, had deliberated and found an unexpected support in the mass of the nation—the peasants and small traders—all of whom threw themselves on a sudden upon the political stage, after the barriers of the July monarchy had fallen down.

The second period, from May 4, 1848, to the end of May, 1849, is the period of the constitution, of the founding of the bourgeois republic. Immediately after the February days, not only was the dynastic opposition surprised by the republicans, and the republicans by the Socialists, but all France was surprised by Paris. The national assembly, that met on May 4, 1848, to frame a constitution, was the outcome of the national elections; it represented the nation. It was a living protest against the assumption of the February days, and it was intended to bring the results of the revolution back to the bourgeois measure. In vain did the proletariat of Paris, which forthwith understood the character of this national assembly, endeavor, a few days after its meeting, on May 15, to deny its existence by force, to dissolve it, to disperse the organic apparition, in which the reacting spirit of the nation was threatening them, and thus reduce it back to its separate component parts. As is known, the 15th of May had no other result than that of removing Blanqui and his associates, i.e., the real leaders of the proletarian party, from the public scene for the whole period of the cycle which we are here considering.

Upon the bourgeois monarchy of Louis Philippe, only the bourgeois republic could follow; that is to say, a limited portion of the bourgeoisie having ruled under the name of the king, now the whole bourgeoisie was to rule under the name of the people. The demands of the Parisian proletariat are utopian tom-fooleries that have to be done away with. To this declaration of the constitutional national assembly, the Paris proletariat answers with the June insurrection, the most colossal event in the history of European civil wars. The bougeois republic won. On its side stood the aristocracy of finance, the industrial bougeoisie; the middle class; the small traders' class; the army; the slums, organized as Guarde Mobile; the intellectual celebrities, the parsons' class, and the rural population. On the side of the Parisian proletariat stood none but itself. Over 3,000 insurgents were massacred, after the victory 15,000 were transported without trial. With this defeat, the proletariat steps to the background on the revolutionary stage. It always seeks to crowd forward, so soon as the movement seems to acquire new impetus, but with ever weaker effort and ever smaller results.

. . .

The more important leaders of the Proletariat, in its councils, and the press, fall one after another victims of the courts, and ever more questionable figures step to the front. *It partly throws itself upon doctrinaire experiments, "co-operative banking" and "labor exchange" schemes; in other words, it goes into movements, in which it gives up the task of revolutionizing the old world with its own large collective weapons and on the contrary, seeks to bring about its emancipation, behind the back of society, in private ways, within the narrow bounds of its own class conditions, and, consequently, inevitably fails.* The proletariat seems to be able neither to find again the revolutionary magnitude within itself nor to draw new energy from the newly formed alliances until *all the classes,* with whom it contended in June, shall lie prostrate along with itself. But in all these defeats, the proletariat succumbs at least with the honor that attaches to great historic struggles; not France alone, all Europe trembles before the June earthquake, while the successive defeats inflicted upon the higher classes are bought so easily that they need the brazen exaggeration of the victorious party itself to be at all able to pass muster as an event; and these defeats become more disgraceful the further removed the defeated party stands from the proletariat.

True enough, the defeat of the June insurgents prepared, leveled the ground, upon which the bourgeois republic could be founded and erected; but it, at the same time, showed that there are in Europe other issues besides that of "Republic or Monarchy." It revealed the fact that here the Bourgeois Republic meant the unbridled despotism of one class over another. It proved that, with nations enjoying an older civilization, having developed class distinctions, modern conditions of production, an intellectual consciousness, wherein all traditions of old have been dissolved through the work of centuries, that with such countries the republic means only the *political revolutionary form of bourgeois society,* not its *conservative form of existence,* as is the case in the United States of America, where, true enough, the classes already exist, but have not yet acquired permanent character, are in constant flux and reflux, constantly changing their elements and yielding them up to one another; where the modern means of production, instead of coinciding with a stagnant population, rather compensate for the relative scarcity of heads and hands; and, finally, where the feverishly youthful life of material production, which has to appropriate a new world to itself, has so far left neither time nor opportunity to abolish the illusions of old.[3]

All classes and parties joined hands in the June days in a "Party of Order" against the class of the proletariat, which was designated as the "Party of Anarchy," of Socialism, of Communism. They claimed to have "saved" society against the "enemies of society." They gave out the slogans of the old social order—"Property, Family, Religion, Order"—as the pass-words for their army, and cried out to the counter-revolutionary crusaders: "In this sign thou wilt conquer!" From that moment on, so soon as any of the numerous parties, which had marshalled themselves under this sign against the June insurgents, tries, in turn, to take the revolutionary field in the interest of its own class, it goes down in its turn before the cry: "Property, Family, Religion, Order." Thus it happens that "society is saved" as often as the circle of its ruling class is narrowed, as often as a more exclusive interest asserts itself over the general. Every demand for the most simple bourgeois financial reform, for the most ordinary liberalism, for the most commonplace republicanism, for the flattest democracy, is forthwith punished as an "assault upon society," and is branded as "Socialism." Finally the High Priests of "Religion and Order" themselves are kicked off their tripods; are fetched out of their beds in the dark, hurried into patrol wagons, thrust into jail or sent into exile; their temple is razed to the ground, their mouths are sealed, their pen is broken, their law torn to pieces in the name of Religion, of Family, of Property, and of Order. Bougeois, fanatic on the point of "order," are shot down on their own balconies by drunken soldiers, forfeit their family property, and their houses are bombarded for pastime—all in the name of Property, of Family, of Religion, and of Order. Finally, the refuse of bourgeois society constitutes the "holy phalanx of Order," and the hero Crapulinsky makes his entry into the Tuileries as the "Savior of Society."

. . .

[3] This was written at the beginning of 1852.

Before we follow this parliamentary history any further, a few observations are necessary, in order to avoid certain common deceptions concerning the whole character of the epoch that lies before us. According to the view of the democrats, the issue, during the period of the legislative National Assembly, was, the same as during the period of the constitutive assembly, simply the struggle between republicans and royalists; the movement itself was summed up by them in the catch-word *Reaction*—night, in which all cats are grey, and allows them to drawl out their drowsy commonplaces. Indeed, at first sight, the party of *Order* presents the appearance of a tangle of royalist factions, that, not only intrigue against each other, each aiming to raise its own Pretender to the throne, and exclude the Pretender of the opposite party, but also are all united in a common hatred for and common attacks against the "Republic." On its side, the *Mountain* appears, in counter-distinction to the royalist conspiracy, as the representative of the "Republic." The party of *Order* seems constantly engaged in a "Reaction," which, neither more nor less than in Prussia, is directed against the press, the right of association and the like, and is enforced by brutal police interventions on the part of the bureaucracy, the police and the public prosecutor—just as in Prussia; the *Mountain,* on the contrary, is engaged with equal assiduity in parrying these attacks, and thus in defending the "eternal rights of man"—as every so-called people's party has more or less done for the last hundred and fifty years. At a closer inspection, however, of the situation and of the parties, this superficial appearance, which veils the *Class Struggle,* together with the peculiar physiognomy of this period, vanishes wholly.

Legitimists and Orleanists constituted, as said before, the two large factions of the party of Order. What held these two factions to their respective Pretenders, and inversely kept them apart from each other, what else was it but the lily and the tricolor, the House of Bourbon and the House of Orleans, different shades of royalty? Under the Bourbons, *Large Landed Property* ruled together with its parsons and lackeys; under the Orleanist, it was the high finance, large industry, large commerce, *i.e., Capital,* with its retinue of lawyers, professors and orators. The Legitimate kingdom was but the political expression for the hereditary rule of the landlords, as the

July monarchy was but the political expression for the usurped rule of the bourgeois upstarts. What, accordingly, kept these two factions apart was no so-called set of principles, it was their material conditions for life—two different sorts of property—; it was the old antagonism of the City and the Country, the rivalry between Capital and Landed property. That simultaneously old recollections; personal animosities, fears and hopes; prejudices and illusions; sympathies and antipathies; convictions, faith and principles bound these factions to one House or the other, who denies it? Upon the several forms of property, upon the social conditions of existence, a whole superstructure is reared of various and peculiarly shaped feelings, illusions, habits of thought and conceptions of life. The whole class produces and shapes these out of its material foundation and out of the corresponding social conditions. The individual unit to whom they flow through tradition and education, may fancy that they constitute the true reasons for and premises of his conduct. Although Orleanists and Legitimists, each of these factions, sought to make itself and the other believe that what kept the two apart was the attachment of each to its respective royal House; nevertheless, facts proved later that it rather was their divided interest that forbade the union of the two royal Houses. As, in private life, the distinction is made between what a man thinks of himself and says, and that which he really is and does, so, all the more, must the phrases and notions of parties in historic struggles be distinguished from their real organism, and their real interests, their notions and their reality. Orleanists and Legitimists found themselves in the republic beside each other with equal claims. Each side wishing, in opposition of the other, to carry out the restoration of its own royal House, meant nothing else than that each of the two great *Interests* into which the bourgeoisie is divided—Land and Capital—sought to restore its own supremacy and the subordinacy of the other. We speak of two bourgeois interests because large landed property, despite its feudal coquetry and pride of race, has become completely bourgeois through the development of modern society. Thus did the Tories of England long fancy that they were enthusiastic for the Kingdom, the Church and the beauties of the old English Constitution, until the day of danger wrung from them the admission that their enthusiasm was only for *Ground-Rent.*

. . .

However, against the allied bourgeois, a coalition was made between the small traders and the workingmen—the so-called *Social Democratic* party. The small traders found themselves ill rewarded after the June days of 1848; they saw their material interests endangered, and the democratic guarantees, that were to uphold their interest, made doubtful. Hence, they drew closer to the workingmen. On the other hand, their parliamentary representatives—the *Mountain*—, after being shoved aside during the dictatorship of the bourgeois republicans, had, during the last half of the term of the constitutive convention, regained their lost popularity through the struggle with Bonaparte and the royalist ministers. They had made an alliance with the Socialist leaders. During February, 1849, reconciliation banquets were held. A common program was drafted, joint election committees were empaneled, and fusion candidates were set up. The revolutionary point was thereby broken off from the social demands of the proletariat, and a democratic turn given to them; while, from the democratic claims of the small traders' class, the mere political form was rubbed off and the Socialist point was pushed forward. Thus came the *Social Democracy* about. The new *Mountain,* the result of this combination, contained, with the exception of some figures from the working class and some Socialist sectarians, the identical elements of the old Mountain, only numerically stronger. In the course of events it had, however, changed, together with the class that it represented. The peculiar character of the Social Democracy is summed up in this: that democratic-republican institutions are demanded as the means, not to remove the two extremes—Capital and Wage-slavery—, but in order to weaken their antagonism and transform them into a harmonious whole. However different the methods may be that are proposed for the accomplishment of this object, however much the object itself may be festooned with more or less revolutionary fancies, the substance remains the same. This substance is the transformation of society upon democratic lines, but a transformation within the boundaries of the small traders' class. No one must run away with the narrow notion that the small traders' class means on principle to enforce a selfish class interest. It believes rather that the special conditions for its own emancipation are the general conditions under which alone modern society can be saved and the class struggle avoided. Likewise must we avoid running away with the notion that the Democratic Representatives are all "shopkeepers," or enthuse for these. They may—by education and individual standing—be as distant from them as heaven is from earth. That which makes them representatives of the small traders' class is that they do not intellectually leap the bounds which that class itself does not leap in practical life; that, consequently, they are theoretically driven to the same problems and solutions, to which material interests and social standing practically drive the latter. Such, in fact, is at all times the relation of the "political" and the "literary" representatives of a class to the class they represent.

After the foregoing explanations, it goes without saying that, while the Mountain is constantly wrestling for the republic and the so-called "rights of man," neither the republic nor the "rights of man" is its real goal, as little as an army, whose weapons it is sought to deprive it of and that defends itself, steps on the field of battle simply in order to remain in possession of its implements of warfare.

The party of Order provoked the Mountain immediately upon the convening of the assembly. The bourgeoisie now felt the necessity of disposing of the democratic small traders' class, just as a year before it had understood the necessity of putting an end to the revolutionary proletariat.

. . .

Seldom was an act announced with greater noise than the campaign contemplated by the Mountain; seldom was an event trumpeted ahead with more certainty and longer beforehand than the "inevitable victory of the democracy." This is evident: the democrats believe in the trombones before whose blasts the walls of Jericho fall together; as often as they stand before the walls of despotism, they seek to imitate the miracle. If the Mountain wished to win in parliament, it should not appeal to arms; if it called to arms in parliament, it should not conduct itself parliamentarily on the street; if the friendly demonstration was meant seriously, it was silly not to foresee that it would meet with a warlike reception; if it was intended for actual war, it was rather original to lay aside the weapons with which war had to be conducted. But the revolutionary threats of the middle class and of their democratic representatives are mere attempts to frighten an adversary; when they have run themselves into a blind alley, when they have sufficiently compromised themselves and are compelled to execute their threats, the thing is done in a hesitating manner that avoids nothing so much as the means to the end, and catches at pretexts to succumb. The bray of the overture, that announces the fray, is lost in a timid growl so soon as this is to start; the actors cease to take themselves seriously, and the performance falls flat like an inflated balloon that is pricked with a needle.

No party exaggerates to itself the means at its disposal more than the democratic, none deceives itself with greater heedlessness on the situation. A part of the Army voted for it, thereupon the Mountain is of the opinion that the Army would revolt in its favor. And by what occasion? By an occasion, that, from the standpoint of the troops, meant nothing else than that the revolutionary soldiers should take the part of the soldiers of Rome against French soldiers. On the other hand, the memory of June, 1848, was still too fresh not to keep alive a deep aversion on the part of the proletariat towards the National Guard, and a strong feeling of mistrust on the part of the leaders of the secret societies for the democratic leaders. In order to balance these differences, great common interests at stake were needed. The violation of an abstract constitutional paragraph could not supply such interests. Had not the constitution been repeatedly violated, according to the assurances of the democrats themselves? Had not the most popular papers branded them as a counter-revolutionary artifice? But the democrat—by reason of his representing the middle class, that is to say, a *Transition Class,* in which the interests of two other classes are mutually dulled—, imagines himself above all class contrast. The democrats grant that opposed to them stands a privileged class, but they, together with the whole remaining mass of the nation, constitute the "PEOPLE." What they represent is the "people's rights"; their interests are the "people's interests." Hence, they do not consider that, at an impending struggle, they need to examine the interests and attitude of the different classes. They need not too seriously weigh their own means. All they have to do is to give the signal in order to have the "people" fall upon the "oppressors" with all its inexhaustible resources. If, thereupon, in the execution, their interests turn out to be uninteresting, and their power to be impotence, it is ascribed either to depraved sophists, who split up the "undivisible people" into several hostile camps; or to the army being too far brutalized and blinded to appreciate the pure aims of the democracy as its own best; or to some detail in the execution that wrecks the whole plan; or, finally, to an unforeseen accident that spoiled the game this time. At all events, the democrat comes out of the disgraceful defeat as immaculate as he went innocently into it, and with the refreshed conviction that he must win; not that he himself and his party must give up their old standpoint, but that, on the contrary, conditions must come to his aid.

. . .

All the same, the revolution is thoroughgoing. It still is on its passage through purgatory. It does its work methodically. Down to December 2, 1851, it had fulfilled one-half of its programme, it now fulfils the other half. It first ripens the power of the Legislature into fullest maturity in order to be able to overthrow it. Now that it has accomplished that, the revolution proceeds to ripen the power of the Executive into equal maturity; it reduces this power to its purest expression; isolates it; places it before itself as the sole subject for reproof in order to concentrate against it all the revolutionary forces of destruction. When the revolution shall have accomplished this second part of its preliminary programme, Europe will jump up from her seat to exclaim: "Well hast thou grubbed, old mole!"

The Executive power, with its tremendous bureaucratic and military organization; with its wide-spreading and artificial machinery of government—an army of office-holders, half a million strong, together with a military force of another million men—; this fearful body of parasites, that coils itself like a snake around French society, stopping all its pores, originated at the time of the absolute monarchy, along with the decline of feudalism, which it helped to hasten. The princely privileges of the landed proprietors and cities were transformed into so many attributes of the Executive power; the feudal dignitaries into paid office-holders; and the confusing design of conflicting mediaeval seigniories, into the well regulated plan of a government, work is subdivided and centralized as in the factory. The first French revolution, having as a mission to sweep away all local, territorial, urban and provincial special privileges, with the object of establishing the civic unity of the nation, was bound to develop what the absolute monarchy had begun—the work of centralization, together with the range, the attributes and the menials of government. Napoleon completed this governmental machinery. The Legitimist and the July Monarchy contribute nothing thereto, except a greater subdivision of labor, that grew in the same measure as the division and subdivision of labor within bourgeois society raised new groups and interests, *i.e.,* new material for the administration of government. Each *Common* interest was in turn forthwith removed from society, set up against it as a higher *Collective* interest, wrested from the individual activity of the members of society, and turned into a subject for governmental administration,—from the bridges, the school house and the communal property of a village community, up to the railroads, the national wealth and the national University of France. Finally, the parliamentary republic found itself, in its struggle against the revolution, compelled, with its repressive measures, to strengthen the means and the centralization of the government. Each overturn, instead of breaking up, carried this machine to higher perfection. The parties, that alternately wrestled for supremacy, looked upon the possession of this tremendous governmental structure as the principal spoils of their victory.

Nevertheless, under the absolute monarchy, during the first revolution, and under Napoleon, the bureaucracy was only the means whereby to prepare the class rule of the bourgeoisie; under the restoration, under Louis Philippe, and under the parliamentary republic, it was the instrument of the ruling class, however eagerly this class strained after autocracy. Not before the advent of the second Bonaparte does the government seem to have made itself fully independent. The machinery of government has by this time so thoroughly fortified itself against society, that the chief of the "Society of December 10" is thought good enough to be at its head; a fortune-hunter, run in from abroad, is raised on its shield by a drunken soldiery, bought by himself with liquor and sausages, and whom he is forced ever again to throw sops to. Hence the timid despair, the sense of crushing humiliation and degradation that oppresses the breast of France and makes her to choke. She feels dishonored.

And yet the French Government does not float in the air. Bonaparte represents an economic class, and that the most numerous in the commonweal of France—the *Allotment Farmer.*[4]

. . .

The allotment farmers are an immense mass, whose individual members live in identical conditions, without, however, entering into manifold relations with one another. Their method of production isolates them from one another, instead of drawing them into mutual intercourse. This isolation is promoted by the poor means of communication in France, together with the poverty of the farmers themselves. Their field of production, the small allotment of land that each cultivates, allows no room for a division of labor, and no opportunity for the application of science; in other words, it shuts out manifoldness of development, diversity of talent, and the luxury of social relations. Every single farmer family is almost self-sufficient; itself produces directly the greater part of what it consumes; and it earns its livelihood more by means of an interchange with nature than by intercourse with society. We have the allotted patch of land, the farmer and his family; alongside of that another allotted patch of land, another farmer and another family. A bunch of these makes up a village; a bunch of villages makes up a Department. Thus the large mass of the French nation is constituted by the simple addition of equal magnitudes—much as a bag with potatoes constitutes a potato-bag. In so far as millions of families live under economic conditions that separate their mode

[4] The first French Revolution distributed the bulk of the territory of France, held at the time by the feudal lords, in small patches among the cultivators of the soil. This allotment of lands created the French farmer class.

of life, their interests and their culture from those of the other classes, and that place them in an attitude hostile toward the latter, they constitute a class; in so far as there exists only a local connection among these farmers, a connection which the individuality and exclusiveness of their interests prevent from generating among them any unity of interest, national connections, and political organization, they do not constitute a class. Consequently, they are unable to assert their class interests in their own name, be it by a parliament or by convention. They can not represent one another, they must themselves be represented. Their representative must at the same time appear as their master, as an authority over them, as an unlimited governmental power, that protects them from above, bestows rain and sunshine upon them. Accordingly, the political influence of the allotment farmer finds its ultimate expression in an Executive power that subjugates the common-weal to its own autocratic will.

. . .

But this should be well understood: The Bonaparte dynasty does not represent the revolutionary, it represents the conservative farmer; it does not represent the farmer, who presses beyond his own economic conditions, his little allotment of land, it represents him rather who would confirm these conditions; it does not represent the rural population, that, thanks to its own inherent energy, wishes, jointly with the cities to overthrow the old order, it represents, on the contrary, the rural population that, hide-bound in the old order, seeks to see itself, together with its allotments, saved and favored by the ghost of the Empire; it represents, not the intelligence, but the superstition of the farmer; not his judgment, but his bias; not his future, but his past; not his modern Cevennes;[7] but his modern Vendée.[8]

The three years' severe rule of the parliamentary republic had freed a part of the French farmers from the Napoleonic illusion, and, though even only superficially; had revolutionized them. The

[7] The Cevennes were the theater of the most numerous revolutionary uprisings of the farmer class.

[8] La Vendée was the theater of protracted reactionary uprisings of the farmer class under the first Revolution.

bourgeoisie threw them, however, violently back every time that they set themselves in motion. Under the parliamentary republic, the modern wrestled with the traditional consciousness of the French farmer. The process went on in the form of a continuous struggle between the school teachers and the parsons;—the bourgeoisie knocked the school teachers down. For the first time, the farmer made an effort to take an independent stand in the government of the country; this manifested itself in the prolonged conflicts of the Mayors with the Prefects;—the bourgeoisie deposed the Mayors. Finally, during the period of the parliamentary republic, the farmers of several localities rose against their own product, the Army;—the bourgeoisie punished them with states of siege and executions. And this is the identical bourgeoisie, that now howls over the "stupidity of the masses," over the "vile multitude," which, it claims, betrayed it to Bonaparte. Itself has violently fortified the imperialism of the farmer class; it firmly maintained the conditions that constitute the birth-place of this farmer-religion. Indeed, the bourgeoisie has every reason to fear the stupidity of the masses—so long as they remain conservative; and their intelligence —so soon as they become revolutionary.

. . .

The economic development of the allotment system has turned bottom upward the relation of the farmer to the other classes of society. Under Napoleon, the parceling out of the agricultural lands into small allotments supplemented in the country the free competition and the incipient large production of the cities. The farmer class was the ubiquitous protest against the aristocracy of land, just then overthrown. The roots that the system of small allotments cast into the soil of France, deprived feudalism of all nutriment. Its boundary-posts constituted the natural buttress of the bourgeoisie against every stroke of the old overlords. But in the course of the nineteenth century, the City Usurer stepped into the shoes of the Feudal Lord, the Mortgage substituted the Feudal Duties formerly yielded by the soil, bourgeois Capital took the place of the aristocracy of Landed Property. The former allotments are now only a pretext that allows the capitalist class to draw profit, interest and rent from agricultural lands, and to leave to the farmer himself the task of seeing to it that he knock out his wages. The mortgage indebtedness that burdens the soil of France imposes upon the French farmer class the payment of an interest as great as the annual interest on the whole British national debt. In this slavery of capital, whither its development drives it irresistibly, the allotment system has transformed the mass of the French nation into troglodytes. Sixteen million farmers (women and children included), house in hovels most of which have only one opening, some two, and the few most favored ones three. Windows are to a house what the five senses are to the head. The bourgeois social order, which, at the beginning of the century, placed the State as a sentinel before the newly instituted allotment, and that manured this with laurels, has become a vampire that sucks out its heart-blood and its very brain, and throws it into the alchemist's pot of capital. The "Code Napoleon" is now but the codex of execution, of sheriff's sales and of intensified taxation. To the four million (children, etc., included) official paupers, vagabonds, criminals and prostitutes, that France numbers, must be added five million souls who hover over the precipice of life, and either sojourn in the country itself, or float with their rags and their children from the country to the cities, and from the cities back to the country. Accordingly, the interests of the farmers are no longer, as under Napoleon, in harmony but in conflict with the interests of the bourgeoisie, *i.e.,* with capital; they find their natural allies and leaders among the urban proletariat, whose mission is the overthrow of the bourgeois social order. . . .

. . .

It is evident that all the "idées Napoléoniennes" are the ideas of the undeveloped and youthfully fresh allotment; they are an absurdity for the allotment that now survives. They are only the hallucinations of its death struggle; words turned to hollow phrases, spirits turned to spooks. But this parody of the Empire was requisite in order to free the mass of the French nation from the weight of tradition, and to elaborate sharply the contrast between Government and Society. Along with the progressive decay of the allotment, the governmental structure, reared upon it, breaks down. The centralization of Government, required by modern society, rises only upon the ruins of the military and bureaucratic governmental machinery that was forged in contrast to feudalism.

The conditions of the French farmers' class solve to us the riddle of the general elections of December 20 and 21, that led the second Bonaparte to the top of Sinai, not to receive, but to decree laws.

The bourgeoisie had now, manifestly, no choice but to elect Bonaparte. When, at the Council of Constance, the puritans complained of the sinful life of the Popes, and moaned about the need of a reform in morals, Cardinal d'Ailly thundered into their faces: "Only the devil in his own person can now save the Catholic Church, and you demand angels." So, likewise, did the French bourgeoisie cry out after the "coup d'état": "Only the chief of the 'Society of December 10' can now save bourgeois society; only theft can save property, only perjury religion, only bastardy the family, only disorder order!"

Bonaparte, as autocratic Executive power, fulfills his mission to secure "bourgeois order." But the strength of this bourgeois order lies in the middle class. He feels himself the representative of the middle class, and issues his decrees in that sense. Nevertheless, he is something only because he has broken the political power of this class, and daily breaks it anew. Hence he feels himself the adversary of the political and the literary power of the middle class. But, by protecting their material, he nourishes anew their political power. Consequently, the cause must be kept alive, but the result, wherever it manifests itself, swept out of existence. But this procedure is impossible without slight mistakings of causes and effects, seeing that both, in their mutual action and reaction, lose their distinctive marks. Thereupon, new decrees, that blur the line of distinction. Bonaparte, furthermore, feels himself, as against the bourgeoisie, the representative of the farmer and the people in general, who, within bourgeois society, is to render the lower classes of society happy. To this end, new decrees, intended to exploit the "true Socialists," together with their governmental wisdom. But, above all, Bonaparte feels himself the chief of the "Society of December 10," the representative of the slum-proletariat, to which he himself, his immediate surroundings, his Government, and his army alike belong, the main object with all of whom is to be good to themselves, and draw Californian tickets out of the national treasury. And he affirms his chieftainship of the "Society of December 10" with decrees, without decrees, and despite decrees.

This contradictory mission of the man explains the contradictions of his own Government, and that confused groping about, that now seeks to win, then to humiliate now this class and then that, and finishes by arraying against itself all the classes; whose actual insecurity constitutes a highly comical contrast with the imperious, categoric style of the Government acts, copied closely from the Uncle.

Industry and commerce, *i.e.,* the business of the middle class, are to be made to blossom in hot-house style under the "strong Government." Loans for a number of railroad grants. But the Bonapartist slum-proletariat is to enrich itself. Peculation is carried on with railroad concessions on the Bourse by the initiated; but no capital is forthcoming for the railroads. The bank then pledges itself to make advances upon railroad stock; but the bank is itself to be exploited; hence, it must be cajoled; it is released of the obligation to publish its reports weekly. Then follows a leonine treaty between the bank and the Government. The people are to be occupied: public works are ordered; but the public works raise the tax rates upon the people; thereupon the taxes are reduced by an attack upon the national bond-holders through the conversion of the five per cent. "rentes" [9] into four-and-halves. Yet the middle class must again be tipped: to this end, the tax on wine is doubled for the people, who buy it at retail, and is reduced to one-half for the middle class, that drink it at wholesale. Genuine labor organizations are dissolved, but promises are made of future wonders to accrue from organization. The farmers are to be helped: mortgage-banks are set up that must promote the indebtedness of the farmer and the concentration of property; but again, these banks are to be utilized especially to the end of squeezing money out of the confiscated estates of the House of Orleans; no capitalist will listen to this scheme, which, moreover, is not mentioned in the decree; the mortgage bank remains a mere decree, etc., etc.

[9] The name of the French national bonds.

Bonaparte would like to appear as the patriarchal benefactor of all classes; but he can give to none without taking from the others.

. . .

Harassed by the contradictory demands of his situation, and compelled, like a sleight-of-hands performer, to keep, by means of constant surprises, the eyes of the public riveted upon himself as the substitute of Napoleon, compelled, consequently, every day to accomplish a sort of "coup" on a small scale, Bonaparte throws the whole bourgeois social system into disorder; he broaches everything that seemed unbroachable by the revolution of 1848; he makes one set of people patient under the revolution, and another anxious for it; and he produces anarchy itself in the name of order, by rubbing off from the whole machinery of Government the veneer of sanctity, by profanating it, by rendering it at once nauseating and laughable. He rehearses in Paris the cult of the sacred coat of Trier with the cult of the Napoleonic Imperial mantle. But, when the Imperial Mantle shall have finally fallen upon the shoulders of Louis Bonaparte, then will also the iron statue of Napoleon drop down from the top of the Vendôme column.[16]

—Marx, *The Eighteenth Brumaire of Louis Bonaparte,* pp. 9–23, 46–49, 51–53, 55–58, 141–48, 149–51, 154–57, 159–60

[16] A prophecy that a few years later, after Bonaparte's coronation as Emperor, was literally fulfilled. By order of the Emperor Louis Napoleon, the military statue of the first Napoleon that originally surmounted the Vendome column, was taken down and replaced by one of first Napoleon in imperial robes.

V

Superstructure and Substructure

Introduction

Marx views the superstructure—ideology, the state, law, the family, and religion—as a reflection of the underlying modes of production. The substructure not only produces social institutions but belief systems as well. Man's mind and the world that he believes in is, logically, a reflection of the "real" world in which he lives. From this vantage point, Marx is able to criticize politics, ethics, bourgeois democracy and beliefs as simply reflections of class-bound self-interest.

Marx's analysis enables him to strip away the metaphysical cloak from institutions generally believed to be sacred and natural, eternal and inevitable, and reveals them in their arbitrary, conditional and temporary forms. He sees the state as protector of bourgeois interests rather than as a neutral umpire of disputes, and religious belief as a diversion from the problems of economic and social misery rather than as an expression of reverent awe before the mysteries of life and death. By proclaiming these shattering truths, Marx performs the historic role of the intellectual as revolutionary. By showing that there is nothing inevitable about the conditions under which men live and by uncovering the "true" nature of institutions, he can arouse and educate the proletariat to the possibilities of action.

Marx's analysis also paves the way for his conception of utopia. Societies, having no class structure, need not be oppressive. An economy of abundance without a division of labor does not require a coercive state and law. It does not require resignation to the horrors of this life through belief in an idealized afterlife. Nor, finally, does it require an exploitative family structure. Family life, in fact all social life, would become spontaneous and affectionate once its base in economic exploitation is removed.

By showing that ideologies and institutions are founded on society's economic base, Marx demonstrates how they support the stability of the capitalist structure. Not only does the state reflect the interests of the ruling class, but it helps contain conflict in the society. It would be erroneous to think of the state as simply an instrument of bourgeois power. The state offers the appearance of impartiality by seemingly standing above society. It moderates conflict, "keeping it within the bounds of 'order'." The exercise of direct coercion is unnecessary if people believe government to be an impartial arbiter of conflict.

Although women are "prostituted" in the bourgeois family and the masses are subjected to poverty and degradation, these conditions do not cause revolutions. The bourgeois ideology that supports family and religious institutions provides a convincing rationale for accepting the world as it is.

Institutions create their own ideology. Their rationalizations (which is what ideology means to Marx) hide the true discontent that lies just beneath the surface. Only the proletariat, because of their suffering, and because of the instruction provided by revolutionary intellectuals, are able to perceive the world as it actually is.

The appendix on the "Jewish question" provides an interesting illustration of how Marx sees even the democratic and civilizing nineteenth-century trend toward equal rights for all as nothing more than an adaptation of social organization to a market economy. Men are freed, in capitalism, only to become additional means of production. Thus they never are truly emancipated. Neither Jews nor Christians can ever become free in a bourgeois society. The solution to the "Jewish question" and the elimination of the Jewish religion, of which Christianity is the highest expression, can only come with the death of the bourgeois society.

●

Ideology

. . . In acquiring new productive forces men change their mode of production, and in changing their mode of production, their manner of gaining a living, they change all their social relations. The windmill gives you society with the feudal lord; the steam-mill, society with the industrial capitalist.

The same men who establish social relations conformably with their material productivity, produce also the principles, the ideas, the categories, conformably with their social relations.

Thus these ideas, these categories, are not more eternal than the relations which they express. They are *historical and transitory products.*

There is a continual movement of growth in the productive forces, of destruction in the social relations, of formation in ideas; there is nothing immutable but the abstraction of the movement—*mors immortalis.*

—Marx, *The Poverty of Philosophy,* p. 119

The ideas of the ruling class are in every epoch the ruling ideas: i.e. the class, which is the ruling material force of society, is at the same time its ruling intellectual force. The class which has the means of material production at its disposal, has control at the same time over the means of mental production, so that thereby, generally speaking, the ideas of those who lack the means of mental production are subject to it. The ruling ideas are nothing more than the ideal expression of the dominant material relationships, the dominant material relationships grasped as ideas; hence of the relationships which make the one class the ruling one, therefore the ideas of its dominance. The individuals composing the ruling class possess among other things consciousness, and therefore think. In so far, therefore, as they rule as a class and determine the extent and compass of an epoch, it is self-evident that they do this in their whole range, hence among other things rule also as thinkers, as producers of ideas, and regulate the production and distribution of the ideas of their age: thus their ideas are the ruling ideas of the epoch. For instance, in an age and in a country where royal power, aristocracy and bourgeoisie are contending for mastery and where, therefore, mastery is shared, the doctrine of the separation of powers proves to be the dominant idea and is expressed as an "eternal law." The division of labour, which we saw above as one of the chief forces of history up till now, manifests itself also in the ruling class as the division of mental and material labour, so that inside this class one part appears as the thinkers of the class (its active, conceptive ideologists, who make the perfecting of the illusion of the class about itself their chief source of livelihood), while the others' attitude to these ideas and illusions is more passive and receptive, because they are in reality the active members of this class and have less time to make up illusions and ideas about themselves. Within this class this cleavage can even develop into a certain opposition and hostility between the two parts, which, however, in the case of a practical collision, in which the class itself is endangered, automatically comes to nothing, in which case there also vanishes the semblance that the ruling ideas were not the ideas of the ruling class and had a power distinct from the power of this class. The existence of revolutionary ideas in a particular period presupposes the existence of a revolutionary class; about the premises for the latter sufficient has already been said above.

—Marx and Engels, *The German Ideology*, pp. 39–40

The State and Law

The Relation of State and Law to Property

The first form of property, in the ancient world as in the Middle Ages, is tribal property, determined with the Romans chiefly by war, with the Germans by the rearing of cattle. In the case of the ancient peoples, since several tribes live together in one town, the tribal property appears as State property, and the right of the individual to it as mere *"possession"* which, however, like tribal property as a whole, is confined to landed property only. Real private property began with the ancients, as with modern nations, with personal movable property—(slavery and community) (*dominium ex jure Quiritium*). In the case of the nations which grew out of the Middle Ages, tribal property evolved through various stages—feudal landed property, corporative movable property, manufacture-capital—to modern capital, determined by big industry and universal competition, i.e. pure private property, which has cast off all semblance of a communal institution and has shut out the State from any influence on the development of property. To this modern private property corresponds the modern State, which, purchased gradually by the owners of property by means of taxation, has fallen entirely into their hands through the national debt, and its existence has become wholly dependent on the commercial credit which the owners of property, the bourgeois, extend to it in the rise and fall of State funds on the stock exchange. By the mere fact that it is a *class* and no longer an *estate,* the bourgeoisie is forced to organize itself no longer locally, but nationally, and to give a general form to its mean average interest. Through the emancipation of private property from the community, the State has become a separate entity, beside and outside civil society; but it is nothing more than the form of organization which the bourgeois necessarily adopt both for internal and external purposes, for the mutual guarantee of their property and interests. The independence of the State is only found nowadays in those countries where the estates have not yet completely developed into classes, where the estates, done away with in more advanced countries, still have a part to play, and where there exists a mixture; countries, that is to say in which no one section of the population can achieve dominance over the others. This is the case particularly in Germany. The most perfect example of the modern State is North America. The modern French, English and American writers all express the opinion that the State exists only for the sake of private property, so that this fact has penetrated into the consciousness of the normal man.

Since the State is the form in which the individuals of a ruling class assert their common interests, and in which the whole civil society of an epoch is epitomized, it follows that in the formation of all communal institutions the State acts as intermediary, that these institutions receive a political form. Hence the illusion that law is based on the will, and indeed on the will divorced from its real basis—on free will. Similarly, the theory of law is in its turn reduced to the actual laws.

Civil law develops simultaneously with private property out of the disintegration of the natural community. With the Romans the development of private property and civil law had no further industrial and commercial consequences, because their whole mode of production did not alter. With modern peoples, where the feudal community was disintegrated by industry and trade, there began with the rise of private property and civil law a new phase, which was capable of further development. The very first town which carried on an extensive trade in the Middle Ages, Amalfi, also developed maritime law. As soon as industry and trade developed private property further, first in Italy and later in other countries, Roman civil law was adopted again in a perfected form and raised to authority. When later the bourgeoisie had acquired so much power that the princes took up their interests in order to overthrow the feudal nobility by means of the bourgeoisie, there began in all countries—in France in the sixteenth century—the real development of law, which in all countries except England proceeded on the basis of the Roman Codex. In England too, Roman legal principles had to be introduced to further the development of civil law (especially in the case of personal movable property). It must not be forgotten that law has just as little an independent history as religion.

In civil law the existing property relationships are declared to be the result of the general will. The *jus utendi et abutendi* itself asserts on the one hand the fact that private property has become entirely independent of the community, and on the other the illusion that private property itself is based on the private will, the arbitrary disposal of the thing. In practice, the *abuti* has very definite economic limitations for the owner of private property, if he does not wish to see his property and hence his *jus abutendi* pass into other hands, since actually the thing, considered merely with reference to his will, is not a thing at all, but only becomes true property in intercourse, and independently of the right to the thing (a *relationship,* which the philosophers call an idea). This juridical illusion, which reduces law to the mere will, necessarily leads, in the further development of property relationships, to the position that a man may have a title to a thing without really having the thing. If, for instance, the income from a piece of land is lost owing to competition, then the proprietor has certainly his legal title to it along with the *jus utendi et abutendi.* But he can do nothing with it; he owns nothing as a landed proprietor if he has not enough capital besides to cultivate his ground. This illusion of the jurists also explains the fact that for them, as for every codex, it is altogether fortuitous that individuals enter into relationships among themselves (e.g. contracts); it explains why they consider that these relationships can be entered into or not at will, and that their content rests purely on the individual free will of the contracting parties. Whenever, through the development of industry and commerce, new forms of intercourse have been evolved, (e.g. assurance companies etc.) the law has always been compelled to admit them among the modes of acquiring property.

. . .

This crystallization of social activity, this consolidation of what we ourselves produce into an objective power above us, growing out of our control, thwarting our expectations, bringing to naught our calculations, is one of the chief factors in historical development up till now. And out of this very contradiction between the interest of the individual and that of the community the latter takes an independent form as the STATE, divorced from the real interests of individual and community, and at the same time as an illusory communal life, always based, however, on the real ties existing in every family and tribal conglomeration (such as flesh and blood, language, division of labour on a larger scale, and other interests) and especially, as we shall enlarge upon later, on the classes, already determined by the division of labour, which in every such mass of men separate out, and of which one dominates all the others. It follows from this that all struggles within the State, the struggle between democracy, aristocracy and monarchy, the struggle for the franchise, etc., etc., are merely the illusory forms in which the real struggles of the different classes are fought out among one another (of this the German theoreticians have not the faintest inkling, although they have received a sufficient introduction to the subject in *The German-French Annals* and *The Holy Family*).

—Marx and Engels, *The German Ideology*, pp. 58–62, 22–23

The state presents itself to us as the first ideological power over man. Society creates for itself an organ for the safeguarding of its common interests against internal and external attacks. This organ is the state power. Hardly come into being, this organ makes itself independent *vis-a-vis* society; and, indeed, the more so, the more it becomes the organ of a particular class, the more it directly enforces the supremacy of that class. The fight of the oppressed class against the ruling class becomes necessarily a political fight, a fight first of all against the political dominance of this class. The consciousness of the interconnection between this political struggle and its economic basis becomes dulled and can be lost altogether. While this is not wholly the case with the participants, it almost always happens with the historians. Of the ancient sources on the struggles within the Roman Republic only Appian tells us clearly and distinctly what was at issue in the last resort—namely, landed property.

But once the state has become an independent power *vis-a-vis* society, it produces forthwith a further ideology. It is indeed among professional politicians, theorists of public law and jurists of private law that the connection with economic facts gets lost for fair. Since in each particular case the economic facts must assume the form of juristic motives in order to receive legal sanction; and since, in so doing, consideration of course has to be given to the whole legal system already in operation, the juristic form is, in consequence, made everything and the economic content nothing. Public law and private law are treated as independent spheres, each having its own independent historical development, each being capable of and needing a systematic presentation by the consistent elimination of all inner contradictions.

—Engels, "Ludwig Feuerbach and the End of Classical German Philosophy," *MESW II,* pp. 360–97

The state is . . . by no means a power forced on society from without; just as little is it "the reality of the ethical idea," "the image and reality of reason," as Hegel maintains. Rather, it is a product of society at a certain stage of development; it is the admission that this society has become entangled in an insoluble contradiction with itself, that it is cleft into irreconcilable antagonisms which it is powerless to dispel. But in order that these antagonisms, classes with conflicting economic interests, might not consume themselves and society in sterile struggle, a power seemingly standing above society became necessary for the purpose of moderating the conflict, of keeping it within the bounds of "order"; and this power, arisen out of society, but placing itself above it, and increasingly alienating itself from it, is the state.

In contradistinction to the old gentile organization, the state, first, divides its subjects *according to territory*. As we have seen, the old gentile associations, built upon and held together by ties of blood, became inadequate, largely because they presupposed that the members were bound to a given territory, a bond which had long ceased to exist. The territory remained, but the people had become mobile. Hence, division according to territory was taken as the point of departure, and citizens were allowed to exercise their public rights and duties wherever they settled, irrespective of gens and tribe. This organization of citizens according to locality is a feature common to all states. That is why it seems natural to us; but we have seen what long and arduous struggles were needed before it could replace, in Athens and Rome, the old organization according to gentes.

The second is the establishment of a *public power* which no longer directly coincided with the population organizing itself as an armed force. This special public power is necessary, because a self-acting armed organization of the population has become impossible since the cleavage into classes. The slaves also belonged to the population; the 90,000 citizens of Athens formed only a privileged class as against the 365,000 slaves. The people's army of the Athenian democracy was an aristocratic public power against the slaves, whom it kept in check; however, a gendarmerie also became necessary to keep the citizens in check, as we related above. This public power exists in every state; it consists not merely of armed people but also of material adjuncts, prisons and institutions of coercion of all kinds, of which gentile society knew nothing. It may be very insignificant, almost infinitesimal, in societies where class antagonisms are still undeveloped and in out-of-the-way places as was the case at certain times and in certain regions in the United States of America. It grows stronger, however, in proportion as class antagonisms within the state become more acute, and as adjacent states become larger and more populated. We have only to look at our present-day Europe, where class struggle and rivalry in conquest have screwed up the public power to such a pitch that it threatens to devour the whole of society and even the state.

In order to maintain this public power, contributions from the citizens become necessary—*taxes*. These were absolutely unknown in gentile society; but we know enough about them today. As civilization advances, these taxes become inadequate; the state makes drafts on the future, contracts loans, *public debts*. Old Europe can tell a tale about these, too.

In possession of the public power and of the right to levy taxes, the officials, as organs of society, now stand *above* society. The free, voluntary respect that was accorded to the organs of the gentile constitution does not satisfy them, even if they could gain it; being the vehicles of a power that is becoming alien to society, respect for them must be enforced by means of exceptional laws by virtue of which they enjoy special sanctity and inviolability. The shabbiest police servant in the civilized state has more "authority" than all the organs of gentile society put together; but the most powerful prince and the greatest statesman, or general, of civilization may well envy the humblest gentile chief for the uncoerced and undisputed respect that is paid to him. The one stands in the midst of society, the other is forced to attempt to represent something outside and above it.

As the state arose from the need to hold class antagonisms in check, but as it arose, at the same time, in the midst of the conflict of these classes, it is, as a rule, the state of the most powerful, economically dominant class, which, through the medium of the state, becomes also the politically dominant class, and thus acquires new means of holding down and exploiting the oppressed class. Thus, the state of antiquity was above all the state of the slave owners for the purpose of holding down the slaves, as the feudal state was the organ of the nobility for holding down the peasant serfs and bondsmen, and the modern representative state is an instrument of exploitation of wage labour by capital. By way of exception, however, periods occur in which the warring classes balance each other so nearly that the state power, as ostensible mediator, acquires, for the moment, a certain degree of independence of both. Such was the absolute monarchy of the seventeenth and eighteenth centuries, which held the balance between the nobility and the class of burghers; such was the Bonapartism of the First, and still more of the Second French Empire, which played off the proletariat against the bourgeoisie and the bourgeoisie against the proletariat. The latest performance of this kind, in which ruler and ruled appear equally ridiculous, is the new German Empire of the Bismarck nation: here capitalists and workers are balanced against each other and equally cheated for the benefit of the impoverished Prussian cabbage junkers.

In most of the historical states, the rights of citizens are, besides, apportioned according to their wealth, thus directly expressing the fact that the state is an organization of the possessing class for its protection against the non-possessing class. It was so already in the Athenian and Roman classification according to property. It was so in the mediaeval feudal state, in which the alignment of political power was in conformity with the amount of land owned. It is seen in the electoral qualifications of the modern representative states. Yet this political recognition of property distinctions is by no means essential. On the contrary, it marks a low stage of state development. The highest form of the state, the democratic republic, which under our modern conditions of society is more and more becoming an inevitable necessity, and is the form of state in which alone the last decisive struggle between proletariat and bourgeoisie can be fought out—the democratic republic officially knows nothing any more of property distinctions. In it wealth exercises its power indirectly, but all the more surely. On the one hand, in the form of the direct corruption of officials, of which America provides the classical example; on the other hand, in the form of an alliance between government and Stock Exchange, which become the easier to achieve the more the public debt increases and the more joint-stock companies concentrate in their hands not only transport but also production itself, using the Stock Exchange as their centre. The latest French republic as well as the United States is a striking example of this; and good old Switzerland has contributed its share in this field. But that a democratic republic is not essential for this fraternal alliance between government and Stock Exchange is proved by England and also by the new German Empire, where one cannot tell who was elevated more by universal suffrage, Bismarck or Bleichröder. And lastly, the possessing class rules directly through the medium of universal suffrage. As long as the oppressed class, in our case, therefore, the proletariat, is not yet ripe to emancipate itself, it will in its majority regard the existing order of society as the only one possible and, politically, will form the tail of the capitalist class, its extreme Left wing. To the extent, however, that this class matures for its self-emancipation, it constitutes itself as its own party and elects its own representatives, and not those of the capitalists. Thus, universal suffrage is the gauge of the maturity of the working class. It cannot and never will be anything more in the present-day state; but that is sufficient. On the day the thermometer of universal suffrage registers boiling point among the workers, both they and the capitalists will know what to do.

The state, then, has not existed from all eternity. There have been societies that did without it, that had no conception of the state and state power. At a certain stage of economic development, which was necessarily bound up with the cleavage of society into classes, the state became a necessity owing to this cleavage. We are now rapidly approaching a stage in the development of production at which the existence of these classes not only will have ceased to be a necessity, but will become a positive hindrance to production. They will fall as inevitably as they arose at an earlier stage. Along with them the state will inevitably fall. The society that will organize production on the basis of a free and equal association of the producers will put the whole machinery of state where it will then belong: into the Museum of Antiquities, by the side of the spinning wheel and the bronze axe.

—Engels, "The Origin of the Family, Private Property and the State," *MESW II,* pp. 318–22

It is always the direct relation of the owners of the conditions of production to the direct producers, which reveals the innermost secret, the hidden foundation of the entire social construction, and with it of the political form of the relations between sovereignty and dependence, in short, of the corresponding form of the state.

—Marx, *Capital:* Vol. III, p. 919

The reaction of the state power upon economic development can be of three kinds: it can run in the same direction, and then development is more rapid; it can oppose the line of development, in which case nowadays it will go to pieces in the long run in every great people; or it can prevent the economic development from proceeding along certain lines, and prescribe other lines. This case ultimately reduces itself to one of the two previous ones. But it is obvious that in cases two and three the political power can do great damage to the economic development and cause a great squandering of energy and material.

Then there is also the case of the conquest and brutal destruction of economic resources, by which, in certain circumstances, a whole local or national economic development could formerly be ruined. Nowadays such a case usually has the opposite effect, at least with great peoples: in the long run the vanquished often gains more economically, politically and morally than the victor.

Similarly with law. As soon as the new division of labour which creates professional lawyers becomes necessary, another new and independent sphere is opened up which, for all its general dependence on production and trade, has also a special capacity for reacting upon these spheres. In a modern state, law must not only correspond to the general economic condition and be its expression, but must also be an *internally coherent* expression which does not, owing to inner contradictions, reduce itself to nought. And in order to achieve this, the faithful reflection of economic conditions suffers increasingly. All the more so the more rarely it happens that a code of law is the blunt, unmitigated, unadulterated expression of the domination of a class—this in itself would offend the "conception of right." Even in the *Code Napoleon* the pure, consistent conception of right held by the revolutionary bourgeoisie of 1792–96 is already adulterated in many ways, and, in so far as it is embodied there, has daily to undergo all sorts of attenuations owing to the rising power of the proletariat. This does not prevent the *Code Napoleon* from being the statute book which serves as the basis of every new code of law in every part of the world. Thus to a great extent the course of the "development of right" consists only, first, in the attempt to do away with the contradictions arising from the direct translation of economic relations into legal principles, and to establish a harmonious system of law, and then in the repeated breaches made in this system by the influence and compulsion of further economic development, which involves it in further contradictions. (I am speaking here for the moment only of civil law.)

The reflection of economic relations as legal principles is necessarily also a topsy-turvy one: it goes on without the person who is acting being conscious of it; the jurist imagines he is operating with *a priori* propositions, whereas they are really only economic reflexes; so everything is upside down. And it seems to me obvious that this inversion, which, so long as it remains unrecognized, forms what we call *ideological outlook,* reacts in its turn upon the economic basis and may, within certain limits, modify it. The basis of the right of inheritance—assuming that the stages reached in the development of the family are the same—is an economic one. Nevertheless, it would be difficult to prove, for instance, that the absolute liberty of the testator in England and the severe restrictions in every detail imposed upon him in France are due to economic causes alone. Both react back, however, on the economic sphere to a very considerable extent, because they influence the distribution of property.

—Engels to C. Schmidt (London, October 27, 1890), *Selected Correspondence,* pp. 503–505

. . . it is necessary to be entirely innocent of all historical knowledge not to know that in all times sovereigns have had to submit to the economic conditions and have never made laws for these. Legislation, political as well as civil, could do no more than give expression to the will of the economic conditions.

. . .

In England trade combination is permitted by law, and it is the economic system which has forced Parliament to give this legal authorisation. In 1825 when, under the minister Huskisson, Parliament had to modify the law in order to bring it more into accord with a state of things resulting from free competition, it was necessary to abolish the laws which prohibited the combination of workmen. The more modern industry and competition develop, the more elements are there which provoke and support competition, and as soon as combinations have become an economic fact, acquiring greater consistency day by day, they will not be slow in becoming a legal fact.

—Marx, *The Poverty of Philosophy,* pp. 90, 185–86

Religion

All religion, however, is nothing but the fantastic reflection in men's minds of those external forces which control their daily life, a reflection in which the terrestrial forces assume the form of supernatural forces. In the beginnings of history it was the forces of nature which were first so reflected, and which in the course of further evolution underwent the most manifold and varied personifications among the various peoples. This early process has been traced back by comparative mythology, at least in the case of the Indo-European peoples, to its origin in the Indian Vedas, and in its further evolution it has been demonstrated in detail among the Indians, Persians, Greeks, Romans, Germans and, so far as material is available, also among the Celts, Lithuanians and Slavs. But it is not long before, side by side with the forces of nature, social forces begin to be active—forces which confront man as equally alien and at first equally inexplicable, dominating him with the same apparent natural necessity as the forces of nature themselves. The fantastic figures, which at first only reflected the mysterious forces of nature, at this point acquire social attributes, become representatives of the forces of history.[1] At a still further stage of evolution, all the natural and social attributes of the numerous gods are transferred to *one* almighty god, who is but a reflection

[1] This two-fold character assumed later on by the divinities was one of the causes of the subsequently wide-spread confusion of mythologies—a cause which comparative mythology has overlooked, as it pays attention exclusively to their character as reflections of the forces of nature. Thus in some Germanic tribes the war-god is called Tyr (Old Nordic) or Zio (Old High German), corresponds therefore to the Greek Zeus, Latin Jupiter for Diu-piter; in other Germanic tribes, Er, Eor, corresponds therefore to the Greek Ares, Latin Mars [*note by Engels*].

of the abstract man. Such was the origin of monotheism, which was historically the last product of the vulgarized philosophy of the later Greeks and found its incarnation in the exclusively national god of the Jews, Jehovah. In this convenient, handy and universally adaptable form, religion can continue to exist as the immediate, that is, the sentimental form of men's relation to the alien, natural and social, forces which dominate them, so long as men remain under the control of these forces. However, we have seen repeatedly that in existing bourgeois society men are dominated by the economic conditions created by themselves, by the means of production which they themselves have produced, as if by an alien force. The actual basis of the reflective activity that gives rise to religion therefore continues to exist, and with it the religious reflection itself. And although bourgeois political economy has given a certain insight into the causal connection of this alien domination, this makes no essential difference. Bourgeois economics can neither prevent crises in general, nor protect the individual capitalists from losses, bad debts and bankruptcy, nor secure the individual workers against unemployment and destitution. It is still true that man proposes and God (that is, the alien domination of the capitalist mode of production) disposes. Mere knowledge, even if it went much further and deeper than that of bourgeois economic science, is not enough to bring social forces under the domination of society. What is above all necessary for this, is a social *act.* And when this act has been accomplished, when society, by taking possession of all means of production and using them on a planned basis, has freed itself and all its members from the bondage in which they are now held by these means of production which they themselves have produced but which confront them as an irresistible alien force; when therefore man no longer merely proposes, but also disposes—only then will the last alien force which is still reflected in religion vanish; and with it will also vanish the religious reflection itself, for the simple reason that then there will be nothing left to reflect.

—Engels, *Anti-Dühring,* pp. 438–40

The religious world is but the reflex of the real world. And for a society based upon the production of commodities, in which the producers in general enter into social relations with one another by treating their products as commodities and values, whereby they reduce their individual private labour to the standard of homogeneous human labour—for such a society, Christianity with its *cultus* of abstract man, more especially in its bourgeois developments, Protestantism, Deism, &c., is the most fitting form of religion.

—Marx, *Capital:* Vol. I, p. 91

We will now in addition deal only briefly with religion, since the latter stands furthest away from material life and seems to be most alien to it. Religion arose in very primitive times from erroneous, primitive conceptions of men about their own nature and external nature surrounding them. Every ideology, however, once it has arisen, develops in connection with the given concept-material, and develops this material further; otherwise it would not be an ideology, that is, occupation with thoughts as with independent entities, developing independently and subject only to their own laws. That the material life conditions of the persons inside whose heads this thought process goes on in the last resort determine the course of this process remains of necessity unknown to these persons, for otherwise there would be an end to all ideology. These original religious notions, therefore, which in the main are common to each group of kindred peoples, develop, after the group separates, in a manner peculiar to each people, according to the conditions of life falling to their lot.

—Engels, "Ludwig Feuerbach and the End of Classical German Philosophy," *MESW II,* pp. 397–98

For Germany the criticism of religion has essentially ended and the criticism of religion is the prerequisite for all criticism. The profane existence of error is endangered after its divine *oratio pro aris et focis* is refuted. The person who has found only the reflection of himself in the fancied reality of heaven, where he was looking for a superman, will no longer feel inclined to find only the *appearance* of himself, only the inhuman person, where he seeks and must seek his true reality.

The foundation of irreligious criticism is this: *Man makes religion;* religion does not make man. And indeed religion is the self-consciousness and the self-realization of the man who either has not yet attained selfhood or has already lost it again. But *man* is not an abstract being, sitting around outside the world. Man is the *world of man,* the state, society. This state and this society produce religion, a *perverse world-consciousness,* because they are a *perverse world.* Religion is the general theory of this world, its encyclopaedic compendium, its logic in popular form, its spiritual point-d'honneur, its enthusiasm, its moral sanction, its solemn complement, its general reason for solace and justification. It is the *realization* in the imagination of the human being, because the *human being* has no true reality. The struggle against religion is thus indirectly the struggle against *that* world, of which religion is the spiritual *aroma.*

Religious misery is at one and the same time the *expression* of real misery and the *protestation* against real misery. Religion is the sigh of the oppressed creature, the mind of a heartless world, as it is the spirit of unspiritual conditions. It is the opiate of the people.

The removal of religion as the illusory happiness of the people is the requirement for their real happiness. The demand that they give up the illusions concerning their condition is *the demand that they give up a condition that requires illusions.* The criticism of religion is therefore basically the criticism of the *vale of tears* whose *halo* is religion.

Criticism has plucked and spoiled the imaginary flowers in the chain, not so that man might bear the chain without imagination and consolation, but so that he might throw off the chain and pick the living flower. The criticism of religion undeceives man, so that he may think, act and shape his reality like a person who has been disillusioned and thus come to his senses, so that he may revolve about himself and thus about his real sun. Religion is only the illusory sun that revolves about man so long as he does not revolve about himself.

It is therefore the *task of history,* after the *world beyond truth* has disappeared, to establish the *truth of this world.* It is first and foremost the *task of philosophy,* which is in the service of history, after the saint-image of man's self-alienation has been unmasked, to unmask the self-alienation in its *unholy forms.* The criticism of heaven thus changes into the criticism of (this) earth, the criticism of religion into the criticism of justice, the criticism of theology into the criticism of politics.

—Marx and Engels, *Towards the Criticism of Hegel's Philosophy of Right,* pp. 378–79

Marriage and Family Life

We have, then, three chief forms of marriage, which, by and large, conform to the three main stages of human development. For savagery—group marriage; for barbarism—pairing marriage; for civilization—monogamy, supplemented by adultery and prostitution. In the upper stage of barbarism, between pairing marriage and monogamy, there is wedged in the dominion exercised by men over female slaves, and polygamy.

As our whole exposition has shown, the advance to be noted in this sequence is linked with the peculiar fact that while women are more and more deprived of the sexual freedom of group marriage, the men are not. Actually, for men, group marriage exists to this day. What for a woman is a crime entailing dire legal and social consequences, is regarded in the case of a man as being honourable or, at most, as a slight moral stain that one bears with pleasure. The more the old traditional hetaerism is changed in our day by capitalist commodity production and adapted to it, and the more it is transformed into unconcealed prostitution, the more demoralizing are its effects. And it demoralizes the men far more than it does the women. Among women, prostitution degrades only those unfortunates who fall into its clutches; and even these are not degraded to the degree that is generally believed. On the other hand, it degrades the character of the entire male world. Thus, in nine cases out of ten, a long engagement is practically a preparatory school for conjugal infidelity.

We are now approaching a social revolution in which the hitherto existing economic foundations of monogamy will disappear just as certainly as will those of its supplement—prostitution. Monogamy arose out of the concentration of considerable wealth in the hands of one person—and that a man—and out of the desire to bequeath this wealth to this man's children and to no one else's. For this purpose monogamy was essential on the woman's part, but not on the man's; so that this monogamy of the women in no way hindered the overt or covert polygamy of the man. The impending social revolution, however, by transforming at least the far greater part of permanent inheritable wealth—the means of production—into social property, will reduce all this anxiety about inheritance to a minimum. Since monogamy arose from economic causes, will it disappear when these causes disappear?

One might not unjustly answer: far from disappearing, it will only begin to be completely realized. For with the conversion of the means of production into social property, wage labour, the proletariat, also disappears, and therewith, also, the necessity for a certain—statistically calculable—number of women to surrender themselves for money. Prostitution disappears; monogamy, instead of declining, finally becomes a reality—for the men as well.

At all events, the position of the men thus undergoes considerable change. But that of the women, of *all* women, also undergoes important alteration. With the passage of the means of production into common property, the individual family ceases to be the economic unit of society. Private housekeeping is transformed into a social industry. The care and education of the children becomes a public matter. Society takes care of all children equally, irrespective of whether they are born in wedlock or not. Thus, the anxiety about the "consequences," which is today the most important social factor —both moral and economic—that hinders a girl from giving herself freely to the man she loves, disappears. Will this not be cause enough for a gradual rise of more unrestrained sexual intercourse, and along with it, a more lenient public opinion regarding virginal honour and feminine shame? And finally, have we not seen that monogamy and prostitution in the modern world, although opposites, are nevertheless inseparable opposites, poles of the same social conditions? Can prostitution disappear without dragging monogamy with it into the abyss?

Here a new factor comes into operation, a factor that, at most, existed in embryo at the time when monogamy developed, namely, individual sex love.

. . .

Our sex love differs materially from the simple sexual desire, the *eros,* of the ancients. First, it presupposes reciprocal love on the part of the loved one; in this respect, the woman stands on a par with the man; whereas in the ancient *eros,* the woman was by no means always consulted. Secondly, sex love attains a degree of intensity and permanency where the two parties regard non-possession or separation as a great, if not the greatest, misfortune; in order to possess each other they take great hazards, even risking life itself—what in antiquity happened, at best, only in cases of adultery. And finally, a new moral standard arises for judging sexual intercourse. The question asked is not only whether such intercourse was legitimate or illicit, but also whether it arose from mutual love or not? It goes without saying that in feudal or bourgeois practice this new standard fares no better than all the other moral standards—it is simply ignored. But it fares no worse, either. It is recognized in theory, on paper, like all the rest. And more than this cannot be expected for the present.

Where antiquity broke off with its start towards sex love, the Middle Ages began, namely, with adultery. We have already described chivalrous love, which gave rise to the Songs of the Dawn. There is still a wide gulf between this kind of love, which aimed at breaking up matrimony, and the love destined to be its foundation, a gulf never completely bridged by the age of chivalry. Even when we pass from the frivolous Latins to the virtuous Germans, we find, in the *Nibelungenlied,* that Kriemhild—although secretly in love with Siegfried every whit as much as he is with her—nevertheless, in reply to Gunther's intimation that he has plighted her to a knight whom he does not name, answers simply: "You have no need to ask; as you command, so will I be for ever. He whom you, my lord, choose for my husband, to him will I gladly plight my troth." It never even occurs to her that her love could possibly be considered in this matter. Gunther seeks the hand of Brunhild without ever having seen her, and Etzel does the same with Kriemhild. The same occurs in the *Gudrun,* where Sigebant of Ireland seeks the hand of Ute the Norwegian, Hetel of Hegelingen that of Hilde of Ireland; and lastly, Siegfried of Morland, Hartmut of Ormany and Herwing of Seeland seek the hand of Gudrun; and here for the first time it happens that Gudrun, of her own free will, decides in favour of the last named. As a rule, the bride of a young prince is selected by his parents; if these are no longer alive, he chooses her himself with the counsel of his highest vassal chiefs, whose word carries great weight in all cases. Nor can it be otherwise. For the knight, or baron, just as for the prince himself, marriage is a political act, an opportunity for the accession of power through new alliances; the interest of the *House* and not individual inclination are the decisive factor. How can love here hope to have the last word regarding marriage?

It was the same for the guildsman of the mediaeval towns. The very privileges which protected him—the guild charters with their special stipulations, the artificial lines of demarcation which legally separated him from other guilds, from his own fellow guildsmen and from his journeymen and apprentices—considerably restricted the circle in which he could hope to secure a suitable spouse. And the question as to who was the most suitable was definitely decided under this complicated system, not by individual inclination, but by family interest.

Up to the end of the Middle Ages, therefore, marriage, in the overwhelming majority of cases, remained what it had been from the commencement, an affair that was not decided by the two principal parties. In the beginning one came into the world married, married to a whole group of the opposite sex. A similar relation probably existed in the later forms of group marriage, only with an ever increasing narrowing of the group. In the pairing family it is the rule that the mothers arrange their children's marriages; and here also, considerations of new ties of relationship that are to strengthen the young couple's position in the gens and tribe are the decisive factor. And when, with the predominance of private property over common property, and with the interest in inheritance, father right and monogamy gain the ascendancy, marriage becomes more than ever dependent on economic considerations. The *form* of marriage by purchase disappears, the transaction itself is to an ever increasing degree carried out in such a way that not only the woman but the man also is appraised, not by his personal qualities but by his possessions. The idea that the mutual inclinations of the principal parties should be the overriding reason for matrimony had been unheard of in the practice of the ruling classes from the very beginning. Such things took place, at best, in romance only, or—among the oppressed classes, which did not count.

This was the situation found by capitalist production when, following the era of geographical discoveries, it set out to conquer the world through world trade and manufacture. One would think that this mode of matrimony should have suited it exceedingly, and such was actually the case. And yet—the irony of world history is unfathomable—it was capitalist production that had to make the decisive breach in it. By transforming all things into commodities, it dissolved all ancient traditional relations, and for inherited customs and historical rights it substituted purchase and sale, "free" contract. And H. S. Maine, the English jurist, believed that he made a colossal discovery when he said that our entire progress in comparison with previous epochs consists in our having evolved from status to contract, from an inherited state of affairs to one voluntarily contracted—a statement which, in so far as it is correct, was contained long ago in the *Communist Manifesto.*

But the closing of contracts presupposes people who can freely dispose of their persons, actions and possessions, and who meet each other on equal terms. To create such "free" and "equal" people was precisely one of the chief tasks of capitalist production. Although in the beginning this took place only in a semi-conscious manner, and in religious guise to boot, nevertheless, from the time of the Lutheran and Calvinistic Reformation it became a firm principle that a person was completely responsible for his actions only if he possessed full freedom of the will when performing them, and that it was an ethical duty to resist all compulsion to commit unethical acts. But how does this fit in with the previous practice of matrimony? According to bourgeois conceptions, matrimony was a contract, a legal affair, indeed the most important of all, since it disposed of the body and mind of two persons for life. True enough, formally the bargain was struck voluntarily; it was not done without the consent of the parties; but how this consent was obtained, and who really arranged the marriage was known only too well. But if real freedom to decide was demanded for all other contracts, why not for this one? Had not the two young people about to be paired the right freely to dispose of themselves, their bodies and its organs? Did not sex love become the fashion as a consequence of chivalry, and was not the love of husband and wife its correct bourgeois form, as against the adulterous love of the knights? But if it was the duty of married people to love each other, was it not just as much the duty of lovers to marry each other and nobody else? And did not the right of these lovers stand higher than that of parents, relatives and other traditional marriage brokers and matchmakers? If the right of free personal investigation unceremoniously forced its way into church and religion, how could it halt at the intolerable claim of the older generation to dispose of body and soul, the property, the happiness and unhappiness of the younger generation?

These questions were bound to arise in a period which loosened all the old social ties and which shook the foundations of all traditional conceptions. . . .

Thus it happened that the rising bourgeoisie, particularly in the Protestant countries, where the existing order was shaken up most of all, increasingly recognized freedom of contract for marriage also and carried it through in the manner described above. Marriage romained [*sic*] class marriage, but, within the confines of the class, the parties were accorded a certain degree of freedom of choice. And on paper, in moral theory as in poetic description, nothing was more unshakably established than that every marriage not based on mutual sex love and on the really free agreement of man and wife was immoral. In short, love marriage was proclaimed a human right; not only as man's right (*droit de l'homme*) but also, by way of exception, as woman's right (*droit de la femme*).

But in one respect this human right differed from all other so-called human rights. While, in practice, the latter remained limited to the ruling class, the bourgeoisie—the oppressed class, the proletariat, being directly or indirectly deprived of them—the irony of history asserts itself here once again. The ruling class continues to be dominated by the familiar economic influences and, therefore, only in exceptional cases can it show really voluntary marriages; whereas, as we have seen, these are the rule among the dominated class.

Thus, full freedom in marriage can become generally operative only when the abolition of capitalist production, and of the property relations created by it, has removed all those secondary economic considerations which still exert so powerful an influence on the choice of a partner. Then, no other motive remains than mutual affection.

Since sex love is by its very nature exclusive—although this exclusiveness is fully realized today only in the woman—then marriage based on sex love is by its very nature monogamy. . . .

With the disappearance of the economic considerations which compelled women to tolerate the customary infidelity of the men—the anxiety about their own livelihood and even more about the future of their children—the equality of woman thus achieved will, judging from all previous experience, result far more effectively in the men becoming really monogamous than in the women becoming polyandrous.

What will most definitely disappear from monogamy, however, is all the characteristics stamped on it in consequence of its having arisen out of property relationships. These are, first, the dominance of the man, and secondly, the indissolubility of marriage. The predominance of the man in marriage is simply a consequence of his economic predominance and will vanish with it automatically. The indissolubility of marriage is partly the result of the economic conditions under which monogamy arose, and partly a tradition from the time when the connection between these economic conditions and monogamy was not yet correctly understood and was exaggerated by religion. Today it has been breached a thousandfold. If only marriages that are based on love are moral, then, also, only those are moral in which love continues. The duration of the urge of individual sex love differs very much according to the individual, particularly among men; and a definite cessation of affection, or its displacement by a new passionate love, makes separation a blessing for both parties as well as for society. People will only be spared the experience of wading through the useless mire of divorce proceedings.

Thus, what we can conjecture at present about the regulation of sex relationships after the impending effacement of capitalist production is, in the main, of a negative character, limited mostly to what will vanish. But what will be added? That will be settled after a new generation has grown up: a generation of men who never in all their lives have had occasion to purchase a woman's surrender either with money or with any other means of social power, and of women who have never been obliged to surrender to any man out of any consideration other than that of real love, or to refrain from giving themselves to their beloved for fear of the economic consequences. Once such people appear, they will not care a rap about what we today think they should do. They will establish their own practice and their own public opinion, conformable therewith, on the practice of each individual—and that's the end of it.

—Engels, "The Origin of the Family, Private Property and the State," *MESW II*, pp. 233–41

Appendix: Civil Liberties—The Jewish Question

German Jews seek emancipation. What kind of emancipation? Civil and political emancipation.

Bruno Bauer answers them as follows: No one in Germany is politically emancipated. We non-Jews are unfree. How can we free you? You Jews are being egotists when you demand special emancipation as Jews. You should, rather, be working as Germans for the political emancipation of Germany and as men for the emancipation of mankind. You should learn to regard the peculiar form of your oppression not as an exception to, but as a confirmation of, the rule.

. . .

When the Jew demands emancipation from the Christian state, he asks that the Christian state give up its religious prejudice. Does he, the Jew, give up *his* religious prejudice? What right, therefore, has he to demand of others the abdication of their religion?

The Christian state cannot by its very nature emancipate the Jew; but, Bauer adds, the Jew cannot, by *his* very nature, be emancipated. As long as the state remains Christian and the Jew Jewish, the one is as incapable of granting emancipation as the other is of receiving it.

The Christian state can behave toward the Jew only in the manner of a Christian state, that is, in a privilege-conferring manner. It permits the separation of the Jew from its other subjects but makes him feel the pressure of the groups from which it has separated him, all the more acutely in that he represents religious opposition to the ruling religion. But the Jew, in turn, can behave toward the state only in a Jewish manner, that is, as a stranger.

. . .

How does Bauer solve the Jewish question? His formulation of the question itself contains his solution. An analysis of the Jewish question provides the answer to it. His analysis can be summarized as follows:

We must emancipate ourselves before we can emancipate others.

The stiffest form of opposition between Jew and Christian is religious. How is it to be resolved? By making it impossible. How can this be achieved? By abolishing religion. As soon as Jew and Christian recognize their respective religions as different stages in the evolution of the human spirit, as successive snakeskins shed by history—man being the snake that bore them all—they will no longer stand in a religious relationship to each other, but in a critical, scientific, human relationship. Science is their ground of unity, and contradictions in science are resolved by science itself.

. . .

Let us see how Bauer views the duty of the state.

"France," he says, "has recently offered us, with regard to the Jewish question—and with regard to all other political questions—the spectacle of a life which is free but which revokes its freedom by law, that is, it proclaims freedom a mere appearance and contradicts free law by deeds . . ."

. . .

When will the Jewish question be solved in France?

"The Jew would cease being a Jew if he stopped letting his Law prevent him fulfilling his duties toward the state and his fellow citizens—for instance, if he went to the Chamber of Deputies on the Sabbath and took part in public debates. All religious privileges, including the monopoly of a privileged church, would have to be abolished, and if a man, or some men, or the overwhelming majority of men, still believed it necessary to fulfill religious duties, such fulfillment would be left a purely private matter. . . ."

. . .

Thus Bauer asks, on the one hand, that the Jew give up Judaism, and man generally give up religion, in order to achieve political emancipation. On the other hand, he holds that the political abolition of religion means the abolition of religion as such.

. . .

The Jewish question receives a different formulation depending on the country in which the Jew finds himself. In Germany, where there is no political state as such, the Jewish question is a purely theological one. The Jew finds himself in religious opposition to a state which believes that Christianity is its basis. This state is a theologian *ex professo*. Criticism here is twofold, of both Christian and Jewish theology. And so we are still operating, however critically, in the sphere of theology.

In France, a constitutional state, the Jewish question is a constitutional one, a question of the incompleteness of political emancipation. Since France maintains the appearance of a state religion, even though by the empty and self-contradictory formula of "the religion of the majority," the relation of the Jew to the state still maintains the appearance of a religious, a theological opposition.

It is only in the free states of North America—or at least in some of them—that the Jewish question loses its theological character and becomes a truly secular one. Only where the political state exists in completely realized form can the relation of the Jew, and of the religious man generally, to the state appear in all its purity and peculiarity. Analysis of this relationship ceases to be theological as soon as the state ceases to stand in a theological relation to religion and replaces that relationship with a political one. Criticism then becomes a criticism of the political state.

. . .

. . . The question is: What is the relation of full political emancipation to religion? If we find even in the land of full political emancipation that religion not only exists, but blossoms fresh and strong, we have proof that the existence of religion is not opposed to the full development of the state. But since the existence of religion is the existence of a defect, the source of this defect can be sought only in the nature of the state. We hold that religion is no longer the operating cause but the result of human limitation. We therefore derive the religious small-mindedness of free citizens from their general small-mindedness. We do not maintain that they must abolish their religious limitations in order to abolish their human limitations. We do not turn secular human problems into religious ones; we turn religious questions into secular ones. History has too long been dissolved into superstitions: we now dissolve superstitions into history. The question of the relationship of political emancipation to religion becomes for us a question of the relationship of political emancipation to human emancipation. We criticize the religious weakness of the political state by criticizing, rather, its defective worldly constitution. We resolve the contradiction between the state and a particular religion, such as Judaism, into a contradiction between the state and certain secular elements, religion in general and the state's own assumptions.

The political emancipation of the Jew, the Christian or the religious man in general is a question of the emancipation of the state from Judaism, Christianity and religion in general. The state emancipates itself from religion, both as to form and content, by emancipating itself from any state religion—that is, by professing no religion except its own statehood. Political emancipation from religion is not emancipation from religion carried out without opposition because political emancipation is not human emancipation carried out without opposition.

The limit of political emancipation lies in the fact that the state can free itself from a limitation without its citizens becoming free from it, and that the state can be a free state without the man in it being a free man. . . .

. . . The state is the intermediary between man and his freedom. As Christ is the intermediary whom the Christian burdens with his divinity and all his religious ties, so the state is the intermediary whom man burdens with his entire non-divinity and his complete absence of ties.

The political triumph of man over religion shares all the advantages and disadvantages of political triumph generally. Thus, for example, the state annuls private property: man proclaims politically that private property is abolished as soon as he abolishes the property qualifications for the vote, as has been done in several American states. Politically speaking, Hamilton judges this fact quite correctly: "The great mass has won a victory over the owners of property and wealth." Is not private property as an idea abolished when the non-owner becomes legislator for the owner? The property qualification for the vote is the ultimate political form of the recognition of private property.

But political annulment of private property does not abolish the existence of private property; on the contrary, it necessarily assumes that existence. The state in its own way abolished differences of birth, status, education and occupation when it proclaims that these differences are nonpolitical; when it makes every member of the people without regard to such differences an equal participant in popular sovereignty; when it judges all the elements making up the actual life of the people from the point of view of the state itself. Nonetheless the state permits private property, education and occupation to continue in themselves, that is, as private property, education and occupation, and to make their particular natures felt. Far from abolishing these activities, the state exists only through assuming their existence. It recognizes itself as a political organism and makes its over-all character felt only in opposition to these, its particular elements. . . .

. . . Where the state has achieved true form, man leads a double life, not only in his thoughts and consciousness but in reality as well. It is both a heavenly and an earthly life—life in a political community, where he feels himself a member of the community, and life in bourgeois society, where he is active as a private individual, uses other men as means to an end and reduces himself to the same role of plaything of powers outside himself. Spiritually speaking, the state is to bourgeois society as heaven is to earth. It opposes it just as religion opposes and overcomes the secular world, by creating it, recognizing it, and letting itself be ruled by it. In bourgeois society man is a secular being. There, where he counts as an individual to himself and to others, he is an untrue phenomenon. In the state, however, where man counts merely as one of his kind, he is an imaginary link in an imagined chain of sovereignty, robbed of his individual life and endowed with an unreal generality.

The conflict in which man as believer in a particular religion finds himself, with his own citizenship and with other members of the community, is reduced to the secular split between the political state and bourgeois society.

. . .

Man emancipates himself from religion politically by relegating it from public to private law. It is no longer the spirit of the state, where man, in community with other men, behaves as a member of his kind, observing special forms in a special sphere. It has become the spirit of bourgeois society, of the sphere of egotism, of the *bellum omnium contra omnes*. It is no longer the essence of community but the essence of differentiation. It has become an expression of the differentiation of man from his communal nature, from himself and from other men—which was its original function. It is now only the abstract confession of a particular peculiarity, of a personal whim. The infinite splits of religion in the United States give it even the external appearance of a purely individual affair. It has been exiled from the sphere of the community as such and has been thrust among a crowd of private interests of which it is but one. But let there be no mistake about the limit of political emancipation. The splitting of man into private and public man, the dislocation of religion from the state in bourgeois society, is not a stage in political emancipation but its completion. It no more abolishes the true religiosity of man than it intends to abolish it.

• • •

The so-called Christian state is a Christian denial of the state, not in any way the political fulfillment of Christianity. The state that continues to profess Christianity as a religion does not yet profess it in political form because it still behaves religiously toward religion. This means that it is not a genuine fulfillment of the human basis of religion, because it is still the product of unreality, of the imaginary shape of the human nucleus. The so-called Christian state is the imperfect state, and it treats Christianity as a supplementation and sanctification of its imperfection. It treats religion as a means to an end and becomes thereby hypocritical. There is a great difference between a perfect state that counts religion as one of its assumptions because of a lack in the nature of the state, and an imperfect state which proclaims religion to be its very foundation because of a lack in its own make-up. In the latter case religion becomes imperfect politics; in the former the inability of religion to offer a perfect policy is immediately apparent. The so-called Christian state needs the Christian religion to complete itself as a state. The democratic state, the true state, requires no religion in order to be politically complete. It can indeed forego all religion because it achieves the human basis of religion in a worldly way. The so-called Christian state, on the other hand, behaves religiously toward politics and politically toward religion. Where it reduces the forms of politics to appearances, it likewise reduces religion to an appearance.

• • •

We have shown that political emancipation from religions permits religion to continue, though not privileged religion. The contradiction with his civil duties in which the adherent of any particular religion finds himself is merely one aspect of the general secular contradiction between the political state and bourgeois society. The perfect Christian state professes itself a state which ignores the religion of its citizens. The emancipation of the state from religion is not the emancipation of man from religion.

We do not, therefore, say to the Jews as Bauer does: "You cannot be politically emancipated unless you emancipate yourselves from Judaism." We say, rather, to them: Since you can become politically emancipated without abandoning Judaism completely, political emancipation will not bring you human emancipation. If you want to emancipate yourselves politically without emancipating yourselves humanly, the contradiction lies not merely in you; it lies also in the nature of political emancipation. If you are bound by this, then you share the general fetters. Just as the state dabbles in religion when it behaves toward the Jews in a Christian fashion, so the Jew dabbles in politics whenever he demands political rights.

. . .

Why, then, is the Jew, according to Bauer, incapable of receiving human rights? "As long as he remains a Jew, the limited nature of his Jewishness wins out over the human nature that would link him as a man to other men, and separates him from non-Jews." But the human right of liberty is not based on the link between man and man, but rather on the separation of man from man. It is the right to this separation, the right to the individual limited to himself.

. . .

None of the so-called human rights, therefore, goes beyond the egotistical man, the man who, in bourgeois society, is separated from the community and withdrawn into himself, his private interest and his private will. Man is not conceived here as a member of his species; rather, the life of the species, that is, society, is conceived as a framework imposed upon individuals, a limitation of their original independence. The only bonds that hold them together are natural necessity, private interests, the conservation of property and their egotistical desires.

It is rather curious that a people just beginning to free itself, to break down the barriers between its individual members and form a political community, should solemnly proclaim the granting of rights to egotistical man, separated from his fellow men and from his community (Declaration of 1791).

. . .

The recognition of the freedom of egotistical man, however, is the recognition of the unrestrained movement of spiritual and material elements that form its content.

Man, therefore, was not freed from his religion but received religious freedom. He was not freed from property but received freedom of property. He was not freed from professional egotism but received freedom to practice it professionally.

The constitution of the political state is the dissolution of bourgeois society into separate individuals, whose relationship is based on rights, whereas that of the men in estates and guilds was based on privilege. But man, as a member of bourgeois society, as unpolitical man, necessarily appears to be "natural man." . . . Finally, man as a member of bourgeois society counts himself truly man, *homme* as distinguished from *citoyen,* because he is man in his sensual, individual and immediate existence while political man is abstract and artificial man, man as an allegorical and moral being. Real man is recognized in the shape of the egotistical *homme,* true man in the shape of the abstract *citoyen.*

. . .

All emancipation is a reduction of the human world, of human relations, to man himself.

Political emancipation is the reduction of man, on the one hand, to the status of membership in bourgeois society, to the egotistical and independent individual, and on the other to the status of citizen, to the moral person.

Human emancipation is achieved only when the individual gives up being an abstract citizen and becomes a member of his species as individual man in his daily life and work and situation, when he recognizes and organizes his *"forces propres,"* his own strength, as part of the forces of society, which are then no longer separated from him as a political power.

—Marx, *A World Without Jews,*
pp. 1–16, 21–22, 26–28, 33–34

In *Deutsch-Französische Jahrbücher* is proved, on the contrary, that Jewry has maintained itself and developed *through* history, *in* and *with* history, and that that development is to be perceived not by the eye of the theologian, but by the eye of the man of the world, because it is to be found, not in *religious theory,* but only in *commercial* and *industrial practice.* It is explained why practical Jewry reaches perfection only in the perfection of the *Christian* world; why, indeed, it is the perfect *practice* of the *Christian world itself.* The existence of the *present-day* Jew is not explained by his religion, as though the latter were some independent being existing apart, but the survival of the Jewish religion is explained by practical factors of civil society which are *fantastically* reflected in that religion. The emancipation of the Jews to make human beings of them, or the human emancipation of Jewry, is therefore not conceived, as by Herr Bauer, as the special task of the Jews, but as the general practical task of the whole world today, which is *Jewish* to the core. It was proved that the task of abolishing the essence of Jewry is in truth the task of abolishing *Jewry in civil society,* abolishing the inhumanity of today's practice of life, the summit of which is the *money system.*

. . .

The *Jews* (like the Christians) are fully *politically emancipated* in various states. Both Jews and Christians are far from being *humanly* emancipated. Hence there must be a *difference* between *political* and *human* emancipation. The essence of *political* emancipation, i.e., of the developed, modern state, must therefore be studied. On the other hand, states which cannot yet *politically* emancipate the Jews must be rated by comparison with accomplished political states and must be considered as under-developed.

That was the point of view from which the "*political* emancipation" of the Jews should have been dealt with and is dealt with in *Deutsch-Französische Jahrbücher.*

Herr Bauer offers the following defence of "Criticism's" *Die Judenfrage:*

"The Jews were shown that they laboured under an illusion as to the *system* of which they demanded to be freed."

Herr Bauer *did* show that the illusion of the *German* Jews was to demand the right to take part in general political life in a land where there was no general political life and to demand *political rights* where only political privileges existed. On the other hand,

Herr Bauer was shown that he himself laboured under no less "illusions" as to the "German political system" than the Jews. His illusion was that he explained the position of the Jews in the German states by the alleged inability of *"the Christian state"* to emancipate the Jews politically. He argued in the teeth of facts and construed the state of *privilege,* the *Christian-German* state, as the Absolute Christian state. It was proved to him, on the contrary, that the politically perfect, modern state that knows no religious privileges is also the perfect *Christian* state, and that hence the perfect Christian state, not only *can* emancipate the Jews but has emancipated them and by its very nature must emancipate them.

"The Jews are shown . . . that they had the greatest illusions concerning themselves when they wanted to demand *freedom* and the *recognition of free humanity,* whereas for them it was only, and could only be, a question of a special *privilege.*"

Freedom! Recognition of free humanity! Special privilege! Edifying words by which certain questions can be apologetically bypassed!

Freedom? It was a matter of *political* freedom. Herr Bauer was shown that if the Jew demands freedom and nevertheless will not renounce his religion, he is *"indulging in politics"* and sets no condition contrary to *political* freedom. Herr Bauer was shown that it is by no means contrary to political emancipation to *divide* man into the non-religious *citizen* and the religious *private individual.* He was shown that as the state emancipates itself from religion by emancipating itself from *state religion* and leaving religion to itself within civil society, so the individual emancipates himself *politically* from religion when his attitude to it is no longer as to a *public* but as to a *private matter*. Finally, it was shown that the *terroristic* attitude of the French *Revolution* to *religion,* far from refuting this conception, bears it out.

Instead of studying the real attitude of the *modern* state to religion, Herr Bauer thought it necessary to imagine a *Critical* state, a state which is nothing else but the *critic of theology inflated to the size of a state* in Herr Bauer's imagination.

. . .

. . . "Free humanity" which the Jews did not just mean to aim at but really did aim at, is the same "free humanity" which found *classic* recognition in what are called the universal *Rights of Man.* Herr Bauer himself dealt with the Jews' desire for the recognition of their free humanity explicitly as the desire to obtain the universal *Rights of Man.*

In *Deutsch-Französische Jahrbücher* it was expounded to Herr Bauer that this "free humanity" and the "recognition" of it are nothing but the recognition of the *selfish civil individual* and the *uncurbed* movement of the spiritual and material elements which are the content of his life situation, the content of civil life *today;* that the *Rights of Man* do not, therefore, free man from religion but give him *freedom of religion;* that they do not free him from property, but procure for him *freedom of property;* that they do not free him from the filth of gain but give him *freedom of choice of a livelihood.*

He was shown that the *recognition of the Rights of Man* by the *modern state* means nothing more than did the *recognition of slavery* by the *state of old.* In the same way, in other words, as the state of old had slavery as its *natural basis,* the *modern state* has civil society and the *man* of civil society, i.e., the independent man depending on other men only by private interest and *unconscious* natural necessity, the slave of earning his living and his own as well as other men's *selfish* need. The modern state has recognized this as its natural basis in the *universal rights of man.* It did not create it. As it was the product of civil society driven beyond its bounds by its own development, it now recognizes the womb it was born of and its basis by the *declaration* of the *rights of man.* Hence, the *political* emancipation of the Jews and the granting to them of the *"rights of man"* is an act the two sides of which are mutually interdependent. Herr *Riesser* correctly expressed the meaning of the Jews' desire for recognition of their free humanity when he demanded, among other things, the freedom of movement, sojourn, travel, earning one's living, etc. These manifestations of *"free humanity"* are explicitly recognized as such in the French Declaration of the Rights of Man. The Jew has all the more right to the recognition of his "free humanity" as "free civil society" is thoroughly commercial and Jewish and the Jew is a necessary link in it.

. . .

Herr Bauer thinks that by the abolition of *privileges* the *object* of privilege will also be abolished. Concerning the statement of Monsieur Martin (*du Nord*) he says:

"There is no more religion when *there is no more privileged religion.* Take away from religion its exclusive force and it no longer exists."

As *industrial activity* is not abolished by the abolition of the *privileges of the trades,* guilds and corporations, but, on the contrary, real *industry* begins only after the abolition of these privileges; as *ownership of the land* is not abolished when *privileges* of land ownership are abolished, but, on the contrary, begins its universal movement with the abolition of privileges and the free division and free alienation of land; as *trade* is not abolished by the abolition of *trade privileges* but finds its true materialization in free trade; so religion develops in its *practical* universality only where there is no *privileged* religion (cf. the North American States).

The modern *"public system,"* the developed modern state, is not based, as Criticism thinks, on a society of privileges, but on a society in which *privileges are abolished* and *dissolved;* on developed *civil society* based on the vital elements which were still politically fettered in the privilege system and have been set free. Here "*no privileged exclusivity*" stands opposed either to any other exclusivity or to the public system. Free industry and free trade abolish privileged exclusivity and thereby the struggle between the privileged exclusivities. In its place they set man free from privilege—which isolates from the social whole but at the same time joins in a narrower exclusivity—man, no longer bound to other men even by the *semblance* of common ties. Thus they produce the universal struggle of man against man, individual against individual. In the same way *civil society* as a whole is this war among themselves of all those individuals no longer isolated from the others by anything else but their *individuality,* and the universal uncurbed movement of the elementary forces of life freed from the fetters of privilege. The contradiction between the *democratic representative state* and *civil society* is the perfection of the *classic* contradiction between public *commonwealth* and *slavedom*. In the modern world each one is *at the same time* a member of slavedom and of the public commonwealth. Precisely the *slavery of civil society* is in *appearance* the greatest *freedom* because it is in appearance the perfect *independence* of the individual. Indeed, the individual considers as his *own* freedom the movement, no longer curbed or fettered by a common tie or by man, the movement of his alienated life elements, like property, industry, religion, etc.; in reality, this is the perfection of his slavery and his inhumanity. *Right* has here taken the place of *privilege*.

It is therefore only here, where we find no contradiction between free theory and the practical import of privilege, but, on the contrary, the practical abolition of privilege, *free* industry, *free* trade, etc., conforming to "free theory," where the public system is *not* faced with any privileged exclusivity, where the contradiction expounded by Criticism is *abolished;* here only do *we find the accomplished modern state.*

—Marx and Engels, *The Holy Family or Critique of Critical Critique,* pp. 147–48, 149–51, 152–53, 156–57

VI

From Capitalism to Communism

Introduction

The first section of this chapter traces the capitalist economy from its origins to a prediction of its ultimate extinction. Despite the pain and suffering caused by capitalist development, writes Marx, it creates an enormous potential for wealth and well-being in the form of a huge stock of highly productive capital equipment. However, because production is for profit rather than for use, capitalism fails to make available to the great masses of people the goods it could produce. Impoverished and largely unemployed labor constitutes an inadequate market. With an inadequate market, profits fall. Without the prospect of profits, production and the accumulation of capital cease. With production immobilized and with the ownership of productive equipment in the hands of relatively few remaining monopolists, the proletariat is discontent and ripe for revolution. The dictatorship of the proletariat replaces the bourgeois state, which, after a transitional period, is replaced by true communism.

The second section, entitled "Political Upheaval," deals with the political transition to communism. Is violent revolution inevitable? The answer is that the use of force depends upon the degree of resistance to peaceful change. In democratic countries the vote makes peaceable revolution possible. Marx believed dispossessed property holders might even be compensated. In authoritarian countries, such as the Germany of Marx's day, violence would undoubtedly be necessary.

"The revolutionary dictatorship of the proletariat" emerges with the downfall of the bourgeois state. This transitional government is formed, according to Engels, by "election on the basis of universal suffrage." Officials are subject to recall by the electorate. (The model for Engels's conception of the dictatorship of the proletariat is to be found in the Paris Commune. See the Appendix to Chapter VI.)

In the third and fourth sections of this chapter, communism is seen as a solution to the twin problems of self-alienation and the exploitation of man by man, and the abolition of the private property system is the key. In Chapter II we saw that the necessity to work ("forced labor") implied a division of labor that eventually evolved into the private property and class system. Here we see the end to "forced labor." With the productive capacity of the economy fully developed under capitalism, "forced labor" is ended by seizing the means of production and operating them on a "rational" basis.

The nationalization of industry at once abolishes the division of labor, along with all its evils. There then occurs a "re-integration or return of man to himself" as a "social" *(i.e., human) being. Man's true (good) nature re-emerges. "Communism is the riddle of history solved. . . ."*

The fourth and final section of Chapter VI describes some elements of a communist society. Marx provides no blueprint of the communist social order but does show some ways, largely of an economic nature, in which it would differ from a bourgeois order. The solution to the problem of alienation—an individual and psychological matter—is optimistically achieved with a solution to economic, political, and social problems. In a communist society, without private property, the chaos of the competitive and individualistic market is replaced by overall "planning." Wage labor and exploitation cease to exist, for they serve no private gain. Class harmony replaces class conflict. With the elimination of class antagonism, bourgeois institutions change their form. The "political authority of the state dies out." The bourgeois family is reformed and religion disappears. The income that would flow "from each according to his ability . . ." would be distributed "to each according to his needs!"

●

The Decline of Capitalism

The most favorable condition for the workingman is the growth of capital. This must be admitted: when capital remains stationary, commerce and manufacture are not merely stationary but decline, and in this case the workman is the first victim. He will suffer before the capitalist. And in the case of the growth of capital, under the circumstances, which, as we have said, are the best for the workingman, what will be his lot? He will suffer just the same. The growth of capital implies the accumulation and the concentration of capital. This centralisation involves a greater division of labor and a greater use of machinery. The greater division of labor destroys the especial skill of the laborer; and by putting in the place of this skilled work labor which anyone can perform it increases competition among the workers.

This competition becomes more fierce as the division of labor enables a single man to do the work of three. Machinery accomplishes the same result on a much larger scale. The accumulation of productive capital forces the industrial capitalist to work with constantly increasing means of production, ruins the small manufacturer, and throws him into the ranks of the proletariat. Then, the rate of interest falling in proportion as capital accumulates, the people of small means and retired tradespeople, who can no longer live upon their small incomes, will be forced to look out for some business again and ultimately to swell the number of proletarians. Finally, the more productive capital grows, the more it is compelled to produce for a market whose requirements it does not know,—the more supply tries to force demand, and consequently crises increase in frequency and in intensity. But every crisis in turn hastens the concentration of capital, adds to the proletariat. Thus, as productive capital grows, competition among the workers grows too, and grows in a far greater proportion. The reward of labor is less for all, and the burden of labor is increased for at least some of them.

—Marx, *The Poverty of Philosophy*, pp. 218–19

A fall in the rate of profit and a hastening of accumulation are in so far only different expressions of the same process as both of them indicate the development of the productive power. Accumulation in its turn hastens the fall of the rate of profit, inasmuch as it implies the concentration of labor on a large scale and thereby a higher composition of capital. On the other hand, a fall in the rate of profit hastens the concentration of capital and its centralisation through the expropriation of the smaller capitalists, the expropriation of the last survivors of the direct producers who still have anything to give up. This accelerates on one hand the accumulation, so far as mass is concerned, although the rate of accumulation falls with the rate of profit.

On the other hand, so far as the rate of self-expansion of the total capital, the rate of profit, is the incentive of capitalist production (just as this self-expansion of capital is its only purpose, its fall checks the formation of new independent capitals and thus seems to threaten the development of the process of capitalist production. It promotes overproduction, speculation, crises, surplus-capital along with surplus-population. Those economists who, like Ricardo, regard the capitalist mode of production as absolute, feel nevertheless, that this mode of production creates its own limits, and therefore they attribute this limit, not to production, but to nature (in their theory of rent). But the main point in their horror over the falling rate of profit is the feeling, that capitalist production meets in the development of productive forces a barrier, which has nothing to do with the production of wealth as such; and this peculiar barrier testifies to the finiteness and the historical, merely transitory character of capitalist production. It demonstrates that this is not an absolute mode for the production of wealth, but rather comes in conflict with the further development of wealth at a certain stage.

. . .

The rate of profit, that is, the relative increment of capital, is above all important for all new offshoots of capital seeking an independent location. And as soon as the formation of capital were to fall into the hands of a few established great capitals, which are compensated by the mass of profits for the loss through a fall in the rate of profits, the vital fire of production would be extinguished. It would fall into a dormant state. The rate of profit is the compelling power of capitalist production, and only such things are produced as yield a profit. Hence the fright of the English economists over the decline of the rate of profit. That the bare possibility of such a thing should worry Ricardo, shows his profound understanding of the conditions of capitalist production. The reproach moved against him, that he has an eye only to the development of the productive forces regardless of "human beings," regardless of the sacrifices in human beings and capital *values* incurred, strikes precisely his strong point. The development of the productive forces of social labor is the historical task and privilege of capital. It is precisely in this way that it unconsciously creates the material requirements of a higher mode of production. What worries Ricardo is the fact that the rate of profit, the stimulating principle of capitalist production, the fundamental premise and driving force of accumulation, should be endangered by the development of production itself. And the quantitative proportion means everything here. There is indeed something deeper than this hidden at this point, which he vaguely feels. It is here demonstrated in a purely economic way, that is, from a bourgeois point of view, within the confines of capitalist understanding, from the standpoint of capitalist production itself, that it has a barrier, that it is relative, that it is not an absolute, but only a historical mode of production corresponding to a definite and limited epoch in the development of the material conditions of production.

—Marx, *Capital:* Vol. III, pp. 283, 304–305

And this is the economic constitution of the whole of our present-day society: it is the working class alone which produces all values. For value is only another expression for labour, that expression whereby in our present-day capitalist society is designated the amount of socially necessary labour contained in a particular commodity. These values produced by the workers do not, however, belong to the workers. They belong to the owners of the raw materials, machines, tools and the reserve funds which allow these owners to buy the labour power of the working class. From the whole mass of products produced by it, the working class, therefore, receives back only a part for itself. And as we have just seen, the other part, which the capitalist class keeps for itself and at most has to divide with the class of landowners, becomes larger with every new discovery and invention, while the part falling to the share of the working class (reckoned per head) either increases only very slowly and inconsiderably or not at all, and under certain circumstances may even fall.

But these discoveries and inventions which supersede each other at an ever-increasing rate, this productivity of human labour which rises day by day to an extent previously unheard of, finally gives rise to a conflict in which the present-day capitalist economy must perish. On the one hand are immeasurable riches and a superfluity of products which the purchasers cannot cope with; on the other hand, the great mass of society proletarianized, turned into wage-workers, and precisely for that reason made incapable of appropriating for themselves this superfluity of products. The division of society into a small, excessively rich class and a large, propertyless class of wage-workers results in a society suffocating from its own superfluity, while the great majority of its members is scarcely, or even not at all, protected from extreme want. This state of affairs becomes daily more absurd and—more unnecessary. It *must* be abolished, it *can* be abolished. A new social order is possible in which the present class differences will have disappeared and in which—perhaps after a short transitional period involving some privation, but at any rate of great value morally—through the planned utilization and extension of the already existing enormous productive forces of all members of society, and with uniform obligation to work, the means for existence, for enjoying life, for the development and employment of all bodily and mental faculties will be available in an equal measure and in ever-increasing fulness. And that the workers are becoming more and more determined to win this new social order will be demonstrated on both sides of the ocean by May the First, tomorrow, and by Sunday, May 3.

—Engels, Introduction to "Wage Labour and Capital," *MESW I*, pp. 77–78

The materialist conception of history starts from the proposition that the production of the means to support human life and, next to production, the exchange of things produced, is the basis of all social structure; that in every society that has appeared in history, the manner in which wealth is distributed and society divided into classes or orders is dependent upon what is produced, how it is produced, and how the products are exchanged. From this point of view the final causes of all social changes and political revolutions are to be sought, not in men's brains, not in man's better insight into eternal truth and justice, but in changes in the modes of production and exchange. They are to be sought not in the *philosophy*, but in the *economics* of each particular epoch. The growing perception that existing social institutions are unreasonable and unjust, that reason has become unreason and right wrong, is only proof that in the modes of production and exchange changes have silently taken place with which the social order, adapted to earlier economic conditions, is no longer in keeping. From this it also follows that the means of getting rid of the incongruities that have been brought to light must also be present, in a more or less developed condition, within the changed modes of production themselves. These means are not to be invented by deduction from fundamental principles, but are to be discovered in the stubborn facts of the existing system of production.

What is, then, the position of modern socialism in this connection?

The present structure of society—this is now pretty generally conceded—is the creation of the ruling class of today, of the bourgeoisie. The mode of production peculiar to the bourgeoisie, known, since Marx, as the capitalist mode of production, was incompatible with the feudal system, with the privileges it conferred upon individuals, entire social ranks and local corporations, as well as with the hereditary ties of subordination which constituted the framework of its social organization. The bourgeoisie broke up the feudal system and built upon its ruins the capitalist order of society, the kingdom of free competition, of personal liberty, of the equality, before the law, of all commodity owners, of all the rest of the capitalist blessings. Thenceforward the capitalist mode of production could develop in freedom. Since steam, machinery, and the making of machines by machinery transformed the older manufacture into modern industry, the productive forces evolved under the guidance of the bourgeoisie developed with a rapidity and in a degree unheard of before. But just as the older manufacture, in its time, and handicraft, becoming more developed under its influence, had come into collision with the feudal trammels of the guilds, so now modern industry, in its more complete development, comes into collision with the bounds within which the capitalistic mode of production holds it confined. The new productive forces have already outgrown the capitalistic mode of using them. And this conflict between productive forces and modes of production is not a conflict engendered in the mind of man, like that between original sin and divine justice. It exists, in fact, objectively, outside us, independently of the will and actions even of the men that have brought it on. Modern socialism is nothing but the reflex, in thought, of this conflict in fact; its ideal reflection in the minds, first, of the class directly suffering under it, the working class.

. . .

[After the mediaeval stage of evolution of the production of commodities] . . . came the concentration of the means of production and of the producers in large workshops and manufactories, their transformation into actual socialized means of production and socialized producers. But the socialized producers and means of production and their products were still treated, after this change, just as they had been before, i.e., as the means of production and the products of individuals. Hitherto, the owner of the instruments of labour had himself appropriated the product, because, as a rule, it was his own product and the assistance of others was the exception. Now the owner of the instruments of labour always appropriated to himself the product, although it was no longer *his* product but exclusively the product of the *labour of others.* Thus, the products now produced socially were not appropriated by those who had actually set in motion the means of production and actually produced the commodities, but by the *capitalists.* The means of production, and production itself, had become in essence socialized. But they were subjected to a form of appropriation which presupposes the private production of individuals, under which, therefore, everyone owns his own product and brings it to market. The mode of production is subjected to this form of appropriation, although it abolishes the conditions upon which the latter rests.[1]

This contradiction, which gives to the new mode of production its capitalistic character, *contains the germ of the whole of the social antagonisms of today.* The greater the mastery obtained by the new mode of production over all important fields of production and in all manufacturing countries, the more it reduced individual production to an insignificant residuum, *the more clearly was brought out the incompatibility of socialized production with capitalistic appropriation.*

[1] It is hardly necessary in this connection to point out that, even if the *form* of appropriation remains the same, the *character* of the appropriation is just as much revolutionized as production is by the changes described above. It is, of course, a very different matter whether I appropriate to myself my own product or that of another. Note in passing that wage-labour, which contains the whole capitalistic mode of production in embryo, is very ancient; in a sporadic, scattered form it existed for centuries alongside of slave-labour. But the embryo could duly develop into the capitalistic mode of production only when the necessary historical preconditions had been furnished [*note by Engels*].

The first capitalists found, as we have said, alongside of other forms of labour, wage-labour ready-made for them on the market. But it was exceptional, complementary, accessory, transitory wage-labour. The agricultural labourer, though, upon occasion, he hired himself out by the day, had a few acres of his own land on which he could at all events live at a pinch. The guilds were so organized that the journeyman of today became the master of tomorrow. But all this changed, as soon as the means of production became socialized and concentrated in the hands of capitalists. The means of production, as well as the product, of the individual producer became more and more worthless; there was nothing left for him but to turn wage-worker under the capitalist. Wage-labour, aforetime the exception and accessory, now became the rule and basis of all production; aforetime complementary, it now became the sole remaining function of the worker. The wage-worker for a time became a wage-worker for life. The number of these permanent wage-workers was further enormously increased by the breaking-up of the feudal system that occurred at the same time, by the disbanding of the retainers of the feudal lords, the eviction of the peasants from their homesteads, etc. The separation was made complete between the means of production concentrated in the hands of the capitalists, on the one side, and the producers, possessing nothing but their labour-power, on the other. *The contradiction between socialized production and capitalistic appropriation manifested itself as the antagonism of proletariat and bourgeoisie.*

We have seen that the capitalistic mode of production thrust its way into a society of commodity-producers, of individual producers, whose social bond was the exchange of their products. But every society based upon the production of commodities has this peculiarity: that the producers have lost control over their own social interrelations. Each man produces for himself with such means of production as he may happen to have, and for such exchange as he may require to satisfy his remaining wants. No one knows how much of his particular article is coming on the market, nor how much of it will be wanted. No one knows whether his individual product will meet an actual demand, whether he will be able to make good his costs of production or even to sell his commodity at all. Anarchy reigns in socialized production.

But the production of commodities, like every other form of production, has its peculiar, inherent laws inseparable from it; and these laws work, despite anarchy, in and through anarchy. They reveal themselves in the only persistent form of social interrelations, i.e., in exchange, and here they affect the individual producers as compulsory laws of competition. They are, at first, unknown to these producers themselves, and have to be discovered by them gradually and as the result of experience. They work themselves out, therefore, independently of the producers, and in antagonism to them, as inexorable natural laws of their particular form of production. The product governs the producers.

. . .

But with the extension of the production of commodities, and especially with the introduction of the capitalist mode of production, the laws of commodity production, hitherto latent, came into action more openly and with greater force. The old bonds were loosened, the old exclusive limits broken through, the producers were more and more turned into independent, isolated producers of commodities. It became apparent that the production of society at large was ruled by absence of plan, by accident, by anarchy; and this anarchy grew to greater and greater height. But the chief means by aid of which the capitalist mode of production intensified this anarchy of socialized production was the exact opposite of anarchy. It was the increasing organization of production, upon a social basis, in every individual productive establishment. By this, the old, peaceful, stable condition of things was ended. Wherever this organization of production was introduced into a branch of industry, it brooked no other method of production by its side. The field of labour became a battle-ground. The great geographical discoveries, and the colonization following upon them, multiplied markets and quickened the transformation of handicraft into manufacture. The war did not simply break out between the individual producers of particular localities. The local struggles begat in their turn national conflicts, the commercial wars of the seventeenth and the eighteenth centuries.

Finally, modern industry and the opening of the world market made the struggle universal, and at the same time gave it an unheard-of virulence. Advantages in natural or artificial conditions of production now decide the existence or non-existence of individual capitalists, as well as of whole industries and countries. He that falls is remorselessly cast aside. It is the Darwinian struggle of the individual for existence transferred from Nature to society with intensified violence. The conditions of existence natural to the animal appear as the final term of human development. The contradiction between socialized production and capitalistic appropriation now presents itself as *an antagonism between the organization of production in the individual workshop and the anarchy of production in society generally.*

The capitalistic mode of production moves in these two forms of the antagonism immanent to it from its very origin. It is never able to get out of that "vicious circle" which Fourier had already discovered. What Fourier could not, indeed, see in his time is that this circle is gradually narrowing; that the movement becomes more and more a spiral, and must come to an end, like the movement of the planets, by collision with the centre. It is the compelling force of anarchy in the production of society at large that more and more completely turns the great majority of men into proletarians; and it is the masses of the proletariat again who will finally put an end to anarchy in production. It is the compelling force of anarchy in social production that turns the limitless perfectibility of machinery under modern industry into a compulsory law by which every individual industrial capitalist must perfect his machinery more and more, under penalty of ruin.

But the perfecting of machinery is making human labour superfluous. If the introduction and increase of machinery means the displacement of millions of manual by a few machine-workers, improvement in machinery means the displacement of more and more of the machine-workers themselves. It means, in the last instance, the production of a number of available wage-workers in excess of the average needs of capital, the formation of a complete industrial reserve army, as I called it in 1845,[1] available at the times when industry is working at high pressure, to be cast out upon the street when the inevitable crash comes, a constant dead weight upon the limbs of the working class in its struggle for existence with capital, a regulator for the keeping of wages down to the low level that suits the interests of capital. Thus it comes about, to quote Marx, that machinery becomes the most powerful weapon in the war of capital against the working class; that the instruments of labour constantly tear the means of subsistence out of the hands of the labourer; that the very product of the worker is turned into an instrument for his subjugation. Thus it comes about that the economizing of the instruments of labour becomes at the same time, from the outset, the most reckless waste of labour power, and robbery based upon the normal conditions under which labour functions; that machinery, "the most powerful instrument for shortening labour time, becomes the most unfailing means for placing every moment of the labourer's time and that of his family at the disposal of the capitalist for the purpose of expanding the value of his capital." (*Capital,* English edition, p. 406.) Thus it comes about that the overwork of some becomes the preliminary condition for the idleness of others, and that modern industry, which hunts after new consumers over the whole world, forces the consumption of the masses at home down to a starvation minimum, and in doing thus destroys its own home market. "The law that always equilibrates the relative surplus population, or industrial reserve army, to the extent and energy of accumulation, this law rivets the labourer to capital more firmly than the wedges of Vulcan did Prometheus to the rock. It establishes an accumulation of misery, corresponding with accumulation of capital. Accumulation of wealth at one pole is, therefore, at the same time, accumulation of misery, agony of toil, slavery, ignorance, brutality, mental degradation, at the opposite pole, i.e., on the side of the class that produces *its own product in the form of capital.*" (Marx's *Capital* [Sonnenschein & Co.], p. 661.) And to expect any other division of the products from the capitalistic mode of production is the same

[1] *The Condition of the Working Class in England* (Sonnenschein & Co.), p. 84 [*note by Engels*].

as expecting the electrodes of a battery not to decompose acidulated water, not to liberate oxygen at the positive, hydrogen at the negative pole, so long as they are connected with the battery.

We have seen that the ever-increasing perfectibility of modern machinery is, by the anarchy of social production, turned into a compulsory law that forces the individual industrial capitalist always to improve his machinery, always to increase its productive force. The bare possibility of extending the field of production is transformed for him into a similar compulsory law. The enormous expansive force of modern industry, compared with which that of gases is mere child's play, appears to us now as a *necessity* for expansion, both qualitative and quantitative, that laughs at all resistance. Such resistance is offered by consumption, by sales, by the markets for the products of modern industry. But the capacity for extension, extensive and intensive, of the markets is primarily governed by quite different laws that work much less energetically. The extension of the markets cannot keep pace with the extension of production. The collision becomes inevitable, and as this cannot produce any real solution so long as it does not break in pieces the capitalist mode of production, the collisions become periodic. Capitalist production has begotten another "vicious circle."

. . .

In these crises, the contradiction between socialized production and capitalist appropriation ends in a violent explosion. The circulation of commodities is, for the time being, stopped. Money, the means of circulation, becomes a hindrance to circulation. All the laws of production and circulation of commodities are turned upside down. The economic collision has reached its apogee. *The mode of production is in rebellion against the mode of exchange.*

The fact that the socialized organization of production within the factory has developed so far that it has become incompatible with the anarchy of production in society, which exists side by side with and dominates it, is brought home to the capitalists themselves by the violent concentration of capital that occurs during crises, through the ruin of many large, and a still greater number of small, capitalists. The whole mechanism of the capitalist mode of production breaks down under the pressure of the productive forces, its own creations. It is no longer able to turn all this mass of means of production into capital. They lie fallow, and for that very reason the industrial reserve army must also lie fallow. Means of production, means of subsistence, available labourers, all the elements of production and of general wealth, are present in abundance. But "abundance becomes the source of distress and want" (Fourier), because it is the very thing that prevents the transformation of the means of production and subsistence into capital. For in capitalistic society the means of production can only function when they have undergone a preliminary transformation into capital, into the means of exploiting human labour-power. The necessity of this transformation into capital of the means of production and subsistence stands like a ghost between these and the workers. It alone prevents the coming together of the material and personal levers of production; it alone forbids the means of production to function, the workers to work and live. On the one hand, therefore, the capitalistic mode of production stands convicted of its own incapacity to further direct these productive forces. On the other, these productive forces themselves, with increasing energy, press forward to the removal of the existing contradiction, to the abolition of their quality as capital, to the *practical recognition of their character as social productive forces.*

This rebellion of the productive forces, as they grow more and more powerful, against their quality as capital, this stronger and stronger command that their social character shall be recognized, forces the capitalist class itself to treat them more and more as social productive forces, so far as this is possible under capitalist conditions. The period of industrial high pressure, with its unbounded inflation of credit, not less than the crash itself, by the collapse of great capitalist establishments, tends to bring about that form of the socialization of great masses of means of production which we meet with in the different kinds of joint-stock companies. Many of these means of production and of distribution are, from the outset, so colossal that, like the railways, they exclude all other forms of capitalistic exploitation. At a further stage of evolution this form also becomes insufficient. The producers on a large scale in a particular branch of industry in a particular country unite in a trust, a union for the purpose of regulating production. They determine the total amount to be produced, parcel it out among themselves, and thus enforce the selling price fixed before hand. But trusts of this kind, as soon as business becomes bad, are generally liable to break up, and on this very account compel a yet greater concentration of association. The whole of the particular industry is turned into one gigantic joint-stock company; internal competition gives place to the internal monopoly of this one company. This has happened in 1890 with the English alkali production, which is now, after the fusion of 48 large works, in the hands of one company, conducted upon a single plan, and with a capital of £6,000,000.

In the trusts, freedom of competition changes into its very opposite—into monopoly; and the production without any definite plan of capitalistic society capitulates to the production upon a definite plan of the invading socialistic society. Certainly this is so far still to the benefit and advantage of the capitalists. But in this case the exploitation is so palpable that it must break down. No nation will put up with production conducted by trusts, with so barefaced an exploitation of the community by a small band of dividend-mongers.

In any case, with trusts or without, the official representative of capitalist society—the state—will ultimately have to undertake the direction of production.[1] This necessity for conversion into state

[1] I say "have to." For only when the means of production and distribution have *actually* outgrown the form of management by joint-stock companies, and when, therefore, the taking them over by the state has become *economically* inevitable, only then—even if it is the state of today that effects this—is there an economic advance, the attainment of another step preliminary to the taking over of all productive forces by society itself. But of late, since Bismarck went in for state ownership of industrial establishments, a kind of spurious socialism has arisen, degenerating, now and again, into something of flunkeyism, that without more ado declares *all* state ownership, even of the Bismarckian sort, to be socialistic. Certainly, if the taking over by the state of the tobacco industry is socialistic, then Napoleon and Metternich must be numbered among the founders of socialism. If the Belgian state, for quite ordinary political and financial reasons, itself constructed its chief railway lines; if Bismarck, not under any economic compulsion, took over for the state the chief Prussian lines, simply to be the better able to have them in hand in case of war, to bring up the

property is felt first in the great institutions for intercourse and communication—the post office, the telegraphs, the railways.

If the crises demonstrate the incapacity of the bourgeoisie for managing any longer modern productive forces, the transformation of the great establishments for production and distribution into joint-stock companies, trusts and state property shows how unnecessary the bourgeoisie are for that purpose. All the social functions of the capitalist are now performed by salaried employees. The capitalist has no further social function than that of pocketing dividends, tearing off coupons, and gambling on the Stock Exchange, where the different capitalists despoil one another of their capital. At first the capitalistic mode of production forces out the workers. Now it forces out the capitalists, and reduces them, just as it reduced the workers, to the ranks of the surplus population, although not immediately into those of the industrial reserve army.

But the transformation, either into joint-stock companies and trusts, or into state ownership, does not do away with the capitalistic nature of the productive forces. In the joint-stock companies and trusts this is obvious. And the modern state, again, is only the organization that bourgeois society takes on in order to support the external conditions of the capitalist mode of production against the encroachments as well of the workers as of individual capitalists. The modern state, no matter what its form, is essentially a capitalist machine, the state of the capitalists, the ideal personification of the total national capital. The more it proceeds to the taking over of productive forces, the more does it actually become the national capitalist, the more citizens does it exploit. The workers remain wage-workers—proletarians. The capitalist relation is not done away with. It is rather brought to a head. But, brought to a head, it topples over. State ownership of the productive forces is not

railway employees as voting cattle for the government, and especially to create for himself a new source of income independent of parliamentary votes—this was, in no sense, a socialistic measure, directly or indirectly, consciously or unconsciously. Otherwise, the Royal Maritime Company, the Royal porcelain manufacture, and even the regimental tailor shops of the Army would also be socialistic institutions, or even, as was seriously proposed by a sly dog in Frederick William III's reign, the taking over by the state of the brothels [*note by Engels*].

the solution of the conflict, but concealed within it are the technical conditions that form the elements of that solution.

—Engels, "Socialism: Utopian and Scientific," *MESW II*, pp. 136–37, 139–49

Political Upheaval

An oppressed class is the vital condition of every society based upon the antagonism of classes. The emancipation of the oppressed class therefore necessarily implies the creation of a new society. In order for the oppressed class to be emancipated it is necessary that the productive powers already acquired and the existing social relations should no longer be able to exist side by side. Of all the instruments of production the greatest productive power is the revolutionary class itself. The organisation of the revolutionary elements as a class supposes the existence of all the productive forces which can be engendered in the bosom of the old society.

Is that to say that after the fall of the old society there will be a new class domination, comprised in a new political power? No.

The essential condition of the emancipation of the working class is the abolition of all classes, as the condition of the emancipation of the third estate of the bourgeois order, was the abolition of all estates, all orders.

The working class will substitute, in the course of its development, for the old order of civil society an association which will exclude classes and their antagonism, and there will no longer be political power, properly speaking, since political power is simply the official form of the antagonism in civil society.

In the meantime, the antagonism between the proletariat and the bourgeoisie is a struggle between class and class, a struggle which, carried to its highest expression, is a complete revolution. Would it, moreover, be matter for astonishment if a society, based upon the *antagonism* of classes, should lead ultimately to a brutal *conflict,* to a hand-to-hand struggle as its final *denouement?*

Do not say that the social movement excludes the political movement. There has never been a political movement which was not at the same time social.

It is only in an order of things in which there will be no longer classes or class antagonism that *social evolutions* will cease to be *political revolutions*. Until then, on the eve of each general reconstruction of society, the last word of social science will ever be:—

> "Le combat ou la mort; la lutte sanguinaire ou le neant.
> C'est ainsi que la question est invinciblement posée." *
> George Sand.

—Marx, *The Poverty of Philosophy,* pp. 189–91

The time is rapidly approaching when a thorough examination of England's economic position will impose itself as an irresistible national necessity. The working of the industrial system of this country, impossible without a constant and rapid extension of production, and therefore of markets, is coming to a dead stop. Free trade has exhausted its resources; even Manchester doubts this its quondam economic gospel.[1] Foreign industry, rapidly developing, stares English production in the face everywhere, not only in protected, but also in neutral markets, and even on this side of the Channel. While the productive power increases in a geometric, the extension of markets proceeds at best in an arithmetic ratio. The decennial cycle of stagnation, prosperity, over-production and crisis, ever recurrent from 1825 to 1867, seems indeed to have run its course; but only to land us in the slough of despond of a perma-

* Combat or death; bloody struggle or extinction.
It is thus that the question is irresistibly put.

[1] At the quarterly meeting of the Manchester Chamber of Commerce, held this afternoon, a warm discussion took place on the subject of Free Trade. A resolution was moved to the effect that "having waited in vain 40 years for other nations to follow the Free Trade example of England, this Chamber thinks the time has now arrived to reconsider that position." The resolution was rejected by a majority of one only, the figures being 21 for, and 22 against.—*Evening Standard,* Nov. 1, 1886.

nent and chronic depression. The sighed-for period of prosperity will not come; as often as we seem to perceive its heralding symptoms, so often do they again vanish into air. Meanwhile, each succeeding winter brings up afresh the great question, "what to do with the unemployed"; but while the number of the unemployed keeps swelling from year to year, there is nobody to answer that question; and we can almost calculate the moment when the unemployed, losing patience, will take their own fate into their own hands. Surely, at such a moment, the voice ought to be heard of a man whose whole theory is the result of a life-long study of the economic history and condition of England, and whom that study led to the conclusion that, at least in Europe, England is the only country where the inevitable social revolution might be effected entirely by peaceful and legal means. He certainly never forgot to add that he hardly expected the English ruling classes to submit, without a "pro-slavery rebellion," to this peaceful and legal revolution.

FREDERICK ENGELS.

November 5, 1886.

—Engels, *Capital:* Editor's Preface to Vol. I, pp. 31–32

Force is the midwife of every old society pregnant with a new one. It is itself an economic power.

—Marx, *Capital:* Vol. I, p. 824

. . . The German workers rendered a second great service to their cause in addition to the first, a service performed by their mere existence as the strongest, best disciplined and most rapidly growing Socialist Party. They supplied their comrades in all countries with a new weapon, and one of the sharpest, when they showed them how to make use of universal suffrage.

There had long been universal suffrage in France, but it had fallen into disrepute through the misuse to which the Bonapartist government had put it. After the Commune there was no workers' party to make use of it. It also existed in Spain since the republic, but in Spain boycott of elections was ever the rule of all serious opposition parties. The experience of the Swiss with universal suffrage was also anything but encouraging for a workers' party. The revolutionary workers of the Latin countries had been wont to regard the suffrage as a snare, as an instrument of government trickery. It was otherwise in Germany. The *Communist Manifesto* had already proclaimed the winning of universal suffrage, of democracy, as one of the first and most important tasks of the militant proletariat, and Lassalle had again taken up this point. Now, when Bismarck found himself compelled to introduce this franchise as the only means of interesting the mass of the people in his plans, our workers immediately took it in earnest and sent August Bebel to the first, constituent Reichstag. And from that day on, they have used the franchise in a way which has paid them a thousandfold and has served as a model to the workers of all countries. The franchise has been, in the words of the French Marxist programme, *transforme, de moyen de duperie qu'il a été jusqu'ici, en instrument d'emancipation*—transformed by them from a means of deception, which it was before, into an instrument of emancipation. And if universal suffrage had offered no other advantage than that it allowed us to count our numbers every three years; that by the regularly established, unexpectedly rapid rise in the number of our votes it increased in equal measure the workers' certainty of victory and the dismay of their opponents, and so became our best means of propaganda; that it accurately informed us concerning our own strength and that of all hostile parties, and thereby provided us with a measure of proportion for our actions second to none, safeguarding us from untimely timidity as much as from untimely foolhardiness—if this had been the only advantage we gained from the suffrage, it would still have been much more than enough. But it did more than this by far. In election agitation it provided us with a means, second to none, of getting in touch with the mass of the people where they still stand aloof from us; of forcing all parties to defend their views and actions against our attacks before all the people; and, further, it provided our representatives in the Reichstag with a platform from which they could speak to their opponents in parliament, and to the masses without, with quite other authority and freedom than in the press or at meetings. Of what avail was their Anti-Socialist Law to the government and the bourgeoisie when election campaigning and socialist speeches in the Reichstag continually broke through it?

With this successful utilization of universal suffrage, however, an entirely new method of proletarian struggle came into operation, and this method quickly developed further. It was found that the state institutions, in which the rule of the bourgeoisie is organized, offer the working class still further opportunities to fight these very state institutions. The workers took part in elections to particular Diets, to municipal councils and to trades courts; they contested with the bourgeoisie every post in the occupation of which a sufficient part of the proletariat had a say. And so it happened that the bourgeoisie and the government came to be much more afraid of the legal than of the illegal action of the workers' party, of the results of elections than of those of rebellion.

For here, too, the conditions of the struggle had essentially changed. Rebellion in the old style, street fighting with barricades, which decided the issue everywhere up to 1848, was to a considerable extent obsolete.

Let us have no illusions about it: a real victory of an insurrection over the military in street fighting, a victory as between two armies, is one of the rarest exceptions. And the insurgents counted on it just as rarely. For them it was solely a question of making the troops yield to moral influences which, in a fight between the armies of two warring countries, do not come into play at all or do so to a much smaller extent. If they succeed in this, the troops fail to respond, or the commanding officers lose their heads, and the insurrection wins. If they do not succeed in this, then, even where the military are in the minority, the superiority of better equipment and training, of single leadership, of the planned employment of the military forces and of discipline makes itself felt. The most that an insurrection can achieve in the way of actual tactical operations is the proper construction and defence of a single barricade. Mutual support, the disposition and employment of reserves—in short, concerted and co-ordinated action of the individual detachments, indispensable even for the defence of one section of a town, not to speak of the whole of a large town, will be attainable only to a very limited extent, and most of the time not at all.

. . .

Of course, our foreign comrades do not thereby in the least renounce their right to revolution. The right to revolution is, after all, the only *really* "historical right," the only right on which all modern states without exception rest, . . .

—Engels, Introduction to "The Class Struggles in France 1848–1850," *MESW I*, pp. 128–31, 135

. . . the present legal conditions in Germany are suddenly supposed to suffice for the party to carry out all its demands in a peaceful way. One tells oneself and the party, "today's social order evolves into socialism," without asking oneself whether it therefore does not equally necessarily evolve out of its old social order and does not have to break this old shell just as forcefully as the crab breaks it, as if in Germany it would besides not have to break the chains of a political order that is still half absolute, and on top of that unbelievably confused. One can imagine that the old social order could evolve peacefully into the new in countries in which the people's representation concentrates all power within itself, where according to the constitution one can do what one wishes as soon as one has the majority of the people behind oneself; in democratic republics like France and America, in monarchies like England, where the imminent buying off of the dynasty is discussed daily in the press, and where this dynasty is powerless against the popular will. But to proclaim something like this in Germany, and without any need at that, where the government is almost omnipotent and the Reichstag and all other representative bodies are without real power, means to take the fig leaf off absolutism and to tie it to one's own nakedness.

—Engels, "Zur Kritik des sozialdemokratischen Programmentwurfes 1891" (Toward a Critique of the Social Democratic Program Draft 1891), *Die Neue Zeit*, XX, No. 1, p. 10

We have the economic certainty that the large and intermediate size farmer must inevitably succumb to the competition of the capitalistic enterprise and cheap transoceanic grain production, as the growing indebtedness and generally evident decline of these farmers proves. We can do nothing against this decline except to recommend here also the merger of the farms into cooperative enterprises in which the exploitation of wage labor is abolished more and more, and in which the gradual transformation into branches of the great national productive cooperative, with equal rights and equal responsibilities, can be begun. Once the farmers see the inevitability of the elimination of their present methods of production, once they draw the necessary consequences therefrom, they will come to us, and it will be our duty insofar as it is in our power to ease for them too the transition to the altered method of production. Otherwise we must leave them to their fate and turn to their hired workers, from whom we shall for the rest be able to rely on the fact that the economic development will also make these thick skulls more responsive to reason. The matter is truly uncomplicated only with the great estates. Here we have undisguised capitalistic enterprise, and in such a case no scruples of any case count. Here we have before us masses of agricultural proletarians, and our task is clear. As soon as our party is in possession of the power of the state, it will simply have to expropriate the large estate owners, just like the industrial manufacturers. Whether this expropriation takes place with or without compensation will for the most part depend not on us but on the circumstances in which we come into the possession of power, and notably also on the attitude of the gentlemen great land owners themselves. We do not necessarily under all circumstances consider compensation as inadmissible; Marx has—how very often!—expressed his opinion to me, that we would come off most cheaply if we could buy out the whole gang. But that does not concern us here. The large estates thereby given back to the public we would have to leave to the agricultural laborers, who are to be organized into cooperatives and who are already farming them, for use under the control of the public. Under what modality, about that nothing can yet be ascertained. In any case the transition of the capitalistic enterprise into a public one is here already completely prepared for and can be carried out overnight, just as for instance with Mr. Krupp's or Mr. von Stumm's factory. And the example of these agricultural cooperatives would convince even the last resisting small farmers, and perhaps some large farmers too, of the advantages of the cooperative large enterprise.

—Engels, "Die Bauernfrage in Frankreich und Deutschland" (The Farm Problem in France and Germany), *Die Neue Zeit,* XIII, No. 1, 304–305

Against this transformation of the state and the organs of the state from servants of society into masters of society—an inevitable transformation in all previous states—the Commune made use of two infallible means. In the first place, it filled all posts—administrative, judicial and educational—by election on the basis of universal suffrage of all concerned, subject to the right of recall at any time by the same electors. And, in the second place, all officials, high or low, were paid only the wages received by other workers. The highest salary paid by the Commune to anyone was 6,000 francs. In this way an effective barrier to place-hunting and careerism was set up, even apart from the binding mandates to delegates to representative bodies which were added besides.

This shattering (*Sprengung*) of the former state power and its replacement by a new and truly democratic one is described in detail in the third section of *The Civil War*. But it was necessary to dwell briefly here once more on some of its features, because in Germany particularly the superstitious belief in the state has been carried over from philosophy into the general consciousness of the bourgeoisie and even of many workers. According to the philosophical conception, the state is the "realization of the idea," or the Kingdom of God on earth, translated into philosophical terms, the sphere in which eternal truth and justice is or should be realized. And from this follows a superstitious reverence for the state and everything connected with it, which takes root the more readily since people are accustomed from childhood to imagine that the affairs and interests common to the whole of society could not be looked after otherwise than as they have been looked after in the past, that is, through the state and its lucratively positioned officials. And people think they have taken quite an extraordinarily bold step forward when they have rid themselves of belief in hereditary monarchy and swear by the democratic republic. In reality, however, the state is nothing but a machine for the oppression of one class by another, and indeed in the democratic republic no less than in the monarchy; and at best an evil inherited by the proletariat after its victorious struggle for class supremacy, whose worst sides the victorious proletariat, just like the Commune, cannot avoid having to lop off at once as much as possible until such time as a generation reared in new, free social conditions is able to throw the entire lumber of the state on the scrap heap.

Of late, the Social-Democratic philistine has once more been filled with wholesome terror at the words: Dictatorship of the Proletariat. Well and good, gentlemen, do you want to know what this dictatorship looks like? Look at the Paris Commune. That was the Dictatorship of the Proletariat.

—Engels, Introduction to "The Civil War in France," *MESW I*, p. 484–85

. . . no credit is due to me for discovering the existence of classes in modern society or the struggle between them. Long before me bourgeois historians had described the historical development of this class struggle and bourgeois economists the economic anatomy of the classes. What I did that was new was to prove: 1) that the *existence of classes* is only bound up with *particular historical phases in the development of production,* 2) that the class struggle necessarily leads to the *dictatorship of the proletariat,* 3) that this dictatorship itself only constitutes the transition to the *abolition of all classes* and to a *classless society*.

—Letter from Marx to J. Weydemeyer (March 5, 1852), *Selected Correspondence,* p. 86

Between capitalist and communist society lies the period of the revolutionary transformation of the one into the other. There corresponds to this also a political transition period in which the state can be nothing but *the revolutionary dictatorship of the proletariat.*

—Marx, "Critique of the Gotha Programme," *MESW II,* p. 32–33

First. If anything at all is certain it is that our party and the working class can come to power only under the form of the democratic republic. This is even the specific form for the dictatorship of the proletariat, as the great French revolution has already demonstrated. It is certainly unthinkable that our best people should become ministers under an emperor, like Miquel.

Now it does not seem legally possible that one puts the demand for a republic directly into the program, although that was as possible even under Louis Philippe in France as it now is in Italy. But the fact that one may not even draw up an openly republican party program in Germany proves how colossal the illusion is, as if one could in a comfortable peaceful way there establish the republic, and not only the republic but the communist social order.

—Engels, "Zur Kritik des sozialdemokratischen Programmentwurfes 1891" (Toward a Critique of the Social Democratic Program Draft 1891), *op. cit.*, p. 11

Communism as a Solution to Alienation

(PRIVATE PROPERTY AND COMMUNISM. VARIOUS STAGES OF DEVELOPMENT OF COMMUNIST VIEWS. CRUDE, EQUALITARIAN COMMUNISM AND COMMUNISM AS SOCIALISM COINCIDING WITH HUMANENESS)

Re. p. XXXIX. The antithesis of *propertylessness* and *property,* so long as it is not comprehended as the antithesis of *labour* and *capital,* still remains an antithesis of indifference, not grasped in its *active connection,* its *internal* relation—an antithesis not yet grasped as a *contradiction.* It can find expression in this *first* form even without the advanced development of private property (as in ancient Rome, Turkey, etc.). It does not yet *appear* as having been established by private property itself. But labour, the subjective essence of private property as exclusion of property, and capital, objective labour as exclusion of labour, constitute *private property* as its developed state of contradiction—hence a dynamic relationship moving inexorably to its resolution.

Re. the same page. The transcendence of self-estrangement follows the same course as self-estrangement. *Private property* is first considered only in its objective aspect—but nevertheless with labour as its essence. Its form of existence is therefore *capital,* which is to be annulled "as such" (Proudhon). Or a *particular form* of labour—labour levelled down, parcelled, and therefore unfree—is conceived as the source of private property's *perniciousness* and of its existence in estrangement from men; for instance, *Fourier,* who, like the physiocrats, also conceived *agricultural labour* to be at least the *exemplary* type, whilst *Saint-Simon* declares in contrast that *industrial labour* as such is the essence, and now also aspires to the *exclusive* rule of the industrialists and the improvement of the workers' condition. Finally, *communism* is the *positive* expression of annulled private property—at first as *universal* private property. By embracing this relation as a *whole,* communism is:

(1) In its first form only a *generalisation* and *consummation* of this relationship. It shows itself as such in a twofold form: on the one hand, the dominion of *material* property bulks so large that it wants to destroy *everything* which is not capable of being possessed by all as *private property.* It wants to abstract *by force* from talent, etc. For it the sole purpose of life and existence is direct, physical *possession.* The category of *labourer* is not done away with, but extended to all men. The relationship of private property persists as the relationship of the community to the world of things. Finally, this movement of counterposing universal private property to private property finds expression in the bestial form of counterposing to *marriage* (certainly a *form of exclusive private property*) the *community of women,* in which a woman becomes a piece of *communal* and *common* property. It may be said that this idea of the

community of women gives away the *secret* of this as yet completely crude and thoughtless communism. Just as the woman passes from marriage to general prostitution,[1] so the entire world of wealth (that is, of man's objective substance) passes from the relationship of exclusive marriage with the owner of private property to a state of universal prostitution with the community. In negating the *personality* of man in every sphere, this type of communism is really nothing but the logical expression of private property, which is this negation. General *envy* constituting itself as a power is the disguise in which *avarice* re-establishes itself and satisfies itself, only in *another* way. The thoughts of every piece of private property—inherent in each piece as such—are *at least* turned against all *wealthier* private property in the form of envy and the urge to reduce to a common level, so that this envy and urge even constitute the essence of competition. The crude communism is only the consummation of this envy and of this levelling-down proceeding from the *preconceived* minimum. It has a *definite, limited* standard. How little this annulment of private property is really an appropriation is in fact proved by the abstract negation of the entire world of culture and civilisation, the regression to the *unnatural* simplicity of the *poor and undemanding* man who has not only failed to go beyond private property, but has not yet even attained to it.

The community is only a community of *labour,* and an equality of *wages* paid out by the communal capital—the *community* as the universal capitalist. Both sides of the relationship are raised to an *imagined* universality—*labour* as a state in which every person is put, and *capital* as the acknowledged universality and power of the community.

In the approach to *woman* as the spoil and handmaid of communal lust is expressed the infinite degradation in which man exists for himself, for the secret of this approach has its *unambiguous,* decisive, *plain* and undisguised expression in the relation of *man* to *woman* and in the manner in which the *direct* and *natural* procre-

[1] Prostitution is only a *specific* expression of the *general* prostitution of the *labourer,* and since it is a relationship in which not the prostitute alone, but also the one who prostitutes, fall—and the latter's abomination is still greater—the capitalist, etc., also comes under this head.

ative relationship is conceived. The direct, natural, and necessary relation of person to person is the *relation of man to woman.* In this *natural* relationship of the sexes man's relation to nature is immediately his relation to man, just as his relation to man is immediately his relation to nature—his own *natural* function. In this relationship, therefore, is *sensuously manifested,* reduced to an observable *fact,* the extent to which the human essence has become nature to man, or to which nature has to him become the human essence of man. From this relationship one can therefore judge man's whole level of development. It follows from the character of this relationship how much *man* as a *species being,* as *man,* has come to be himself and to comprehend himself; the relation of man to woman is *the most natural* relation of human being to human being. It therefore reveals the extent to which man's *natural* behavior has become *human,* or the extent to which the *human* essence in him has become a *natural* essence—the extent to which his *human nature* has come to be *nature to him.* In this relationship is revealed, too, the extent to which man's *need* has become a *human* need; the extent to which, therefore, the *other* person as a person has become for him a need—the extent to which he in his individual existence is at the same time a social being. The first positive annulment of private property—*crude* communism—is thus merely one *form* in which the vileness of private property, which wants to set itself up as the *positive community, comes to the surface.*

(2) Communism (α) of a political nature still—democratic or despotic; (β) with the annulment of the state, yet still incomplete, and being still affected by private property (i.e., by the estrangement of man). In both forms communism already knows itself to be re-integration or return of man to himself, the transcendence of human self-estrangement; but since it has not yet grasped the positive essence of private property, and just as little the *human* nature of need, it remains captive to it and infected by it. It has, indeed, grasped its concept, but not its essence.

(3) *Communism* as the *positive* transcendence of *private property,* as *human self-estrangement,* and therefore as the real *appropriation of the human* essence by and for man; communism therefore as the complete return of man to himself as a *social* (i.e., human)

being—a return become conscious, and accomplished within the entire wealth of previous development. This communism, as fully-developed naturalism, equals humanism, and as fully-developed humanism equals naturalism; it is the *genuine* resolution of the conflict between man and nature and between man and man—the true resolution of the strife between existence and essence, between objectification and self-confirmation, between freedom and necessity, between the individual and the species. Communism is the riddle of history solved, and it knows itself to be this solution.

The entire movement of history is, therefore, both its *actual* act of genesis (the birth act of its empirical existence) and also for its thinking consciousness the *comprehended* and *known* process of its *coming-to-be*. That other, still immature communism, meanwhile, seeks an *historical* proof for itself—a proof in the realm of the existent—amongst disconnected historical phenomena opposed to private property, tearing single phases from the historical process and focusing attention on them as proofs of its historical pedigree (a horse ridden hard especially by Cabet, Villegardelle, etc.). By so doing it simply makes clear that by far the greater part of this process contradicts its claims, and that, if it has once been, precisely its being in the *past* refutes its pretension to being *essential.*

That the entire revolutionary movement necessarily finds both its empirical and its theoretical basis in the movement of *private property*—in that of the economy, to be precise—is easy to see.

This *material,* immediately *sensuous* private property is the material sensuous expression of *estranged human* life. Its movement—production and consumption—is the *sensuous* revelation of the movement of all production hitherto—i.e., the realisation or the reality of man. Religion, family, state, law, morality, science, art, etc., are only *particular* modes of production, and fall under its general law. The positive transcendence of *private property* as the appropriation of *human* life is, therefore, the positive transcendence of all estrangement—that is to say, the return of man from religion, family, state, etc., to his *human,* i.e., *social* mode of existence. Religious estrangement as such occurs only in the realm of *consciousness,* of man's inner life, but economic estrangement is that of *real life;* its transcendence therefore embraces both aspects. It is evident that the *initial* stage of the movement amongst the various peoples depends on whether the true and for them *authentic* life of the people manifests itself more in consciousness or in the external world—is more ideal or real. Communism begins from the outset (*Owen*) with atheism; but atheism is at first far from being *communism;* indeed, it is still mostly an abstraction.

The philanthropy of atheism is therefore at first only *philosophical,* abstract, philanthropy, and that of communism is at once *real* and directly bent on *action.*

We have seen how on the premise of positively annulled private property man produces man—himself and the other man; how the object, being the direct embodiment of his individuality, is simultaneously his own existence for the other man, the existence of the other man, and that existence for him. Likewise, however, both the material of labour and man as the subject, are the point of departure as well as the result of the movement (and precisely in this fact, that they must constitute the *point of departure,* lies the historical *necessity* of private property). Thus the *social* character is the general character of the whole movement: *just as* society itself produces *man as man,* so is society *produced* by him. Activity and consumption, both in their content and in their *mode of existence,* are *social: social* activity and *social* consumption; the *human* essence of nature first exists only for *social* man; for only here does nature exist for him as a *bond* with *man*—as his existence for the other and the other's existence for him—as the life-element of the human world; only here does nature exist as the *foundation* of his own *human* existence. Only here has what is to him his *natural* existence become his *human* existence, and nature become man for him. Thus *society* is the consummated oneness in substance of man and nature—the true resurrection of nature—the naturalism of man and the humanism of nature both brought to fulfillment.

Social activity and social consumption exist by no means *only* in the form of some *directly* communal activity and directly *communal* consumption, although *communal* activity and *communal* consumption—i.e., activity and consumption which are manifested and directly confirmed in *real association* with other men—will occur wherever such a *direct* expression of sociality stems from the true character of the activity's content and is adequate to the nature of consumption.

But again when I am active *scientifically,* etc.,—when I am engaged in activity which I can seldom perform in direct community with others—then I am *social,* because I am active as a *man.* Not only is the material of my activity given to me as a social product (as is even the language in which the thinker is active): my *own* existence *is* social activity, and therefore that which I make of myself, I make of myself for society and with the consciousness of myself as a social being.

My *general* consciousness is only the *theoretical* shape of that of which the *living* shape is the *real* community, the social fabric, although at the present day *general* consciousness is an abstraction from real life and as such antagonistically confronts it. Consequently, too, the *activity* of my general consciousness, as an activity, is my *theoretical* existence as a social being.

What is to be avoided above all is the re-establishing of "Society" as an abstraction *vis-à-vis* the individual. The individual is *the social being.* His life, even if it may not appear in the direct form of a *communal* life carried out together with others—is therefore an expression and confirmation of *social life.* Man's individual and species life are not *different,* however much—and this is inevitable—the mode of existence of the individual is a more *particular,* or more *general* mode of the life of the species, or the life of the species is a more *particular* or more *general* individual life.

In his *consciousness of species* man confirms his real *social life* and simply repeats his real existence in thought, just as conversely the being of the species confirms itself in species-consciousness and is for *itself* in its generality as a thinking being.

Man, much as he may therefore be a *particular* individual (and it is precisely his particularity which makes him an individual, and a real *individual* social being), is just as much the *totality*—the ideal totality—the subjective existence of thought and experienced society present for itself; just as he exists also in the real world as the awareness and the real enjoyment of social existence, and as a totality of human life-activity.

Thinking and being are thus no doubt *distinct,* but at the same time they are in *unity* with each other.

Death seems to be a harsh victory of the species over the *definite* individual and to contradict their unity. But the determinate individual is only a *determinate species being,* and as such mortal.

(4) Just as *private property* is only the sensuous expression of the fact that man becomes *objective* for himself and at the same time becomes to himself a strange and inhuman object; just as it expresses the fact that the assertion of his life is the alienation of his life, that his realisation is his loss of reality, is an *alien* reality: conversely, the positive transcendence of private property—i.e., the *sensuous* appropriation for and by man of the human essence and of human life, of objective man, of human *achievements*—is not to be conceived merely in the sense of *direct,* one-sided *gratification*—merely in the sense of *possessing,* of *having.* Man appropriates his total essence in a total manner, that is to say, as a whole man. Each of his *human* relations to the world—seeing, hearing, smelling, tasting, feeling, thinking, being aware, sensing, wanting, acting, loving—in short, all the organs of his individual being, like those organs which are directly social in their form, are in their *objective* orientation or in their *orientation to the object,* the appropriation of that object, the appropriation of the *human* world; their orientation to the object is the *manifestation of the human world;*[1] it is human *efficaciousness* and human *suffering,* for suffering, apprehended humanly, is an enjoyment of self in man.

Private property has made us so stupid and one-sided that an object is only *ours* when we have it—when it exists for us as capital, or when it is directly possessed, eaten, drunk, worn, inhabited, etc., —in short, when it is *used* by us. Although private property itself again conceives all these direct realisations of possession as *means of life,* and the life which they serve as means is the *life of private property*—labour and conversion into capital.

In place of *all* these physical and mental senses there has therefore come the sheer estrangement of *all* these senses—the sense of

[1] For this reason it is just as highly varied as the *determinations* of human *essence* and *activities.*

having. The human being had to be reduced to this absolute poverty in order that he might yield his inner wealth to the outer world. (On the category of *"having,"* see Hess in the *Twenty-One Sheets.*)

The transcendence of private property is therefore the complete *emancipation* of all human senses and attributes; but it is this emancipation precisely because these senses and attributes have become, subjectively and objectively, *human.* The eye has become a *human* eye, just as its *object* has become a social, *human* object—an object emanating from man for man. The *senses* have therefore become directly in their practice theoreticians. They relate themselves to the *thing* for the sake of the thing, but the thing itself is an *objective human* relation to itself and to man,[1] and vice versa. Need or enjoyment have consequently lost their *egotistical* nature, and nature has lost its mere *utility* by use becoming *human* use.

In the same way, the senses and enjoyments of other men have become my *own* appropriation. Besides these direct organs, therefore, social organs develop in the *form* of society; thus, for instance, activity in direct association with others, etc., has become an organ for *expressing* my own *life,* and a mode of appropriating *human* life.

It is obvious that the *human* eye gratifies itself in a way different from the crude, non-human eye; the human *ear* different from the crude ear, etc.

To recapitulate; man is not lost in his object only when the object becomes for him a *human* object or objective man. This is possible only when the object becomes for him a *social* object, he himself for himself a social being, just as society becomes a being for him in this object.

On the one hand, therefore, it is only when the objective world becomes everywhere for man in society the world of man's essential powers—human reality, and for that reason the reality of his *own* essential powers—that all *objects* become for him the *objectification of himself,* become objects which confirm and realise his individuality, become *his* objects: that is, *man himself* becomes the object. The manner in which they become *his* depends on the *nature of the objects* and on the nature of the *essential power* correspond-

[1] In practice I can relate myself to a thing humanly only if the thing relates itself to the human being humanly.

ing *to it;* for it is precisely the *determinateness* of this relationship which shapes the particular, *real* mode of affirmation. To the *eye* an object comes to be other than it is to the *ear,* and the object of the eye is another object than the object of the *ear.* The peculiarity of each essential power is precisely its *peculiar essence,* and therefore also the peculiar mode of its objectification, of its *objectively actual* living *being.* Thus man is affirmed in the objective world not only in the act of thinking, but with *all* his senses.

On the other hand, looking at this in its subjective aspect: just as music alone awakens in man the sense of music, and just as the most beautiful music has *no* sense for the unmusical ear—is no object for it, because my object can only be the confirmation of one of my essential powers and can therefore only be so for me as my essential power is present for itself as a subjective capacity, because the sense of an object for me goes only so far as *my* senses go (has only sense for a sense corresponding to that object)—for this reason the *senses* of the social man are *other* senses than those of the non-social man. Only through the objectively unfolded richness of man's essential being is the richness of subjective *human* sensibility (a musical ear, an eye for beauty of form—in short, *senses* capable of human gratifications, senses confirming themselves as essential powers of *man*) either cultivated or brought into being. For not only the five senses but also the so-called mental senses—the practical senses (will, love, etc.)—in a word, *human* sense—the humanness of the senses—comes to be by virtue of its object, by virtue of *humanised* nature. The *forming* of the five senses is a labour of the entire history of the world down to the present.

The *sense* caught up in crude practical need has only a *restricted* sense. For the starving man, it is not the human form of food that exists, but only its abstract being as food; it could just as well be there in its crudest form, and it would be impossible to say wherein this feeding-activity differs from that of *animals.* The care-burdened man in need has no sense for the finest play; the dealer in minerals sees only the mercantile value but not the beauty and the unique nature of the mineral: he has no mineralogical sense. Thus, the objectification of the human essence both in its theoretical and practical aspects is required to make man's *sense human,* as well as to create the *human sense* corresponding to the entire wealth of human and natural substance.

Just as resulting from the movement of *private property,* of its wealth as well as its poverty—or of its material and spiritual wealth and poverty—the budding society finds to hand all the material for this *development:* so *established* society produces man in this entire richness of his being—produces the *rich* man *profoundly endowed with all the senses*—as its enduring reality.

It will be seen how subjectivism and objectivism, spiritualism and materialism, activity and suffering, only lose their antithetical character, and thus their existence, as such antitheses in the social condition; it will be seen how the resolution of the *theoretical* antitheses is *only* possible *in a practical* way, by virtue of the practical energy of man. Their resolution is therefore by no means merely a problem of knowledge, but a *real* problem of life, which *philosophy* could not solve precisely because it conceived this problem as *merely* a theoretical one.

It will be seen how the history of *industry* and the established *objective* existence of industry are the *open* book of *man's essential powers,* the exposure to the senses of human *psychology*. Hitherto this was not conceived in its inseparable connection with man's *essential being,* but only in an external relation of utility, because, moving in the realm of estrangement, people could only think man's general mode of being—religion or history in its abstract-general character as politics, art, literature, etc.,—to be the reality of man's essential powers and *man's species-activity*. We have before us the *objectified essential powers* of man in the form of *sensuous, alien, useful objects,* in the form of estrangement, displayed in *ordinary material industry* (which can be conceived as a part of that general movement, just as that movement can be conceived as a particular part of industry, since all human activity hitherto has been labour—that is, industry—activity estranged from itself).

A *psychology* for which this, the part of history most contemporary and accessible to sense, remains a closed book, cannot become a genuine, comprehensive and *real* science. What indeed are we to think of a science which *airily* abstracts from this large part of human labour and which fails to feel its own incompleteness, while such a wealth of human endeavour unfolded before it means nothing more to it than, perhaps, what can be expressed in one word—*"need," "vulgar need"*?

The *natural sciences* have developed an enormous activity and have accumulated a constantly growing mass of material. Philosophy, however, has remained just as alien to them as they remain to philosophy. Their momentary unity was only a *chimerical illusion.* The will was there, but the means were lacking. Even historiography pays regard to natural science only occasionally, as a factor of enlightenment and utility arising from individual great discoveries. But natural science has invaded and transformed human life all the more *practically* through the medium of industry; and has prepared human emancipation, however directly and much it had to consummate dehumanisation. *Industry* is the *actual,* historical relation of nature, and therefore of natural science, to man. If, therefore, industry is conceived as the *exoteric* revelation of man's *essential powers,* we also gain an understanding of the ***human*** essence of nature or the *natural* essence of man. In consequence, natural science will lose its abstractly material—or rather, its idealistic—tendency, and will become the basis of *human* science, as it has already become the basis of actual human life, albeit in an estranged form. *One* basis for life and another basis for *science* is *a priori* a lie. The nature which comes to be in human history—the genesis of human society—is man's *real* nature; hence nature as it comes to be through industry, even though in an *estranged* form, is true *anthropological* nature.

Sense-perception (see Feuerbach) must be the basis of all science. Only when it proceeds from sense-perception in the twofold form both of *sensuous* consciousness and of *sensuous* need—that is, only when science proceeds from nature—is it *true* science. All history is the preparation for *"man"* to become the object of *sensuous* consciousness, and for the needs of "man as man" to become [natural, sensuous] needs. History itself is a *real* part of *natural history*—of nature's coming to be man. Natural science will in time subsume under itself the science of man, just as the science of man will subsume under itself natural science: there will be *one* science.

Man is the immediate object of natural science: for immediate, *sensuous nature* for man is, immediately, human sensuousness (the expressions are identical)—presented immediately in the form of the *other* man sensuously present for him. For his own sensuousness first exists as human sensuousness for himself through the *other* man. But *nature* is the immediate object of the *science of man:* the first object of man—man—is nature, sensuousness; and the particular human sensuous essential powers can only find their self-knowledge in the science of the natural world in general, since they can find their objective realisation in *natural* objects only. The element of thought itself—the element of thought's living expression—*language*—is of a sensuous nature. The *social* reality of nature, and *human* natural science, or the *natural science about man,* are identical terms.

It will be seen how in place of the *wealth* and *poverty* of political economy come the *rich human being* and rich *human* need. The *rich* human being is simultaneously the human being *in need of* a totality of human life-activities—the man in whom his own realisation exists as an inner necessity, as *need.* Not only *wealth,* but likewise the *poverty* of man—given socialism—receives in equal measure a *human* and therefore social significance. Poverty is the passive bond which causes the human being to experience the need of the greatest wealth—the *other* human being. The dominion of the objective being in me, the sensuous outburst of my essential activity, is *emotion,* which thus becomes here the *activity* of my being.

(5) A *being* only considers himself independent when he stands on his own feet; and he only stands on his own feet when he owes his *existence* to himself. A man who lives by the grace of another regards himself as a dependent being. But I live completely by the grace of another if I owe him not only the sustenance of my life, but if he has, moreover, *created* my *life*—if he is the *source* of my life; and if it is not of my own creation, my life has necessarily a source of this kind outside it. The *Creation* is therefore an idea very difficult to dislodge from popular consciousness. The self-

mediated being of nature and of man is *incomprehensible* to it, because it contradicts everything *palpable* in practical life.

The creation of the *earth* has received a mighty blow from *geogeny*—i.e., from the science which presents the formation of the earth, the coming-to-be of the earth, as a process, as self-generation. *Generatio aequivoca* is the only practical refutation of the theory of creation.

Now it is certainly easy to say to the single individual what Aristotle has already said. You have been begotten by your father and your mother; therefore in you the mating of two human beings —a species-act of human beings—has produced the human being. You see, therefore, that even physically, man owes his existence to man. Therefore you must not only keep sight of the *one* aspect—the *infinite* progression which leads you further to enquire: "Who begot my father? Who his grandfather?", etc. You must also hold on to the *circular movement* sensuously perceptible in that progression, by which *man* repeats himself in procreation, thus always remaining the subject. You will reply, however: I grant you this circular movement; now grant me the progression which drives me ever further until I ask: Who begot the first man, and nature as a whole? I can only answer you: Your question is itself a product of abstraction. Ask yourself how you arrived at that question. Ask yourself whether your question is not posed from a standpoint to which I cannot reply, because it is a perverse one. Ask yourself whether that progression as such exists for a reasonable mind. When you ask about the creation of nature and man, you are abstracting, in so doing, from man and nature. You postulate them as *non-existent,* and yet you want me to prove them to you as *existing.* Now I say to you: Give up your abstraction and you will also give up your question. Or if you want to hold on to your abstraction, then be consistent, and if you think of man and nature as *non-existent,* then think of yourself as non-existent, for you too are surely nature and man. Don't think, don't ask me, for as soon as you think and ask, your *abstraction* from the existence of nature and man has no meaning. Or are you such an egoist that you postulate everything as nothing, and yet want yourself to be?

You can reply: I do not want to postulate the nothingness of nature. I ask you about *its genesis,* just as I ask the anatomist about the formation of bones, etc.

But since for the socialist man the *entire so-called history of the world* is nothing but the begetting of man through human labour, nothing but the coming-to-be of nature for man, he has the visible, irrefutable proof of his *birth* through himself, of his *process of coming-to-be.* Since the *real existence* of man and nature has become practical, sensuous and perceptible—since man has become for man as the being of nature, and nature for man as the being of man—the question about an *alien* being, about a being above nature and man—a question which implies the admission of the inessentiality of nature and of man—has become impossible in practice. *Atheism,* as the denial of this inessentiality, has no longer any meaning, for atheism is a *negation of God,* and postulates the *existence of man* through this negation; but socialism as socialism no longer stands in any need of such a mediation. It proceeds from the *practically and theoretically sensuous consciousness* of man and of nature as the *essence.* Socialism is man's *positive self-consciousness,* no longer mediated through the annulment of religion, just as *real life* is man's positive reality, no longer mediated through the annulment of private property, through *communism. Communism* is the position as the negation of the negation, and is hence the *actual* phase necessary for the next stage of historical development in the process of human emancipation and recovery. Communism is the necessary pattern and the dynamic principle of the immediate future, but communism as such[1] is not the goal of human development—the structure of human society.

—Marx, *Economic and Philosophic Manuscripts of 1844,* pp. 98–114

. . . In fact, the realm of freedom does not commence until the point is passed where labor under the compulsion of necessity and

[1] Under "communism as such" Marx here means crude, equalitarian communism, such as propounded by Babeuf and his followers.—Ed.

of external utility is required. In the very nature of things it lies beyond the sphere of material production in the strict meaning of the term. Just as the savage must wrestle with nature, in order to satisfy his wants, in order to maintain his life and reproduce it, so civilized man has to do it, and he must do it in all forms of society and under all possible modes of production. With his development the realm of natural necessity expands, because his wants increase; but at the same time the forces of production increase, by which these wants are satisfied. The freedom in this field cannot consist of anything else but of the fact that socialized man, the associated producers, regulate their interchange with nature rationally, bring it under their common control, instead of being ruled by it as by some blind power; that they accomplish their task with the least expenditure of energy and under conditions most adequate to their human nature and most worthy of it. But it always remains a realm of necessity. Beyond it begins that development of human power, which is its own end, the true realm of freedom, which, however, can flourish only upon that realm of necessity as its basis. . . .

—Marx, *Capital:* Vol. III, pp. 954–55

. . . the division of labour offers us the first example of how, as long as man remains in natural society, that is as long as a cleavage exists between the particular and the common interest, as long therefore as activity is not voluntarily, but naturally, divided, man's own deed becomes an alien power opposed to him, which enslaves him instead of being controlled by him. For as soon as labour is distributed, each man has a particular, exclusive sphere of activity, which is forced upon him and from which he cannot escape. He is a hunter, a fisherman, a shepherd, or a critical critic, and must remain so if he does not want to lose his means of livelihood; while in communist society, where nobody has one exclusive sphere of activity but each can become accomplished in any branch he wishes, society regulates the general production and thus makes it possible for me to do one thing to-day and another to-morrow, to hunt in the morning, fish in the afternoon, rear cattle in the evening, criticize after dinner, just as I have a mind, without ever becoming hunter, fisherman, shepherd or critic.

. . .

This "estrangement" (to use a term which will be comprehensible to the philosophers) can, of course, only be abolished given two *practical* premises. For it to become an "intolerable" power, i.e., a power against which men make a revolution, it must necessarily have rendered the great mass of humanity "propertyless," and produced, at the same time, the contradiction of an existing world of wealth and culture, both of which conditions presuppose a great increase in productive power, a high degree of its development. And, on the other hand, this development of productive forces (which itself implies the actual empirical existence of men in their *world-historical,* instead of local, being) is absolutely necessary as a practical premise: firstly, for the reason that without it only *want* is made general, and with want the struggle for necessities and all the old filthy business would necessarily be reproduced; and secondly, because only with this universal development of productive forces is a *universal* intercourse between men established, which produces in all nations simultaneously the phenomenon of the "propertyless" mass (universal competition), makes each nation dependent on the revolutions of the others, and finally has put *world-historical,* empirically universal individuals in place of local ones.

. . .

. . . it is just as empirically established that, by the overthrow of the existing state of society by the communist revolution (of which more below) and the abolition of private property which is identical with it, this power, which so baffles the German theoreticians, will be dissolved; and that then the liberation of each single individual will be accomplished in the measure in which history becomes transformed into world-history. From the above it is clear that the real intellectual wealth of the individual depends entirely on the wealth of his real connections. Only then will the separate individuals be liberated from the various national and local barriers, be brought into practical connection with the material and intellectual production of the whole world and be put in a position to acquire the capacity to enjoy this all-sided production of the whole earth (the creations of man). Universal dependence, this natural form of the world-historical co-operation of individuals, will be transformed by this communist revolution into the control and conscious mastery of these powers, which, born of the action of men on one another, have till now overawed and governed men as powers completely alien to them. . . .

—Marx and Engels, *The German Ideology*, pp. 22, 24–25, 27–28

The Communist State

Let us briefly sum up our sketch of historical evolution.

I. *Mediaeval Society*—Individual production on a small scale. Means of production adapted for individual use; hence primitive, ungainly, petty, dwarfed in action. Production for immediate consumption, either of the producer himself or of his feudal lord. Only where an excess of production over this consumption occurs is such excess offered for sale, enters into exchange. Production of commodities, therefore, only in its infancy. But already it contains within itself, in embryo, *anarchy in the production of society at large*.

II. *Capitalist Revolution*—Transformation of industry, at first by means of simple co-operation and manufacture. Concentration of the means of production, hitherto scattered, into great workshops. As a consequence, their transformation from individual to social means of production—a transformation which does not, on the whole, affect the form of exchange. The old forms of appropriation remain in force. The capitalist appears. In his capacity as owner of the means of production, he also appropriates the products and turns them into commodities. Production has become a *social* act. Exchange and appropriation continue to be *individual* acts, the acts of individuals. *The social product is appropriated by the individual capitalist.* Fundamental contradiction, whence arise all the contradictions in which our present-day society moves, and which modern industry brings to light.

A. Severance of the producer from the means of production. Condemnation of the worker to wage-labour for life. *Antagonism between the proletariat and the bourgeoisie.*

B. Growing predominance and increasing effectiveness of the laws governing the production of commodities. Unbridled competition. *Contradiction between socialized organization in the individual factory and social anarchy in production as a whole.*

C. On the one hand, perfecting of machinery, made by competition compulsory for each individual manufacturer, and complemented by a constantly growing displacement of labourers. *Industrial reserve army.* On the other hand, unlimited extension of production, also compulsory under competition, for every manufacturer. On both sides, unheard-of development of productive forces, excess of supply over demand, over-production, glutting of the markets, crises every ten years, the vicious circle: excess here, of means of production and products—excess there, of labourers, without employment and without means of existence. But these two levers of production and of social well-being are unable to work together, because the capitalist form of production prevents the productive forces from working and the products from circulating, unless they are first turned into capital—which their very superabundance prevents. The contradiction has grown into an absurdity. *The mode of production rises in rebellion against the form of exchange.* The bourgeoisie are convicted of incapacity further to manage their own social productive forces.

D. Partial recognition of the social character of the productive forces forced upon the capitalists themselves. Taking over of the great institutions for production and communication, first by joint-stock companies, later on by trusts, then by the state. The bourgeoisie demonstrated to be a superfluous class. All its social functions are now performed by salaried employees.

III. *Proletarian Revolution*—Solution of the contradictions. The proletariat seizes the public power, and by means of this transforms the socialized means of production, slipping from the hands of the bourgeoisie, into public property. By this act, the proletariat frees the means of production from the character of capital they have thus far borne, and gives their socialized character complete freedom to work itself out. Socialized production upon a predetermined plan becomes henceforth possible. The development of production makes the existence of different classes of society thenceforth an anachronism. In proportion as anarchy in social production vanishes, the political authority of the state dies out. Man, at last the master of his own form of social organization, becomes at the same time the lord over Nature, his own master—free.

To accomplish this act of universal emancipation is the historical mission of the modern proletariat. To thoroughly comprehend the historical conditions and thus the very nature of this act, to impart to the now oppressed proletarian class a full knowledge of the conditions and of the meaning of the momentous act it is called upon to accomplish, this is the task of the theoretical expression of the proletarian movement, scientific socialism.

—Engels, "Socialism: Utopian and Scientific," *MESW II,* pp. 154–55

. . . (Only when production will be under the conscious and prearranged control of society, will society establish a direct relation between the quantity of social labor time employed in the production of definite articles and the quantity of the demand of society for them.) The commodities must then be sold below their market-value, and a portion of them may even become unsaleable. The opposite takes place, if the quantity of social labor employed in the production of a certain kind of commodities is too small to meet the social demand for them. But if quantity of social labor spent in the production of a certain article corresponds to the social demand for it, so that the quantity produced is that which is the ordinary on that scale of production and for that same demand, then the article is sold at its market-value. The exchange, or sale, of commodities at their value is the rational way, the natural law of their equilibrium.

. . .

The general rule in differential rent is that the market-value always stands above the total price of production of the mass of products. For instance, take Table I. The ten quarters of the total product are sold at 600 shillings, because the market price is determined by the price of production of A, which amounts to 60 shillings per quarter. But the actual price of production is:

A	1 qr. = 60 sh.	1 qr. = 60 sh.
B	2 qrs. = 60 sh.	1 qr. = 30 sh.
C	3 qrs. = 60 sh.	1 qr. = 20 sh.
D	4 qrs. = 60 sh.	1 qr. = 15 sh.
	10 qrs. = 240 sh.	Average 1 qr. = 24 sh.

The actual price of production of these 10 quarters is 240 shillings. But they are sold at 600 shillings, 250% too dear. The actual average price for 1 quarter is 24 shillings; the market price is 60 shillings, also 250% too dear.

This is a determination by the market-value, which is enforced on the basis of capitalist production by means of competition; it creates a false social value. This arises from the law of the market-value, to which the products of the soil are subject. The determination of the market-value of the products, including the products of the soil, is a social act, although performed by society unconsciously and unintentionally. It rests necessarily upon the exchange-value of the product, not upon the soil and its differences in fertility.

If we imagine that the capitalistic form of society is abolished and society is organized as a conscious and systematic association, then those 10 quarters represent a quantity of independent labor, which is equal to that contained in 240 shillings. In that case society would not buy this product of the soil at two and a half times the labor time contained in it. The basis of a class of land owners would thus be destroyed. This would have the same effect as a cheapening of the product to the same amount by foreign imports. While it is correct to say that, by retaining the present mode of production but paying the differential rent to the state, the prices of the products of the soil would remain the same, other circumstances remaining unchanged, it is wrong to say that the value of the products would remain the same, if capitalist production were superseded by association. The sameness of the market prices for commodities of the same kind is the way in which the social character of value asserts itself on the basis of capitalist production, as it does of any production resting on the exchange of commodities between individuals. What society in its capacity as a consumer pays too much for the products of the soil, what constitutes a minus for the realisation of its labor time in agricultural production, is now a plus for a portion of society, for the landlords.

—Marx, *Capital:* Vol. III, pp. 221, 773–74

. . . In the case of socialized production, the money-capital is eliminated. Society distributes labor-power and means of production to the different lines of occupation. The producers may eventually receive paper checks, by means of which they withdraw from the social supply of means of consumption a share corresponding to their labor-time. These checks are not money. They do not circulate.

—Marx, *Capital:* Vol. II, p. 412

Let us now picture to ourselves, by way of change, a community of free individuals, carrying on their work with the means of production in common, in which the labour-power of all the different individuals is consciously applied as the combined labour-power of the community. All the characteristics of Robinson's labour are here repeated, but with this difference, that they are social, instead of individual. Everything produced by him was exclusively the result of his own personal labour, and therefore simply an object of use for himself. The total product of our community is a social product. One portion serves as fresh means of production and remains social. But another portion is consumed by the members as means of subsistence. A distribution of this portion amongst them is consequently necessary. The mode of this distribution will vary with the productive organization of the community, and the degree of historical development attained by the producers. We will assume, but merely for the sake of a parallel with the production of commodities, that the share of each individual producer in the means of subsistence is determined by his labour-time. Labour-time would, in that case, play a double part. Its apportionment in accordance with a definite social plan maintains the proper proportion between the different kinds of work to be done and the various wants of the community. On the other hand, it also serves as a measure of the portion of the common labour borne by each individual and of his share in the part of the total product destined for individual consumption. The social relations of the individual producers, with regard both to their labour and to its products, are in this case perfectly simple and intelligible, and that with regard not only to production but also to distribution.

—Marx, *Capital:* Vol. I, pp. 90–91

> 3. "The emancipation of labour demands the promotion of the instruments of labour to the common property of society and the co-operative regulation of the total labour with a fair distribution of the proceeds of labour."

"Promotion of the instruments of labour to the common property" ought obviously to read their "conversion into the common property"; but this only in passing.

What are the "proceeds of labour"? The product of labour or its value? And in the latter case, is it the total value of the product or only that part of the value which labour has newly added to the value of the means of production consumed?

"Proceeds of labour" is a loose notion which Lassalle has put in the place of definite economic conceptions.

What is "a fair distribution"?

Do not the bourgeois assert that the present-day distribution is "fair"? And is it not, in fact, the only "fair" distribution on the basis of the present-day mode of production? Are economic relations regulated by legal conceptions or do not, on the contrary, legal relations arise from economic ones? Have not also the socialist sectarians the most varied notions about "fair" distribution?

To understand what is implied in this connection by the phrase "fair distribution," we must take the first paragraph and this one together. The latter presupposes a society wherein "the instruments of labour are common property and the total labour is cooperatively regulated," and from the first paragraph we learn that "the proceeds of labour belong undiminished with equal right to all members of society."

"To all members of society"? To those who do not work as well? What remains then of the "undiminished proceeds of labour"? Only to those members of society who work? What remains then of the "equal right" of all members of society?

But "all members of society" and "equal right" are obviously mere phrases. The kernel consists in this, that in this communist society every worker must receive the "undiminished" Lassallean "proceeds of labour."

Let us take first of all the words "proceeds of labour" in the sense of the product of labour; then the co-operative proceeds of labour are the *total social product.*

From this must now be deducted:

First, cover for replacement of the means of production used up.

Secondly, additional portion for expansion of production.

Thirdly, reserve or insurance funds to provide against accidents, dislocations caused by natural calamities, etc.

These deductions from the "undiminished proceeds of labour" are an economic necessity and their magnitude is to be determined according to available means and forces, and partly by computation of probabilities, but they are in no way calculable by equity.

There remains the other part of the total product, intended to serve as means of consumption.

Before this is divided among the individuals, there has to be deducted again, from it:

First, the general costs of administration not belonging to production.

This part will, from the outset, be very considerably restricted in comparision with present-day society and it diminishes in proportion as the new society develops.

Secondly, that which is intended for the common satisfaction of needs, such as schools, health services, etc.

From the outset this part grows considerably in comparison with present-day society and it grows in proportion as the new society develops.

Thirdly, funds for those unable to work, etc., in short, for what is included under so-called official poor relief today.

Only now do we come to the "distribution" which the programme, under Lassallean influence, alone has in view in its narrow fashion, namely, to that part of the means of consumption which is divided among the individual producers of the cooperative society.

The "undiminished proceeds of labour" have already unnoticeably become converted into the "diminished" proceeds, although what the producer is deprived of in his capacity as a private individual benefits him directly or indirectly in his capacity as a member of society.

Just as the phrase of the "undiminished proceeds of labour" has disappeared, so now does the phrase of the "proceeds of labour" disappear altogether.

Within the co-operative society based on common ownership of the means of production, the producers do not exchange their products; just as little does the labour employed on the products appear here *as the value* of these products, as a material quality possessed by them, since now, in contrast to capitalist society, individual labour no longer exists in an indirect fashion but directly as a component part of the total labour. The phrase "proceeds of labour," objectionable also today on account of its ambiguity, thus loses all meaning.

What we have to deal with here is a communist society, not as it has *developed* on its own foundations, but, on the contrary, just as it *emerges* from capitalist society; which is thus in every respect, economically, morally and intellectually, still stamped with the birth marks of the old society from whose womb it emerges. Accordingly, the individual producer receives back from society—after the deductions have been made—exactly what he gives to it. What he has given to it is his individual quantum of labour. For example, the social working day consists of the sum of the individual hours of work; the individual labour time of the individual producer is the part of the social working day contributed by him, his share in it. He receives a certificate from society that he has furnished such and such an amount of labour (after deducting his labour for the common funds), and with this certificate he draws from the social stock of means of consumption as much as costs the same amount of labour. The same amount of labour which he has given to society in one form he receives back in another.

Here obviously the same principle prevails as that which regulates the exchange of commodities, as far as this is exchange of equal values. Content and form are changed, because under the altered circumstances no one can give anything except his labour, and because, on the other hand, nothing can pass to the ownership of individuals except individual means of consumption. But, as far as the distribution of the latter among the individual producers is concerned, the same principle prevails as in the exchange of commodity-equivalents: a given amount of labour in one form is exchanged for an equal amount of labour in another form.

Hence, *equal right* here is still in principle—*bourgeois right,* although principle and practice are no longer at loggerheads, while the exchange of equivalents in commodity exchange only exists *on the average* and not in the individual case.

In spite of this advance, this *equal right* is still constantly stigmatized by a bourgeois limitation. The right of the producers is *proportional* to the labour they supply; the equality consists in the fact that measurement is made with an *equal standard,* labour.

But one man is superior to another physically or mentally and so supplies more labour in the same time, or can labour for a longer time; and labour, to serve as a measure, must be defined by its duration or intensity, otherwise it ceases to be a standard of measurement. This *equal* right is an unequal right for unequal labour. It recognizes no class differences, because everyone is only a worker like everyone else; but it tacitly recognizes unequal individual endowment and thus productive capacity as natural privileges. *It is, therefore, a right of inequality, in its content, like every right.* Right by its very nature can consist only in the application of an equal standard; but unequal individuals (and they would not be different individuals if they were not unequal) are measurable only by an equal standard in so far as they are brought under an equal point of view, are taken from one *definite* side only, for instance, in the present case, are regarded *only as workers* and nothing more is seen in them, everything else being ignored. Further, one worker is married, another not; one has more children than another, and so on and so forth. Thus, with an equal performance of labour, and hence an equal share in the social consumption fund, one will in fact receive more than another, one will be richer than another, and so on. To avoid all these defects, right instead of being equal would have to be unequal.

But these defects are inevitable in the first phase of communist society as it is when it has just emerged after prolonged birth pangs from capitalist society. Right can never be higher than the economic structure of society and its cultural development conditioned thereby.

In a higher phase of communist society, after the enslaving subordination of the individual to the division of labour, and therewith also the antithesis between mental and physical labour, has vanished; after labour has become not only a means of life but life's prime want; after the productive forces have also increased with the all-round development of the individual, and all the springs of co-operative wealth flow more abundantly—only then can the narrow horizon of bourgeois right be crossed in its entirety and society inscribe on its banners: From each according to his ability, to each according to his needs!

—Marx, "Critique of the Gotha Programme," *MESW II,* pp. 21–24

The intensity and productiveness of labour being given, the time which society is bound to devote to material production is shorter, and as a consequence, the time at its disposal for the free development, intellectual and social, of the individual is greater, in proportion as the work is more and more evenly divided among all the able-bodied members of society, and as a particular class is more and more deprived of the power to shift the natural burden of labour from its own shoulders to those of another layer of society.

—Marx, *Capital:* Vol. I, p. 581

For socialism, which wants to emancipate human labour-power from its status of a *commodity,* the realization that labour has no value and can have none is of great importance. With this realization all attempts—inherited by Herr Duhring from primitive workers' socialism—to regulate the future distribution of the necessaries of life as a kind of higher wages fall to the ground. And from it comes the further realization that distribution, in so far as it is governed by purely economic considerations, will be regulated by the interests of production, and that production is most encouraged by a mode of distribution which allows *all* members of society to develop, maintain and exercise their capacities with maximum universality. It is true that, to the mode of thought of the educated classes which Herr Duhring has inherited, it must seem monstrous that in time to come there will no longer be any professional porters or architects, and that the man who for half an hour gives instructions as an architect will also act as a porter for a period, until his activity as an architect is once again required. A fine sort of socialism that would be—perpetuating professional porters!

. . .

How then are we to solve the whole important question of the higher wages paid for compound labor? In a society of private producers, private individuals or their families pay the costs of training the qualified worker; hence the higher price paid for qualified labour-power accrues first of all to private individuals; the skilful slave is sold for a higher price, and the skilful wage-earner is paid higher wages. In a socialistically organized society, these costs are borne by society, and to it therefore belong the fruits, the greater values produced by compound labour. The worker himself has no claim to extra pay. And from this, incidentally, follows the moral that at times there is a drawback to the popular demand of the workers for "the full proceeds of labour."

. . .

In making itself the master of all the means of production to use them in accordance with a social plan, society puts an end to the former subjection of men to their own means of production. It goes without saying that society cannot free itself unless every individual is freed. The old mode of production must therefore be revolutionized from top to bottom, and in particular the former division of labour must disappear. Its place must be taken by an organization of production in which, on the one hand, no individual can throw on the shoulders of others his share in productive labour, this natural condition of human existence; and in which, on the other hand, productive labour, instead of being a means of subjugating men, will become a means of their emancipation, by offering each individual the opportunity to develop all his faculties, physical and mental, in all directions and exercise them to the full—in which, therefore, productive labour will become a pleasure instead of being a burden.

Today this is no longer a fantasy, no longer a pious wish. With the present development of the productive forces, the increase in production that will follow from the very fact of the socialization of the productive forces, coupled with the abolition of the barriers and disturbances, and of the waste of products and means of production, resulting from the capitalist mode of production, will suffice, with everybody doing his share of work, to reduce the time required for labour to a point which, measured by our present conceptions, will be small indeed.

Nor is the abolition of the old division of labour a demand which could only be carried through to the detriment of the productivity of labour. On the contrary. Thanks to modern industry it has become a condition of production itself. "The employment of machinery does away with the necessity of crystallizing this distribution after the manner of Manufacture, by the constant annexation of a particular man to a particular function. Since the motion of the whole system does not proceed from the workman, but from the machinery, a change of persons can take place at any time without an interruption of the work. . . . Lastly, the quickness with which machine-work is learnt by young people, does away with the necessity of bringing up for exclusive employment by machinery, a special class of operatives." [1] But while the capitalist mode of employment of machinery necessarily perpetuates the old division of labour with its fossilized specialization, although it has become superfluous from a technical standpoint, the machinery itself rebels against this anachronism. The technical basis of modern industry is revolutionary. "By means of machinery, chemical processes and other methods, it is continually causing changes not only in the technical basis of production, but also in the functions

[1] *Capital,* Vol. I, Moscow 1954, p. 421.

of the labourer, and in the social combinations of the labour process. At the same time, it thereby also revolutionizes the division of labour within the society, and incessantly launches masses of capital and of workpeople from one branch of production to another. Modern industry, by its very nature, therefore necessitates variation of labour, fluency of function, universal mobility of the labourer. . . ." [2]

. . .

Once more, only the abolition of the capitalist character of modern industry can bring us out of this new vicious circle, can resolve this contradiction in modern industry, which is constantly reproducing itself. Only a society which makes it possible for its productive forces to dovetail harmoniously into each other on the basis of one single vast plan can allow industry to be distributed over the whole country in the way best adapted to its own development, and to the maintenance and development of the other elements of production.

Accordingly, abolition of the antithesis between town and country is not merely possible. It has become a direct necessity of industrial production itself, just as it has become a necessity of agricultural production and, besides, of public health. The present poisoning of the air, water and land can be put an end to only by the fusion of town and country; and only such fusion will change the situation of the masses now languishing in the towns, and enable their excrement to be used for the production of plants instead of for the production of disease.

. . .

The abolition of the separation of town and country is therefore not utopian, also, in so far as it is conditioned on the most equal distribution possible of modern industry over the whole country. It is true that in the huge towns civilization has bequeathed us a heritage which it will take much time and trouble to get rid of. But it must and will be got rid of, however protected a process it may be. Whatever destiny may be in store for the German Empire

[2] *Capital,* Vol. I, Moscow 1954, pp. 487–488.

of the Prussian nation, Bismarck can go to his grave proudly aware that the desire of his heart is sure to be fulfilled: the great towns will perish.

—Engels, *Anti-Dühring,* pp. 277–79, 407–409, 411, 412

This solution can only consist in the practical recognition of the social nature of the modern forces of production, and therefore in the harmonizing of the modes of production, appropriation, and exchange with the socialized character of the means of production. And this can only come about by society openly and directly taking possession of the productive forces which have outgrown all control except that of society as a whole. The social character of the means of production and of the products today reacts against the producers, periodically disrupts all production and exchange, acts only like a law of Nature working blindly, forcibly, destructively. But with the taking over by society of the productive forces, the social character of the means of production and of the products will be utilized by the producers with a perfect understanding of its nature, and instead of being a source of disturbance and periodical collapse, will become the most powerful lever of production itself.

Active social forces work exactly like natural forces: blindly, forcibly, destructively, so long as we do not understand, and reckon with, them. But when once we understand them, when once we grasp their action, their direction, their effects, it depends only upon ourselves to subject them more and more to our own will, and by means of them to reach our own ends. And this holds quite especially of the mighty productive forces of today. As long as we obstinately refuse to understand the nature and the character of these social means of action—and this understanding goes against the grain of the capitalist mode of production and its defenders—so long these forces are at work in spite of us, in opposition to us, so long they master us, as we have shown above in detail.

But when once their nature is understood, they can, in the hands of the producers working together, be transformed from master demons into willing servants. The difference is as that between the destructive force of electricity in the lightning of the storm, and electricity under command in the telegraph and the voltaic arc; the difference between a conflagration, and fire working in the service of man. With this recognition, at last, of the real nature of the productive forces of today, the social anarchy of production gives place to a social regulation of production upon a definite plan, according to the needs of the community and of each individual. Then the capitalist mode of appropriation, in which the product enslaves first the producer and then the appropriator, is replaced by the mode of appropriation of the products that is based upon the nature of the modern means of production; upon the one hand, direct social appropriation, as means to the maintenance and extension of production—on the other, direct individual appropriation, as means of subsistence and of enjoyment.

Whilst the capitalist mode of production more and more completely transforms the great majority of the population into proletarians, it creates the power which, under penalty of its own destruction, is forced to accomplish this revolution. Whilst it forces on more and more the transformation of the vast means of production, already socialized, into state property, it shows itself the way to accomplishing this revolution. *The proletariat seizes political power and turns the means of production into state property.*

But, in doing this, it abolishes itself as proletariat, abolishes all class distinctions and class antagonisms, abolishes also the state as state. Society thus far, based upon class antagonisms, had need of the state. That is, of an organization of the particular class which was *pro tempore* the exploiting class, an organization for the purpose of preventing any interference from without with the existing conditions of production, and, therefore, especially, for the purpose of forcibly keeping the exploited classes in the condition of oppression corresponding with the given mode of production (slavery, serfdom, wage-labour). The state was the official representative of society as a whole; the gathering of it together into a visible embodiment. But it was this only in so far as it was the state of that class which itself represented, for the time being, society as a whole: in ancient times, the state of slaveowning citizens; in the

Middle Ages, the feudal lords; in our own time, the bourgeoisie. When at last it becomes the real representative of the whole of society, it renders itself unnecessary. As soon as there is no longer any social class to be held in subjection; as soon as class rule, and the individual struggle for existence based upon our present anarchy in production, with the collisions and excesses arising from these, are removed, nothing more remains to be repressed, and a special repressive force, a state, is no longer necessary. The first act by virtue of which the state really constitutes itself the representative of the whole of society—the taking possession of the means of production in the name of society—this is, at the same time, its last independent act as a state. State interference in social relations becomes, in one domain after another, superfluous, and then dies out of itself; the government of persons is replaced by the administration of things, and by the conduct of processes of production. The state is not "abolished." *It dies out.* This gives the measure of the value of the phrase *"a free state,"* both as to its justifiable use at times by agitators, and as to its ultimate scientific insufficiency; and also of the demands of the so-called anarchists for the abolition of the state out of hand.

Since the historical appearance of the capitalist mode of production, the appropriation by society of all the means of production has often been dreamed of, more or less vaguely, by individuals, as well as by sects, as the ideal of the future. But it could become possible, could become a historical necessity, only when the actual conditions for its realization were there. Like every other social advance, it becomes practicable, not by men understanding that the existence of classes is in contradiction to justice, equality, etc., not by the mere willingness to abolish these classes, but by virtue of certain new economic conditions. The separation of society into an exploiting and an exploited class, a ruling and an oppressed class, was the necessary consequence of the deficient and restricted development of production in former times. So long as the total social labour only yields a produce which but slightly exceeds that barely necessary for the existence of all; so long, therefore, as labour engages all or almost all the time of the great majority of the members of society—so long, of necessity, this society is divided into classes. Side by side with the great majority, exclusively bond slaves to labour, arises a class freed from directly productive labour, which looks after the general affairs of society: the direction of labour, state business, law, science, art, etc. It is, therefore, the law of division of labour that lies at the basis of the division into classes. But this does not prevent this division into classes from being carried out by means of violence and robbery, trickery and fraud. It does not prevent the ruling class, once having the upper hand, from consolidating its power at the expense of the working class, from turning its social leadership into an intensified exploitation of the masses.

But if, upon this showing, division into classes has a certain historical justification, it has this only for a given period, only under given social conditions. It was based upon the insufficiency of production. It will be swept away by the complete development of modern productive forces. And, in fact, the abolition of classes in society presupposes a degree of historical evolution at which the existence, not simply of this or that particular ruling class, but of any ruling class at all, and, therefore, the existence of class distinction itself has become an obsolete anachronism. It presupposes, therefore, the development of production carried out to a degree at which appropriation of the means of production and of the products, and, with this, of political domination, of the monopoly of culture, and of intellectual leadership by a particular class of society, has become not only superfluous but economically, politically, intellectually, a hindrance to development.

This point is now reached. Their political and intellectual bankruptcy is scarcely any longer a secret to the bourgeoisie themselves. Their economic bankruptcy recurs regularly every ten years. In every crisis, society is suffocated beneath the weight of its own productive forces and products, which it cannot use, and stands helpless, face to face with the absurd contradiction that the producers have nothing to consume, because consumers are wanting. The expansive force of the means of production bursts the bonds that the capitalist mode of production had imposed upon them. Their deliverance from these bonds is the one precondition for an unbroken, constantly accelerated development of the productive forces, and therewith for a practically unlimited increase of production itself. Nor is this all. The socialized appropriation of the means of production does away, not only with the present artificial restrictions upon production, but also with the positive waste and devastation of productive forces and products that are at the present time the inevitable concomitants of production, and that reach their height in the crises. Further, it sets free for the community at large a mass of means of production and of products, by doing away with the senseless extravagance of the ruling classes of today and their political representatives. The possibility of securing for every member of society, by means of socialized production, an existence not only fully sufficient materially, and becoming day by day more full, but an existence guaranteeing to all the free development and exercise of their physical and mental faculties—this possibility is now for the first time here, but *it is here.*

With the seizing of the means of production by society, production of commodities is done away with, and, simultaneously, the mastery of the product over the producer. Anarchy in social production is replaced by systematic, definite organization. The struggle for individual existence disappears. Then for the first time man, in a certain sense, is finally marked off from the rest of the animal kingdom, and emerges from mere animal conditions of existence into really human ones. The whole sphere of the conditions of life which environ man, and which have hitherto ruled man, now comes under the dominion and control of man, who for the first time becomes the real, conscious lord of Nature, because he has now become master of his own social organization. The laws of his own social action, hitherto standing face to face with man as laws of Nature foreign to, and dominating him, will then be used with full understanding, and so mastered by him. Man's own social organization, hitherto confronting him as a necessity imposed by Nature and history, now becomes the result of his own free action. The extraneous objective forces that have hitherto governed history pass under the control of man himself. Only from that time will man himself, more and more consciously, make his own history—only from that time will the social causes set in movement by him have, in the main and in a constantly growing measure, the results intended by him. It is the ascent of man from the kingdom of necessity to the kingdom of freedom.

—Engels, "Socialism: Utopian and Scientific," *MESW II,* pp. 149–53

PROLETARIANS AND COMMUNISTS

In what relation do the Communists stand to the proletarians as a whole?

The Communists do not form a separate party opposed to other working-class parties.

They have no interests separate and apart from those of the proletariat as a whole.

They do not set up any sectarian principles of their own, by which to shape and mould the proletarian movement.

The Communists are distinguished from the other working-class parties by this only: 1. In the national struggles of the proletarians of the different countries, they point out and bring to the front the common interests of the entire proletariat, independently of all nationality. 2. In the various stages of development which the struggle of the working class against the bourgeoisie has to pass through, they always and everywhere represent the interests of the movement as a whole.

The Communists, therefore, are on the one hand, practically, the most advanced and resolute section of the working-class parties of every country, that section which pushes forward all others; on the other hand, theoretically, they have over the great mass of the proletariat the advantage of clearly understanding the line of march, the conditions, and the ultimate general results of the proletarian movement.

The immediate aim of the Communists is the same as that of all the other proletarian parties: formation of the proletariat into a class, overthrow of the bourgeois supremacy, conquest of political power by the proletariat.

The theoretical conclusions of the Communists are in no way based on ideas or principles that havc been invented, or discovered, by this or that would-be universal reformer.

They merely express, in general terms, actual relations springing from an existing class struggle, from a historical movement going on under our very eyes. The abolition of existing property relations is not at all a distinctive feature of Communism.

All property relations in the past have continually been subject to historical change consequent upon the change in historical conditions.

The French Revolution, for example, abolished feudal property in favour of bourgeois property.

The distinguishing feature of Communism is not the abolition of property generally, but the abolition of bourgeois property. But modern bourgeois private property is the final and most complete expression of the system of producing and appropriating products, that is based on class antagonisms, on the exploitation of the many by the few.

In this sense, the theory of the Communists may be summed up in the single sentence: Abolition of private property.

We Communists have been reproached with the desire of abolishing the right of personally acquiring property as the fruit of a man's own labour, which property is alleged to be the groundwork of all personal freedom, activity and independence.

Hard-won, self-acquired, self-earned property! Do you mean the property of the petty artisan and of the small peasant, a form of property that preceded the bourgeois form? There is no need to abolish that; the development of industry has to a great extent already destroyed it, and is still destroying it daily.

Or do you mean modern bourgeois private property?

But does wage-labour create any property for the labourer? Not a bit. It creates capital, *i.e.,* that kind of property which exploits wage-labour, and which cannot increase except upon condition of begetting a new supply of wage-labour for fresh exploitation. Property, in its present form, is based on the antagonism of capital and wage-labour. Let us examine both sides of this antagonism.

To be a capitalist, is to have not only a purely personal, but a social *status* in production. Capital is a collective product, and only by the united action of many members, nay, in the last resort, only by the united action of all members of society, can it be set in motion.

Capital is, therefore, not a personal, it is a social power.

When, therefore, capital is converted into common property, into the property of all members of society, personal property is not thereby transformed into social property. It is only the social character of the property that is changed. It loses its class-character.

Let us now take wage-labour.

The average price of wage-labour is the minimum wage, *i.e.,* that quantum of the means of subsistence, which is absolutely requisite to keep the labourer in bare existence as a labourer. What, therefore, the wage-labourer appropriates by means of his labour, merely suffices to prolong and reproduce a bare existence. We by no means intend to abolish this personal appropriation of the products of labour, an appropriation that is made for the maintenance and reproduction of human life, and that leaves no surplus wherewith to command the labour of others. All that we want to do away with, is the miserable character of this appropriation, under which the labourer lives merely to increase capital, and is allowed to live only in so far as the interest of the ruling class requires it.

In bourgeois society, living labour is but a means to increase accumulated labour. In Communist society, accumulated labour is but a means to widen, to enrich, to promote the existence of the labourer.

In bourgeois society, therefore, the past dominates the present; in Communist society, the present dominates the past. In bourgeois society capital is independent and has individuality, while the living person is dependent and has no individuality.

And the abolition of this state of things is called by the bourgeois, abolition of individuality and freedom! And rightly so. The abolition of bourgeois individuality, bourgeois independence, and bourgeois freedom is undoubtedly aimed at.

By freedom is meant, under the present bourgeois conditions of production, free trade, free selling and buying.

But if selling and buying disappears, free selling and buying disappears also. This talk about free selling and buying, and all the other "brave words" of our bourgeoisie about freedom in general, have a meaning, if any, only in contrast with restricted selling and buying, with the fettered traders of the Middle Ages, but have no meaning when opposed to the Communistic abolition of buying and selling, of the bourgeois conditions of production, and of the bourgeoisie itself.

You are horrified at our intending to do away with private property. But in your existing society, private property is already done away with for nine-tenths of the population; its existence for the few is solely due to its non-existence in the hands of those nine-tenths. You reproach us, therefore, with intending to do away with a form of property, the necessary condition for whose existence is the non-existence of any property for the immense majority of society.

In one word, you reproach us with intending to do away with your property. Precisely so; that is just what we intend.

From the moment when labour can no longer be converted into capital, money, or rent, into a social power capable of being monopolised, *i.e.,* from the moment when individual property can no longer be transformed into bourgeois property, into capital, from that moment, you say, individuality vanishes.

You must, therefore, confess that by "individual" you mean no other person than the bourgeois, than the middle-class owner of property. This person must, indeed, be swept out of the way, and made impossible.

Communism deprives no man of the power to appropriate the products of society; all that it does is to deprive him of the power to subjugate the labour of others by means of such appropriation.

It has been objected that upon the abolition of private property all work will cease, and universal laziness will overtake us.

According to this, bourgeois society ought long ago to have gone to the dogs through sheer idleness; for those of its members who work, acquire nothing, and those who acquire anything, do not work. The whole of this objection is but another expression of the tautology: that there can no longer be any wage-labour when there is no longer any capital.

All objections urged against the Communistic mode of producing and appropriating material products, have, in the same way, been urged against the Communistic modes of producing and appropriating intellectual products. Just as, to the bourgeois, the disappearance of class property is the disappearance of production itself, so the disappearance of class culture is to him identical with the disappearance of all culture.

That culture, the loss of which he laments, is, for the enormous majority, a mere training to act as a machine.

But don't wrangle with us so long as you apply, to our intended abolition of bourgeois property, the standard of your bourgeois notions of freedom, culture, law, &c. Your very ideas are but the outgrowth of the conditions of your bourgeois production and bourgeois property, just as your jurisprudence is but the will of your class made into a law for all, a will, whose essential character and direction are determined by the economical conditions of existence of your class.

The selfish misconception that induces you to transform into eternal laws of nature and of reason, the social forms springing from your present mode of production and form of property—historical relations that rise and disappear in the progress of production—this misconception you share with every ruling class that has preceded you. What you see clearly in the case of ancient property, what you admit in the case of feudal property, you are of course forbidden to admit in the case of your own bourgeois form of property.

Abolition of the family! Even the most radical flare up at this infamous proposal of the Communists.

On what foundation is the present family, the bourgeois family, based? On capital, on private gain. In its completely developed form this family exists only among the bourgeoisie. But this state of things finds its complement in the practical absence of the family among the proletarians, and in public prostitution.

The bourgeois family will vanish as a matter of course when its complement vanishes, and both will vanish with the vanishing of capital.

Do you charge us with wanting to stop the exploitation of children by their parents? To this crime we plead guilty.

But, you will say, we destroy the most hallowed of relations, when we replace home education by social.

And your education! Is not that also social, and determined by the social conditions under which you educate, by the intervention, direct or indirect, of society, by means of schools, &c.? The Communists have not invented the intervention of society in education; they do but seek to alter the character of that intervention, and to rescue education from the influence of the ruling class.

The bourgeois clap-trap about the family and education, about the hallowed co-relation of parent and child, becomes all the more disgusting, the more, by the action of Modern Industry, all family ties among the proletarians are torn asunder, and their children transformed into simple articles of commerce and instruments of labour.

But you Communists would introduce community of women, screams the whole bourgeoisie in chorus.

The bourgeois sees in his wife a mere instrument of production. He hears that the instruments of production are to be exploited in common, and, naturally, can come to no other conclusion than that the lot of being common to all will likewise fall to the women.

He has not even a suspicion that the real point aimed at is to do away with the status of women as mere instruments of production.

For the rest, nothing is more ridiculous than the virtuous indignation of our bourgeois at the community of women which, they pretend, is to be openly and officially established by the Communists. The Communists have no need to introduce community of women; it has existed almost from time immemorial.

Our bourgeois, not content with having the wives and daughters of their proletarians at their disposal, not to speak of common prostitutes, take the greatest pleasure in seducing each other's wives.

Bourgeois marriage is in reality a system of wives in common and thus, at the most, what the Communists might possibly be reproached with, is that they desire to introduce, in substitution for a hypocritically concealed, an openly legalised community of women. For the rest, it is self-evident that the abolition of the present system of production must bring with it the abolition of the community of women springing from that system, *i.e.*, of prostitution both public and private.

The Communists are further reproached with desiring to abolish countries and nationality.

The working men have no country. We cannot take from them what they have not got. Since the proletariat must first of all acquire political supremacy, must rise to be the leading class of the nation, must constitute itself *the* nation, it is, so far, itself national, though not in the bourgeois sense of the word.

National differences and antagonisms between peoples are daily more and more vanishing, owing to the development of the bourgeoisie, to freedom of commerce, to the world-market, to uniformity in the mode of production and in the conditions of life corresponding thereto.

The supremacy of the proletariat will cause them to vanish still faster. United action, of the leading civilised countries at least, is one of the first conditions for the emancipation of the proletariat.

In proportion as the exploitation of one individual by another is put an end to, the exploitation of one nation by another will also be put an end to. In proportion as the antagonism between classes within the nation vanishes, the hostility of one nation to another will come to an end.

The charges against Communism made from a religious, a philosophical, and, generally, from an ideological standpoint, are not deserving of serious examination.

Does it require deep intuition to comprehend that man's ideas, views and conceptions, in one word, man's consciousness, changes with every change in the conditions of his material existence, in his social relations and in his social life?

What else does the history of ideas prove, than that intellectual production changes its character in proportion as material production is changed? The ruling ideas of each age have ever been the ideas of its ruling class.

When people speak of ideas that revolutionise society, they do but express the fact, that within the old society, the elements of a new one have been created, and that the dissolution of the old ideas keeps even pace with the dissolution of the old conditions of existence.

When the ancient world was in its last throes, the ancient religions were overcome by Christianity. When Christian ideas succumbed in the 18th century to rationalist ideas, feudal society fought its death battle with the then revolutionary bourgeoisie. The ideas of religious liberty and freedom of conscience merely gave expression to the sway of free competition within the domain of knowledge.

"Undoubtedly," it will be said, "religious, moral, philosophical and juridical ideas have been modified in the course of historical development. But religion, morality, philosophy, political science, and law, constantly survived this change."

"There are, besides, eternal truths, such as Freedom, Justice, etc., that are common to all states of society. But Communism abolishes eternal truths, it abolishes all religion, and all morality, instead of constituting them on a new basis; it therefore acts in contradiction to all past historical experience."

What does this accusation reduce itself to? The history of all past society has consisted in the development of class antagonisms, antagonisms that assumed different forms at different epochs.

But whatever form they may have taken, one fact is common to all past ages, *viz.,* the exploitation of one part of society by the other. No wonder, then, that the social consciousness of past ages, despite all the multiplicity and variety it displays, moves within certain common forms, or general ideas, which cannot completely vanish except with the total disappearance of class antagonisms.

The Communist revolution is the most radical rupture with traditional property relations; no wonder that its development involves the most radical rupture with traditional ideas.

But let us have done with the bourgeois objections to Communism.

We have seen above, that the first step in the revolution by the working class, is to raise the proletariat to the position of ruling class, to win the battle of democracy.

The proletariat will use its political supremacy to wrest, by degrees, all capital from the bourgeoisie, to centralise all instruments of production in the hands of the State, *i.e.,* of the proletariat organised as the ruling class; and to increase the total of productive forces as rapidly as possible.

Of course, in the beginning, this cannot be effected except by means of despotic inroads on the rights of property, and on the conditions of bourgeois production; by means of measures, therefore, which appear economically insufficient and untenable, but which, in the course of the movement, outstrip themselves, necessitate further inroads upon the old social order, and are unavoidable as a means of entirely revolutionising the mode of production.

These measures will of course be different in different countries.

Nevertheless in the most advanced countries, the following will be pretty generally applicable.

1. Abolition of property in land and application of all rents of land to public purposes.

2. A heavy progressive or graduated income tax.

3. Abolition of all right of inheritance.

4. Confiscation of the property of all emigrants and rebels.

5. Centralisation of credit in the hands of the State, by means of a national bank with State capital and an exclusive monopoly.

6. Centralisation of the means of communication and transport in the hands of the State.

7. Extension of factories and instruments of production owned by the State; the bringing into cultivation of waste-lands, and the improvement of the soil generally in accordance with a common plan.

8. Equal liability of all to labour. Establishment of industrial armies, especially for agriculture.

9. Combination of agriculture with manufacturing industries; gradual abolition of the distinction between town and country, by a more equable distribution of the population over the country.

10. Free education for all children in public schools. Abolition of children's factory labour in its present form. Combination of education with industrial production, &c., &c.

When, in the course of development, class distinctions have disappeared, and all production has been concentrated in the hands of a vast association of the whole nation, the public power will lose its political character. Political power, properly so called, is merely the organised power of one class for oppressing another. If the proletariat during its contest with the bourgeoisie is compelled, by the force of circumstances, to organise itself as a class, if, by means of a revolution, it makes itself the ruling class, and, as such, sweeps away by force the old conditions of production, then it will, along with these conditions, have swept away the conditions for the existence of class antagonisms and of classes generally, and will thereby have abolished its own supremacy as a class.

In place of the old bourgeois society, with its classes and class antagonisms, we shall have an association, in which the free development of each is the condition for the free development of all.

—Marx and Engels, "Manifesto of the Communist Party," *MESW I*, pp. 46–54

Appendix: The Paris Commune

On the dawn of the 18th of March, Paris arose to the thunderburst of "Vive la Commune!" What is the Commune, that sphinx so tantalizing to the bourgeois mind?

"The proletarians of Paris," said the Central Committee in its manifesto of the 18th March, "amidst the failures and treasons of the ruling classes, have understood that the hour has struck for them to save the situation by taking into their own hands the direction of public affairs. . . . They have understood that it is their imperious duty and their absolute right to render themselves masters of their own destinies, by seizing upon the governmental power." But the working class cannot simply lay hold of the ready-made state machinery, and wield it for its own purposes.

The centralized State power, with its ubiquitous organs of standing army, police, bureaucracy, clergy, and judicature—organs wrought after the plan of a systematic and hierarchic division of labour,—originates from the days of absolute monarchy, serving nascent middle-class society as a mighty weapon in its struggles against feudalism. Still, its development remained clogged by all manner of mediaeval rubbish, seignorial rights, local privileges, municipal and guild monopolies and provincial constitutions. The gigantic broom of the French Revolution of the eighteenth century swept away all these relics of bygone times, thus clearing simultaneously the social soil of its last hindrances to the superstructure of the modern State edifice raised under the First Empire, itself the offspring of the coalition wars of old semi-feudal Europe against modern France. During the subsequent *regimes* the Government, placed under parliamentary control—that is, under the direct control of the propertied classes—became not only a hotbed of huge national debts and crushing taxes; with its irresistible allurements of place, pelf, and patronage, it became not only the bone of contention between the rival factions and adventurers of the ruling classes; but its political character changed simultaneously with the economic changes of society. At the same pace at which the progress of modern industry developed, widened, intensified the class antagonism between capital and labour, the State power assumed more and more the character of the national power of capital over labour, of a public force organized for social enslavement, of an engine of class despotism. After every revolution marking a progressive phase in the class struggle, the purely repressive character of the State power stands out in bolder and bolder relief. The Revolution of 1830, resulting in the transfer of Government from the landlords to the capitalists, transferred it from the more remote to the more direct antagonists of the working men. The bourgeois Republicans, who, in the name of the Revolution of February, took the State power, used it for the June massacres, in order to convince the working class that "social" republic meant the Republic ensuring their social subjection, and in order to convince the royalist bulk of the bourgeois and landlord class that they might safely leave the cares and emoluments of Government to the bourgeois "Republicans." However, after their one heroic exploit of June, the bourgeois Republicans had, from the front, to fall back to the rear of the "Party of Order"—a combination formed by all the rival fractions and factions of the appropriating class in their now openly declared antagonism to the producing classes.

The proper form of their joint-stock Government was the *Parliamentary Republic,* with Louis Bonaparte for its President. Theirs was a *regime* of avowed class terrorism and deliberate insult toward the "vile multitude." If the Parliamentary Republic, as M. Thiers said, "divided them (the different fractions of the ruling class) least," it opened an abyss between that class and the whole body of society outside their spare ranks. The restraints by which their own divisions had under former *regimes* still checked the State power, were removed by their union; and in view of the threatening upheaval of the proletariat, they now used that State power mercilessly and ostentatiously as the national war-engine of capital against labour. In their uninterrupted crusade against the producing masses they were, however, bound not only to invest the executive with continually increased powers of repression, but at the same time to divest their own parliamentary stronghold—the National Assembly—one by one, of all its own means of defence against the Executive. The Executive, in the person of Louis Bonaparte, turned them out. The natural offspring of the "Party-of-Order" Republic was the Second Empire.

The empire, with the *coup d'etat* for its certificate of birth, universal suffrage for its sanction, and the sword for its sceptre, professed to rest upon the peasantry, the large mass of producers not directly involved in the struggle of capital and labour. It professed to save the working class by breaking down Parliamentarism, and, with it, the undisguised subserviency of Government to the propertied classes. It professed to save the propertied classes by upholding their economic supremacy over the working class; and, finally, it professed to unite all classes by reviving for all the chimera of national glory. In reality, it was the only form of government possible at a time when the bourgeoisie had already lost, and the working class had not yet acquired, the faculty of ruling the nation. It was acclaimed throughout the world as the saviour of society. Under its sway, bourgeois society, freed from political cares, attained a development unexpected even by itself. Its industry and commerce expanded to colossal dimensions; financial swindling celebrated cosmopolitan orgies; the misery of the masses was set off by a shameless display of gorgeous, meretricious and debased luxury. The State power, apparently soaring high above society, was at the same time itself the greatest scandal of that society and the very hotbed of all its corruptions. Its own rottenness, and the rottenness of the society it had saved, were laid bare by the bayonet of Prussia, herself eagerly bent upon transferring the supreme seat of that *regime* from Paris to Berlin. Imperialism is, at the same time, the most prostitute and the ultimate form of the State power which nascent middle-class society had commenced to elaborate as a means of its own emancipation from feudalism, and which full-grown bourgeois society had finally transformed into a means for the enslavement of labour by capital.

The direct antithesis to the empire was the Commune. The cry of "social republic," with which the revolution of February was ushered in by the Paris proletariat, did but express a vague aspiration after a Republic that was not only to supersede the monarchical form of class-rule, but class-rule itself. The Commune was the positive form of that Republic.

Paris, the central seat of the old governmental power, and, at the same time, the social stronghold of the French working class, had risen in arms against the attempt of Thiers, and the Rurals to restore and perpetuate that old governmental power bequeathed to them by the empire. Paris could resist only because, in consequence of the siege, it had got rid of the army, and replaced it by a National Guard, the bulk of which consisted of working men. This fact was now to be transformed into an institution. The first decree of the Commune, therefore, was the suppression of the standing army, and the substitution for it of the armed people.

The Commune was formed of the municipal councillors, chosen by universal suffrage in the various wards of the town, responsible and revocable at short terms. The majority of its members were naturally working men, or acknowledged representatives of the working class. The Commune was to be a working, not a parliamentary, body, executive and legislative at the same time. Instead of continuing to be the agent of the Central Government, the police was at once stripped of its political attributes, and turned into the responsible and at all times revocable agent of the Commune. So were the officials of all other branches of the Administration. From the members of the Commune downwards, the public service had to be done at *workmen's wages*. The vested interests and the representation allowances of the high dignitaries of State disappeared along with the high dignitaries themselves. Public functions ceased to be the private property of the tools of the Central Government. Not only municipal administration, but the whole initiative hitherto exercised by the State was laid into the hands of the Commune.

Having once got rid of the standing army and the police, the physical force elements of the old Government, the Commune was anxious to break the spiritual force of repression, the "parson-power," by the disestablishment and disendowment of all churches as proprietary bodies. The priests were sent back to the recesses of private life, there to feed upon the alms of the faithful in imitation of their predecessors, the Apostles. The whole of the educational institutions were opened to the people gratuitously, and at the same time cleared of all interference of Church and State. Thus, not only was education made accessible to all, but science itself freed from the fetters which class prejudice and governmental force had imposed upon it.

The judicial functionaries were to be divested of that sham independence which had but served to mask their abject subserviency to all succeeding governments to which, in turn, they had taken, and broken, the oaths of allegiance. Like the rest of public servants, magistrates and judges were to be elective, responsible, and revocable.

The Paris Commune was, of course, to serve as a model to all the great industrial centres of France. The communal *regime* once established in Paris and the secondary centres, the old centralized Government would in the provinces, too, have to give way to the self-government of the producers. In a rough sketch of national organization which the Commune had no time to develop, it states clearly that the Commune was to be the political form of even the smallest country hamlet, and that in the rural districts the standing army was to be replaced by a national militia, with an extremely short term of service. The rural communes of every district were to administer their common affairs by an assembly of delegates in the central town, and these district assemblies were again to send deputies to the National Delegation in Paris, each delegate to be at any time revocable and bound by the *mandat imperatif* (formal instructions) of his constituents. The few but important functions which still would remain for a central government were not to be suppressed, as has been intentionally misstated, but were to be discharged by Communal, and therefore strictly responsible agents. The unity of the nation was not to be broken, but, on the contrary, to be organized by the Communal Constitution and to become a reality by the destruction of the State power which claimed to be the embodiment of that unity independent of, and superior to, the nation itself, from which it was but a parasitic excrescence. While the merely repressive organs of the old governmental power were to be amputated, its legitimate functions were to be wrested from an authority usurping pre-eminence over society itself, and restored to the responsible agents of society. Instead of deciding once in three or six years which member of the ruling class was to misrepresent the people in Parliament, universal suffrage was to serve the people, constituted in Communes, as individual suffrage serves every other employer in the search for the workmen and managers in his business. And it is well known that companies, like individuals, in matters of real business generally know how to put the right man in the right place, and, if they for once make a mistake, to redress it promptly. On the other hand, nothing could be more foreign to the spirit of the Commune than to supersede universal suffrage by hierarchic investiture.

It is generally the fate of completely new historical creations to be mistaken for the counterpart of older and even defunct forms of social life, to which they may bear a certain likeness. Thus, this new Commune, which breaks the modern State power, has been mistaken for a reproduction of the mediaeval Communes, which first preceded, and afterwards became the substratum of, that very State power. The Communal Constitution has been mistaken for an attempt to break up into a federation of small States, as dreamt of by Montesquieu and the Girondins, that unity of great nations which, if originally brought about by political force, has now become a powerful coefficient of social production. The antagonism of the Commune against the State power has been mistaken for an exaggerated form of the ancient struggle against over-centralization. Peculiar historical circumstances may have prevented the classical development, as in France, of the bourgeois form of government, and may have allowed, as in England, to complete the great central State organs by corrupt vestries, jobbing councillors, and ferocious poor-law guardians in the towns, and virtually hereditary magistrates in the counties. The Communal Constitution would have restored to the social body all the forces hitherto absorbed by the State parasite feeding upon, and clogging the free movement of, society. By this one act it would have initiated the regeneration of France. The provincial French middle class saw in the Commune an attempt to restore the sway their order had held over the country under Louis Philippe, and which, under Louis Napoleon, was supplanted by the pretended rule of the country over the towns. In reality, the Communal Constitution brought the rural producers under the intellectual lead of the central towns of their districts, and these secured to them, in the working men, the natural trustees of their interests. The very existence of the Commune involved, as a matter of course, local municipal liberty, but no longer as a check upon the, now superseded, State power. It could only enter into the head of a Bismarck, who, when not engaged on his intrigues of blood and iron, always likes to resume his old trade, so befitting his mental calibre, of contributor to *Kladderadatsch* (the Berlin *Punch*), it could only enter into such a head, to ascribe to the Paris Commune aspirations after that caricature of the old French municipal organization of 1791, the Prussian municipal constitution which degrades the town governments to mere secondary wheels in the police-machinery of the Prussian State. The Commune made that catchword of bourgeois revolutions, cheap government, a reality, by destroying the two greatest sources of expenditure—the standing army and State functionarism. Its very existence presupposed the non-existence of monarchy, which, in Europe at least, is the normal incumbrance and indispensable cloak of class-rule. It supplied the Republic with the basis of really democratic institutions. But neither cheap Government nor the "true Republic" was its ultimate aim; they were its mere concomitants.

The multiplicity of interpretations to which the Commune has been subjected, and the multiplicity of interests which construed it in their favour, show that it was a thoroughly expansive political form, while all previous forms of government had been emphatically repressive. Its true secret was this. It was essentially a working-class government, the produce of the struggle of the producing against the appropriating class, the political form at last discovered under which to work out the economic emancipation of labour.

Except on this last condition, the Communal Constitution would have been an impossibility and a delusion. The political rule of the producer cannot coexist with the perpetuation of his social slavery. The Commune was therefore to serve as a lever for uprooting the economical foundations upon which rests the existence of classes, and therefore of class-rule. With labour emancipated, every man becomes a working man, and productive labour ceases to be a class attribute.

It is a strange fact. In spite of all the tall talk and all the immense literature, for the last sixty years, about Emancipation of Labour, no sooner do the working men anywhere take the subject into their own hands with a will, than uprises at once all the apologetic phraseology of the mouthpieces of present society with its two poles of Capital and Wages Slavery (the landlord now is but the sleeping partner of the capitalist), as if capitalist society was still in its purest state of virgin innocence, with its antagonisms still undeveloped, with its delusions still unexploded, with its prostitute realities not yet laid bare. The Commune, they exclaim, intends to abolish property, the basis of all civilization! Yes, gentlemen, the Commune intended to abolish that class-property which makes the labour of the many the wealth of the few. It aimed at the expropriation of the expropriators. It wanted to make individual property a truth by transforming the means of production, land and capital, now chiefly the means of enslaving and exploiting labour, into mere instruments of free and associated labour.—But this is Communism, "impossible" Communism! Why, those members of the ruling classes who are intelligent enough to perceive the impossibility of continuing the present system—and they are many—have become the obtrusive and full-mouthed apostles of co-operative production. If co-operative production is not to remain a sham and a snare; if it is to supersede the Capitalist system; if united co-operative societies are to regulate national production upon a common plan, thus taking it under their own control, and putting an end to the constant anarchy and periodical convulsions which are the fatality of Capitalist production—what else, gentlemen, would it be but Communism, "possible" Communism?

The working class did not expect miracles from the Commune. They have no ready-made utopias to introduce *par decret du peuple.* They know that in order to work out their own emancipation, and along with it that higher form to which present society is irresistibly tending by its own economical agencies, they will have to pass through long struggles, through a series of historic processes, transforming circumstances and men. They have no ideals to realize, but to set free the elements of the new society with which old collapsing bourgeois society itself is pregnant. In the full consciousness of their historic mission, and with the heroic resolve to act up to it, the working class can afford to smile at the coarse invective of the gentlemen's gentlemen with the pen and ink-horn, and at the didactic patronage of well-wishing bourgeois-doctrinaires, pouring forth their ignorant platitudes and sectarian crotchets in the oracular tone of scientific infallibility.

When the Paris Commune took the management of the revolution in its own hands; when plain working men for the first time dared to infringe upon the Governmental privilege of their "natural superiors," and, under circumstances of unexampled difficulty, performed their work modestly, conscientiously, and efficiently,—performed it at salaries the highest of which barely amounted to one-fifth of what, according to high scientific authority, is the minimum required for a secretary to a certain metropolitan school board,—the old world writhed in convulsions of rage at the sight of the Red Flag, the symbol of the Republic of Labour, floating over the Hotel de Ville.

And yet this was the first revolution in which the working class was openly acknowledged as the only class capable of social initiative, even by the great bulk of the Paris middle class—shopkeepers, tradesmen, merchants—the wealthy capitalists alone excepted. The Commune had saved them by a sagacious settlement of that ever-recurring cause of dispute among the middle classes themselves—the debtor and creditor accounts. The same portion of the middle class, after they had assisted in putting down the working men's insurrection of June, 1848, had been at once unceremoniously sacrificed to their creditors by the then Constituent Assembly. But this was not their only motive for now rallying round the working class. They felt that there was but one alternative—the Commune, or the Empire—under whatever name it might reappear. The Empire had ruined them economically by the havoc it made of public wealth, by the wholesale financial swindling it fostered, by the props it lent to the artificially accelerated centralization of capital, and the concomitant expropriation of their own ranks. It had suppressed them politically, it had shocked them morally by its orgies, it had insulted their Voltairianism by handing over the education of their children to the *frères Ignorantins,* it had revolted their national feeling as Frenchmen by precipitating them headlong into a war which left only one equivalent for the ruins it made—the disappearance of the Empire. In fact, after the exodus from Paris of the high Bonapartist and capitalist *boheme,* the true middle-class Party of Order came out in the shape of the "Union Republicaine," enrolling themselves under the colours of the Commune and defending it against the wilful misconstruction of Thiers. Whether the gratitude of this great body of the middle class will stand the present severe trial, time must show.

The Commune was perfectly right in telling the peasants that "its victory was their only hope." Of all the lies hatched at Versailles and re-echoed by the glorious European penny-a-liner, one of the most tremendous was that the Rurals represented the French peasantry.

. . .

The French peasant had elected Louis Bonaparte president of the Republic; but the Party of Order created the Empire. What the French peasant really wants he commenced to show in 1849 and 1850, by opposing his *maire* to the Government's prefect, his schoolmaster to the Government's priest, and himself to the Government's gendarme. All the laws made by the Party of Order in January and February, 1850, were avowed measures of repression against the peasant. The peasant was a Bonapartist, because the great Revolution, with all its benefits to him, was, in his eyes, personified in Napoleon. This delusion, rapidly breaking down under the Second Empire (and in its very nature hostile to the Rurals), this prejudice of the past, how could it have withstood the appeal of the Commune to the living interests and urgent wants of the peasantry?

The Rurals—this was, in fact, their chief apprehension—knew that three months' free communication of Communal Paris with the provinces would bring about a general rising of the peasants, and hence their anxiety to establish a police blockade around Paris, so as to stop the spread of the rinderpest.

If the Commune was thus the true representative of all the healthy elements of French society, and therefore the truly national Government, it was, at the same time, as a working men's Government, as the bold champion of the emancipation of labour, emphatically international. Within sight of the Prussian army, that had annexed to Germany two French provinces, the Commune annexed to France the working people all over the world.

The Second Empire had been the jubilee of cosmopolitan blacklegism, the rakes of all countries rushing in at its call for a share in its orgies and in the plunder of the French people. Even at this moment the right hand of Thiers is Ganesco, the foul Wallachian, and his left hand is Markovsky, the Russian spy. The Commune admitted all foreigners to the honour of dying for an immortal cause. Between the foreign war lost by their treason, and the civil war fomented by their conspiracy with the foreign invader, the bourgeoisie had found the time to display their patriotism by organizing police-hunts upon the Germans in France. The Commune made a German working man its Minister of Labour. Thiers, the bourgeoisie, the Second Empire, had continually deluded Poland by loud professions of sympathy, while in reality betraying her to, and doing the dirty work of, Russia. The Commune honoured the heroic sons of Poland by placing them at the head of the defenders of Paris. And, to broadly mark the new era of history it was conscious of initiating, under the eyes of the conquering Prussians, on the one side, and of the Bonapartist army, led by Bonapartist generals, on the other, the Commune pulled down that colossal symbol of martial glory, the Vendome column.

The great social measure of the Commune was its own working existence. Its special measures could but betoken the tendency of a government of the people by the people. Such were the abolition of the nightwork of journeymen bakers; the prohibition, under penalty, of the employers' practice to reduce wages by levying upon their work-people fines under manifold pretexts,—a process in which the employer combines in his own person the parts of legislator, judge, and executor, and filches the money to boot. Another measure of this class was the surrender, to associations of workmen, under reserve of compensation, of all closed workshops and factories, no matter whether the respective capitalists had absconded or preferred to strike work.

The financial measures of the Commune, remarkable for their sagacity and moderation, could only be such as were compatible with the state of a besieged town. Considering the colossal robberies committed upon the city of Paris by the great financial companies and contractors, under the protection of Haussmann, the Commune would have had an incomparably better title to confiscate their property than Louis Napoleon had against the Orleans family. The Hohenzollern and the English oligarchs, who both have derived a good deal of their estates from Church plunder, were, of course, greatly shocked at the Commune clearing but 8,000 f. out of secularization.

While the Versailles Government, as soon as it had recovered some spirit and strength, used the most violent means against the Commune; while it put down the free expression of opinion all over France, even to the forbidding of meetings of delegates from the large towns; while it subjected Versailles and the rest of France to an espionage far surpassing that of the Second Empire; while it burned by its gendarme inquisitors all papers printed at Paris, and sifted all correspondence from and to Paris; while in the National Assembly the most timid attempts to put in a word for Paris were howled down in a manner unknown even to the *Chambre introuv-*

able of 1816; with the savage warfare of Versailles outside, and its attempts at corruption and conspiracy inside Paris—would the Commune not have shamefully betrayed its trust by affecting to keep up all the decencies and appearances of liberalism as in a time of profound peace? Had the Government of the Commune been akin to that of M. Thiers, there would have been no more occasion to suppress Party-of-Order papers at Paris than there was to suppress Communal papers at Versailles.

It was irritating indeed to the Rurals that at the very same time they declared the return to the church to be the only means of salvation for France, the infidel Commune unearthed the peculiar mysteries of the Picpus nunnery, and of the Church of Saint Laurent. It was a satire upon M. Thiers that, while he showered grand crosses upon the Bonapartist generals in acknowledgement of their mastery in losing battles, signing capitulations, and turning cigarettes at Wilhelmshöhe, the Commune dismissed and arrested its generals whenever they were suspected of neglecting their duties. The expulsion from, and arrest by, the Commune of one of its members who had slipped in under a false name, and had undergone at Lyons six days' imprisonment for simple bankruptcy, was it not a deliberate insult hurled at the forger, Jules Favre, then still the foreign minister of France, still selling France to Bismarck, and still dictating his orders to that paragon Government of Belgium? But indeed the Commune did not pretend to infallibility, the invariable attribute of all governments of the old stamp. It published its doings and sayings, it initiated the public into all its shortcomings.

. . .

Wonderful, indeed, was the change the Commune had wrought in Paris! No longer any trace of the meretricious Paris of the Second Empire. No longer was Paris the rendezvous of British landlords, Irish absentees, American ex-slaveholders and shoddy men, Russian ex-serfowners, and Wallachian boyards. No more corpses at the morgue, no nocturnal burglaries, scarcely any robberies; in fact, for the first time since the days of February, 1848, the streets of Paris were safe, and that without any police of any kind. "We," said a member of the Commune, "hear no longer of assassination, theft and personal assault; it seems indeed as if the police had dragged along with it to Versailles all its Conservative friends." The *cocottes* had refound the scent of their protectors—the absconding men of family, religion, and, above all, of property. In their stead, the real women of Paris showed again at the surface—heroic, noble, and devoted, like the women of antiquity. Working, thinking, fighting, bleeding Paris—almost forgetful, in its incubation of a new society, of the cannibals at its gates—radiant in the enthusiasm of its historic initiative!

Opposed to this new world at Paris, behold the old world at Versailles—that assembly of the ghouls of all defunct *régimes,* Legitimists and Orleanists, eager to feed upon the carcass of the nation,—with a tail of antediluvian Republicans, sanctioning, by their presence in the Assembly, the slaveholders' rebellion, relying for the maintenance of their Parliamentary Republic upon the vanity of the senile mountebank at its head, and caricaturing 1789 by holding their ghastly meetings in the *Jeu de Paume.*[2] There it was, this Assembly, the representative of everything dead in France, propped up to the semblance of life by nothing but the swords of the generals of Louis Bonaparte. Paris all truth, Versailles all lie; and that lie vented through the mouth of Thiers.

Thiers tells a deputation of the mayors of the Seine-et-Oise,—"You may rely upon my word, which I have *never* broken!" He tells the Assembly itself that "it was the most freely elected and most Liberal Assembly France ever possessed"; he tells his motley soldiery that it was "the admiration of the world, and the finest army France ever possessed"; he tells the provinces that the bombardment of Paris by him was a myth: "If some cannon-shots have been fired, it is not the deed of the army of Versailles, but of some insurgents trying to make believe that they are fighting, while they dare not show their faces." He again tells the provinces that "the artillery of Versailles does not bombard Paris, but only cannonades it." He tells the Archbishop of Paris that the pretended executions and reprisals (!) attributed to the Versailles troops were all moon-

[2] *Jeu de Paume:* The tennis court where the National Assembly of 1789 adopted its famous decisions [*note to German edition of 1871*].

shine. He tells Paris that he was only anxious "to free it from the hideous tyrants who oppress it," and that, in fact, the Paris of the Commune was "but a handful of criminals."

The Paris of M. Thiers was not the real Paris of the "vile multitude," but a phantom Paris, the Paris of the *francs-fileurs,* the Paris of the Boulevards, male and female—the rich, the capitalist, the gilded, the idle Paris, now thronging with its lackeys, its blacklegs, its literary *boheme,* and its *cocottes* at Versailles, Saint-Denis, Rueil, and Saint-Germain; considering the civil war but an agreeable diversion, eyeing the battle going on through telescopes, counting the rounds of cannon, and swearing by their own honour and that of their prostitutes, that the performance was far better got up than it used to be at the Porte St. Martin. The men who fell were really dead; the cries of the wounded were cries in good earnest; and, besides the whole thing was so intensely historical.

—Marx, "The Civil War in France," *MESW I,* pp. 516–30

Sources

Anti-Dühring, by Frederick Engels. Moscow: Foreign Language Publishing House, 1954. Originally published in German in 1878, this is a translation of the third German edition (1894).

Capital: A Critique of Political Economy, by Karl Marx. Vols. I, II, and III. Chicago: Charles H. Kerr and Co., 1906. Originally, Volume I (*The Process of Capitalist Production*) was published in German in 1867; Volume II (*The Process of Circulation of Capital*) appeared in 1885, two years after Marx's death; Volume III (*The Process of Capitalist Production as a Whole*) did not appear until 1893.

Economic and Philosophic Manuscripts of 1844, by Karl Marx. Moscow: Foreign Language Publishing House, 1961.

The Eighteenth Brumaire of Louis Bonaparte, by Karl Marx. Chicago: Charles H. Kerr and Co. (3rd ed.), 1913. First published in 1852, this was translated from the German by Daniel DeLeon in 1897.

The German Ideology, by Karl Marx and Frederick Engels. Edited with an introduction by R. Pascal. New York: International Publishers, Inc.,

1939. This work was written in 1845–1846 and published in parts. One section appeared as an article in 1847; others were published in *Dokumente des Sozialismus* by Ed. Bernstein in 1902–1903; and still another part was published by G. Mayer in *Archiv fur Sozial Wissenschaft und Socialpolitik* in 1921. Parts I and III, translated by W. Looch and C. P. Magill, were published as *German Ideology* by Lawrence and Wishart in London in 1938.

The Holy Family or Critique of Critical Critique, by Karl Marx and Frederick Engels. Moscow: Foreign Language Publishing House, 1956. Written in 1844, this was first published in Frankfort a/M. in 1845.

"The Civil War in France," by Karl Marx. Selection taken from *Marx-Engels Selected Works,* Vol. I (hereafter *MESW I*). Moscow: Foreign Language Publishing House, 1958. This was an address to the General Council of the International Working Men's Association, May 30, 1871.

Frederich Engels's introduction to "The Class Struggles in France," by Karl Marx. *MESW I.* Written in 1895 and published in Berlin, this was translated from the extant galleys of the original German text.

Preface to "A Contribution to the Critique of Political Economy," by Karl Marx. *MESW I.* Written in 1859, this was originally published by Otto Meissner in Hamburg in 1894.

Introduction to "The Dialectics of Nature," by Frederick Engels. *MESW I.* Probably written in 1878, this was originally published in German in 1898.

"Manifesto of the Communist Party," by Karl Marx and Frederick Engels. *MESW I.* This work was originally published by J. E. Burghard in London in February, 1848.

"Wage Labour and Capital," by Karl Marx. *MESW I.* Originally published in German in the *Neue Rheinische Zeitung* of April 5–8 and 11, 1849, this was published as a pamphlet in Zurich in 1884.

"Critique of the Gotha Programme," by Karl Marx. Selection taken from *Marx-Engels Selected Works,* Vol. II (hereafter *MESW II*). Moscow: Foreign Language Publishing House, 1958. This was published by Engels in 1891 in *Die Neue Zeit.* The first English translation, by Daniel DeLeon, was published in New York in 1922.

"Ludwig Feuerbach and the End of Classical German Philosophy," by Frederick Engels. *MESW II.* This was originally published in Stuttgart in 1888.

"The Origin of the Family, Private Property and the State," by Frederick Engels. *MESW II.* This was originally published in Zurich in 1844.

"Socialism: Utopian and Scientific," by Frederick Engels. *MESW II.* This was originally published in Paris in 1880.

"Die Bauernfrage in Frankreich and Deutschland," by Frederick Engels. Translated especially for this volume by Eric von Brockdorff. Die Neue Zeit, XIII (1895), No. 1, 304–305. This was written in 1894–1895.

"Zur Kritik des sozialdemokratischen Programmentwurfes 1891," by Frederick Engels. Translated especially for this volume by Eric von Brockdorff. *Die Neue Zeit,* XX (1901), No. 1, 10–11. This was written in 1891.

The Poverty of Philosophy, by Karl Marx. Translated by H. Quelch. Chicago: Charles H. Kerr and Co., 1920. This work first appeared in 1847 as *Misère de la Philosophie.*

Selected Correspondence of Karl Marx and Friedrich Engels. Moscow: Foreign Language Publishing House, n.d. This is a translation from the Russian edition of 1953.

Towards the Criticism of Hegel's Philosophy of Right, by Karl Marx and Friedrich Engels. Introduction by Karl Marx. Translated especially for this volume by Glenn Waas. Historisch-Kritische Gesamtaus gabe East Abt., Bd. 1. Erster Halbd. Frankfort a/M.: Marx-Engels Archiv Verlagsgesellschaft M.B.H., 1927. This was originally published in the *Deutsch-Franzosiche Jahrbucher* by A. Ruge and Karl Marx in Paris in 1843.

"The Jewish Question," from *A World Without Jews,* by Karl Marx. Edited and with an introduction by Dagobert D. Runes. Translated by I. Langnas. New York: The Philosophical Library, 1959. This originally appeared in the *Deutsch-Franzosische Jahrbucher* in 1844.

Index

Also by Robert Freedman:

MARX ON ECONOMICS

EDITED BY ROBERT FREEDMAN

INTRODUCTION BY HARRY SCHWARTZ

The first systematic compilation of Karl Marx's economic theories and critique of capitalism, drawn from all his writings and presented in a logical order with brief summaries of the argument.

HB 39 $2.25